Falling Back into the Arms of God....
Stripped & Broken

The sequel to "Living the Miracle"

My Child, I've Got This"

And "Surprised by God with Pancreatic Cancer"

Falling Back Into The Arms of God…. Stripped & Broken

ISBN-13: 978-1492715252

ISBN-10: 1492715255

Copyright 2013 Susan D. Smith

Cover Design by Susan D. Smith

Printed in the United States of America.

All rights reserved. No part of this book may be used or reproduced in any manner whatsoever without written permission except in the case of brief quotations embodied in critical articles and reviews. For information address the author, Susan D. Smith, 1169 Beckwith Rd., Fayetteville, WV 25840 or at mrssusandsmith@gmail.com.

This book may be purchased online at:

http://amazon.com and other fine book sellers.

Bookstores and churches, etc., may purchase this book at wholesale for resale or distribution.

Zechariah 13:9

⁹ And I will bring the third part through the fire, and will refine them as silver is refined, and will try them as gold is tried: they shall call on my name, and I will hear them: I will say, It is my people: and they shall say, The LORD is my God.

II Corinthians 4:17

For our light affliction, which is but for a moment, worketh for us a far more exceeding and eternal weight of glory;

Falling Back Into The Arms of God
Stripped and broken

Chorus:
Falling back into the arms of God stripped and broken
  Where he understands the pain I feel,
Falling back into the arms of God stripped and broken
  Where He wraps His comforting arms around me,
Falling back into the arms of God stripped and broken,
   Where I learn how much he cares for me...

Verse 1
Standing at the graves stripped and broken,
   Learning to worship God with tears that won't stop
   Learning to worship God when life keeps kicking me
   Learning to worship God when darkness surrounds me
   Learning to worship God...

Verse 2
Standing alone in a crowd
   Learning to worship God in the barren desert of my childless state
   Learning to worship God in the barren desert of lost love
   Learning to worship God in the barren desert of the tombs of my dreams
   Learning to worship God. . . .

Verse 3
 Standing with Jesus never alone
    Where I've learned how to Worship God in the fullness of his joy
    Where I've learned how to Worship God soaring to new heights like an eagle
    Where I've learned how to Worship God with no restrictions
    Where I've learned how to worship God....

Ending Chorus
   Falling back into the arms of God With hands lifted high
     Where I begin to understand the pain he felt,
   Falling back into the arms of God with hands lifted high,
     Where I begin to understand the comfort He has given,
   Falling back into the arms of God with hands lifted high,
     Where I begin to understand the depths of His love for me.

DEDICATION

This book is dedicated to first of all, to my God, the Lord Jesus, who is leading me each and every step of the way.

Then it is dedicated to my husband who passed away August 25, 2013 who encouraged me to follow God and was my staunchest supporter. I can still hear him saying, Go for it, Susie. You've got to obey God.

Then it's dedicated to my children Joseph Smith and Leah Simpson with her husband Evan. They taught me how to love unconditionally and continue to teach me about myself. I love all three of you and am so proud of the successful adults you have become!

Lastly this book is dedicated to the people God has blessed me with in my life of which I will try to name a few below that have obeyed God, praying with me and counseling with me. Many may never know their true impact on my life but God does and after all, that's all that really matters

    My father, Joseph M. Wine who passed away April 7, 2014

    Bishop James Kilgore who passed away February 5, 2014

    My mother, Patricia S. Wine

    Bishop & Sis. Tommy Craft

    Bro. William Mooring

    Bro. & Sister Doug Joseph

    Bro. & Sis. E.S. Harper

    Sister Beverly Haygood

    Sister Regina Horne

    Bro. & Sis. T. L. Dobbs

    Bro. John & Sis. Aurelia Hopkins

    Bro. Howard & Sis. Darlene Watson

    Linda Clark & Tammy Gallaugher (The Memories)

There are many more but these are the ones that stand out to me. Please know that I love everyone who has impacted my life and I could never thank you enough.

Table of Contents

Foreword 13

Have you Considered My Servant? 15

God lowered the hedge 61

Death is Always a Stranger 73

I Worshipped 85

The Stripping! 109

Where is God? 245

BROKEN 315

A Note from the Author 383

Just a few of the curve balls life has thrown me... 390

Foreword

I feel this is an area that is rarely covered in our movement and because it is not, many suffer under misconceptions. The Jews believed strongly that "when you do good, good things happen to you", but we know that is not really the way it is. The disciples asked the Lord "who did sin.."(the man born blind)because they felt some sin has to happen for bad things to come into a life...we know that is not true. Bad things happen to good people, but what do they do when it happens? You are addressing these issues and I think it is great. Instead of "why me" we should be asking "what does this mean".

Bro. Ron Macey
Houston, Texas

The first time I saw Susie she came to Jackson FPC, invited by a friend, to take pictures of our Ladies Tea. From that first meeting, little did we know that we would be there for her during some very difficult times in her life; one being the loss of her husband.

God has certainly worked many miracles in her life and opened doors she didn't know existed. She is a great writer and I'm confident this book will be a blessing to all who read it. Knowing Susie, I'm sure there will be many more adventures in her future.

Sister Diann Craft
Jackson, Mississippi

We will live through times in our lives when The Lord allows us to experience a breaking process. The pain that accompanies the process is acute but God has a purpose beyond our pain. Author Susan D. Wine Smith shares her personal experience in the hope that it will encourage you to keep trusting the Lord Jesus in your darkest hour.

Sis. Aurelia Hopkins
Houston, Texas

Have you Considered My Servant?

Job 1:8-9
"And the Lord said unto Satan, Hast thou considered my servant Job, that there is none like him in the earth, a perfect and an upright man, one that feareth God and escheweth evil?"

Take a step into my life before major tragedy strikes in this chapter.

May 2, 2013
Tomorrow I will be headed from Jackson, Mississippi to East Tennessee to visit my cousin Diane Wine and her mother. Then I will be headed on home. I have missed home so much.

I'm so excited a lot of big doors are opening once again. I am just waiting on phone calls to verify. Please pray that in everything I do and say I follow Jesus because all I want to do is bring glory to God. He's all that matters.

I always spend time talking to God when I drive. My car has become my secret place with Him. It is here where I spend time talking to Him and then listening. I don't know how to describe the sessions we have except to say God is so awesome and the Spirit that flows into my car is unbelievable.

May 3, 2013
God cares so much about the details of our lives. I just went with my cousin, Diane Wine here in Kingsport, Tennessee to an attic sale at her church. They had a box of brand new hose the exact brand and size I purchase. Normally they are eight dollars a pair. I bought nine pair for seven dollars and fifty cents total. Then I had wanted a red trench coat. They had the exact one I had wanted just like new. It makes me want to cry I am so thankful that He loves all of us so much to take care of the details of our lives.

I'm meeting my guys for dinner and then heading on home. How do I explain how I felt when they arrived? They are my world. My heart beats faster when I see them. I know people don't understand why I'm doing what I'm doing but this is so much bigger than me. It's something that drives me.

My husband understands. Sometimes he's the one who encourages me to keep following what God wants. When we follow God it will work out. We may not know how. We may not know when but we know our God will work it all out.

Mike, my husband, had tried to explain to me that one of our dogs, Baby might need to be put down. I didn't want to believe him. No one wants to make that decision.

Our animals are like family members to us. When I got home I saw what he meant. She could barely walk and while she looked healthy she also looked miserable. I knew we'd have to do something but I couldn't deal with that today. I need a few days to get my head around it.

Driving home it felt like my car was trying to slide even on dry roads. I mentioned it to my husband. Of course, he thought, it was just me. However, our son drove my car home and when we got there he told his dad to look at my car and explained what he had felt when driving it. Then he goes out to test drive it and tells me before we go to Morgantown he will be pulling the tires and finding the problem.

May 4, 2013
It was so nice to wake up in our home. My husband helped me unload the car so that I could unpack to repack for us. We are heading to Morgantown, West Virginia where I will be ministering in the morning at Hope Church. Yes, I'm tired but it's a good tired. How do I explain the wonderfulness I feel knowing that I'm obeying God. Are their times I wish I was able to be home more? Absolutely, but for now this is the journey I am on with God.

Wow!!!

My help truly comes from the Lord. Today Mike checked out my car because it felt like it was walking or sliding on the road. He, at first, thought I needed new back tires. Then as he looked closer he found on the left rear tire the hub nut that holds the wheel on with half the threads off the nut.

What that means to all of us who don't understand is my left rear tire could have come off and went flying down the road beside me. That could have been disastrous but you see my help truly comes from God. I am in His hands and He is taking care of me and my family!

I looked at him and said, "Do you remember in Charlotte when guys were coming on the lot during church and loosening the lug nuts on peoples cars during church what you said."

"Yes, I do. The night they did your tires and I found it the next morning I remember telling you I could see angels holding your tires on all the way home."

That's the God we serve. He takes care of us when we don't realize we need taking care of. That's falling back in the arms of God. Sometimes you know you're doing it and other times you don't. When you don't realize it and after the fact you find out about the miracle is when you realize He caught you and took care of you.

You'll never know how I felt getting in the car with my husband. I could relax. He was himself no extra medications today. He was driving and I could focus on the service tomorrow. Since he is a backslider he loves his rock music very loud. So I was armed with my phone, youtube and my ear buds.

As we drove I listened to music and prayed in my mind. Well, that didn't last for long. God swept in the car. I remember Mike reaching for my hand and holding it as I prayed. Tears flowed as I worshipped God. When I finished I looked at my love and he said, "Do you know what you were saying?"

I answered, "Not really. In my mind I was worshipping God and praying for the service tomorrow. "

He then said, "You kept repeating one phrase over and over then you would go on to something else. Do you have any idea what you could have been saying?"

I looked at him and said, "Well, when I pray I always, always tell God how much I love Him. I also always pray for you, J.T. and Leah."

He responded, "It was short so it must have been you telling the Lord you loved him."

I looked at him and said, "I know you're uncomfortable with all of this but you need to know if this continues to move forward like God has shown me then when you travel with me I will be doing a lot of praying. I have to be in tune with God. I can't just get up and minister. I want a Word from God. I want His anointing. I crave it."

He just nodded his head as I continued. "Can you handle this? Can you handle being in church a lot? If you travel with me I don't want you in a motel somewhere when it's time for church. If you're with me, I need you to be with me."

He nodded his head and said, "I don't know that I'm ready yet but I support you in this."

Upon arriving in Morgantown we checked into our hotel and then went for a dinner date. We were just enjoying being together. Then we went shopping where I got him a new suit to go with the shoes I had purchased for him on my way home. It was so nice to see him dressed up. I love my husband but he's a true redneck. He'd rather be in blue jeans with an old shirt and sneakers then all buttoned up in a suit.

Later that evening my friend Ronda Dalton and I got together. We went to the church. As we sat and talked, tears flowed and God moved in. When we get together with friends it should be to talk about the goodness of the Lord, to glorify Him. Yes, we need to have fun but sometimes we need to be sensitive to the Spirit of God that moves in. Instead of avoiding the Spirit of God we need to flow with it.

May 5, 2013
I love church. How do I explain how much I love my God? He's more than my God. He's my best friend.

When we arrived at church early I went to find Bro. Jody Dunham and his father the Bishop they showed me where to go pray until church started. I explained my husband was with me. I'll never forget the welcome they gave Mike. I could hardly believe he was with me on the road even if it was only a three hour ride from home.

There is nothing like finding a place to pray. How do I explain those moments when it's me and my God? I try but words cannot express the completeness I feel when communing with Him. He is the reason I am doing this. He is the reason I go where I go and say what I say. It's all about Him. I love Him so.

The message God gave me for this morning was "Delight myself!" I was building a foundation that God gave me and when I finish I hope you understand. No, I did not read the whole chapter of Psalms 119.

I began by reading in Psalms 119:16 where it says,
16. *"I will delight myself in thy statutes: I will not forget thy word."*
27. *"Make me to understand the way of thy precepts: so shall I talk of thy wondrous works."*

40. *"And I will walk at liberty: for I seek thy precepts: quicken me in thy righteousness."*

Then to verses 45-48; *"And I will walk at liberty: for I seek thy precepts. I will speak of thy testimonies also before kings, and will not be ashamed. I will speak of thy testimonies also before kings, and will not be ashamed. And I will delight myself in thy commandments, which I have loved. My hands also will I lift up unto thy commandments, which I have loved; and I will meditate in thy statutes."*
Now to verses 93-94; *"I will never forget thy precepts: for with them thou hast quickened me. I am thine, save me; for I have sought thy precepts."*
And to verses 97-105; *"Oh, how love I thy law! It is my meditation all the day. Thou through thy commandments hast made me wiser than mine enemies for they are ever with me. I have more understanding then all my teachers: for thy testimonies are my meditation. I understand more than ancients, because I keep thy precepts. I have refrained my feet from every evil way, that I might keep thy word. I have not departed from thy judgments: for thou hast taught me. How sweet are thy words unto my taste! Yea, sweeter than honey to my mouth! Through thy precepts I get understanding: therefore,I hate every false way. Thy word is a lamp unto my feet and a light unto my path"*.

After reading all of this I first want to give you the definition of the term precept as found on www.merriam-webster.com/dictionary it states as follows:

A command or principle intended especially as a general rule of action. An order issued by legally constituted authority to a subordinate official

What I found interesting is it gives the following as an example:
The basic *precepts* of a religion. I was taught by *precept* and by example.

Then I want to define the word statute as Merriam-Webster does below: A law enacted by the legislative branch of a government. An act of a corporation or of its founder intended as a permanent rule. An international instrument setting up an agency and regulating its scope or authority.

When you look at the scriptures I read with the understanding of the words precept and statute suddenly things became much clearer. I realized that when I read Psalms 119:16 that I should delight myself in the laws of God.

We should long after the laws of God. We shouldn't argue the principles and laws but we should seek to understand them and to follow them. Why is it so hard for us? Why do we have so much trouble with laws?

In verse 40 of Psalms 119 it tells us if we *"And I will walk at liberty: for I seek thy precepts: quicken me in thy righteousness."* Don't we want liberty? Isn't liberty freedom? Why then do we have so much trouble with this?

When we delight ourselves in God is when we seek to learn His ways. When we do this we become like Him and this is when we find freedom in Him. People look at the way, we, as, Apostolic people, live a separated life from certain things and do not understand us. All they see are rules. What they don't see is the liberty and protection God gives us as our consecration grows in Him.

You may not understand what I mean by this so let me explain. Growing up I wasn't allowed to go to certain activities and participate in certain things. What I didn't realize that back then was that by not participating in those things I was being protected. You may want to know what things. Well, I went to school, sang in a trio at church, even led song service but until my senior year never participated in school activities. You probably think that's a bit strict.

In this day and age I would agree, however, by allowing our children access to some things we have opened the door for them to be exposed to things we never would have dreamed in our wildest nightmares. Looking back, now, that my children are raised I wish there were some things I would have stood my ground and said, No, you can't but I didn't.

My generation wanted our children to be well rounded. In being well rounded we have lost many of our children. Yes, my children were involved in church activities. They knew how to pray and where the prayer rooms were.

However, by allowing these other activities I allowed exposure to sin and to attitudes that were not godly. My children and I are paying the price along with many others of my generation who thought we were doing the right thing. It was the American way that our children have more than we did. Perhaps more is not better.

I have been blessed to have been raised Apostolic. Because of the way I was raised there are some things I've never done, for example; recreational use of illegal drugs or the abuse of alcohol. Therefore, I don't fight some of the battles others fight because of the things they participated in where they had access to these things.

Now let's look at verse 46 where it talks about, "... *speaking of thy testimonies before kings, and will not be ashamed.*" Could you give your testimony before a king or kings and not be ashamed? You never know when or where God will open a door for you to share what He has done for you. What will you do should that door open for you?

In verse 48-49 it talks about "*...delight myself in thy commandments....I will meditate in thy statutes...*" How long has it been since you delighted in rules? What about spending time thinking about the Word of God? Have you ever sat and just thought about what you read in the Word? I believe God wants us to know His Word as well as some may know sports statistics of players, understanding of the stock market, the latest sales, etc. Think about it. How much time do you spend on these other activities in comparison to how much time you spend in the Word of God learning of Him?

When I think about delighting myself it usually involves Facebook, shopping or food. You see I love all of that. However, I have to be careful because I can spend more time on Facebook than I do with God. I can spend more time thinking about that big juicy T-Bone steak medium rare with mushrooms and stringed onions on top than I do meditating on His Word and with Him.

Think about that steak, the smell when it is cooking on the grill, the mushrooms cooking in butter and garlic, the onions as they are frying. Finally, it comes to the table. Your mouth is watering. You're already happy about the taste of that meal. Then when you put a piece of it in your mouth the taste buds go crazy with the explosion of the different tastes that you love.

That's delight. So what do you delight in?

You may be saying she's shallow if that's all she thinks about. No, there are many more things. However I have to have self-control. I have to limit some things in my life in order to have a closer relationship with God. What price are you willing to pay to be close to God?

Let's skip down to verse 97 and 98 where it talks about how much he loved the law of God. He loved it so much he meditated on it all day. Then he says that by doing so he is wiser than his enemies.

Wow! What a concept. Think about it, to be wiser than your enemies you spend time in the Word of God. Then in verse 99 it talks about having more understanding than all his teachers because he meditates in thy testimonies. Do we know how to share our testimonies? Do we know how to give God glory? Do we know how to explain to our children and to their children what God delivered us from?

We should give God glory every day for being alive. Every day God protects us. You may not have had any disasters or crisis in your life. If you haven't had any problems, be blessed, but for those of us who live in the real world we have challenges sometimes daily. When we face those challenges or obstacles do we know how to teach our children what to do?

Have they heard us talk about the goodness of the Lord? I love getting together with God's people and discussing what He's done for me and for them. I love hearing the stories of miracles. It increases our faith so the next time we need something from God we have the faith that it will happen.

Verse 100 thrills me because it talks about how he knew more than the ancients because he kept the precepts. He obeyed. While there are things I have not experienced in life I do feel I was protected from those things. I did do things I shouldn't have done and it is those things that haunt me.

We all have things that we did when we were younger that we wished we had left alone. If we could really get what the book of Psalms is talking about here, about loving the law, loving the Word and really love it we would be saved so much heartache and heartbreak. No, our lives would not be perfect but because we obeyed God there would be many battles we would not have to fight.

In verse 101 it talks about refraining my feet from every evil way. Have you turned away from all sin? When you do you keep His Word. It's pretty simple. When we spend time in His word as verse 102 tells us is when we find Him teaching us. The

Word is His mind. Therefore, spending time in it is when we are allowing Him to teach us.

The Word of God is described in verse 103 as sweeter than honey. Do you see it that way? If not, why?

Verse 104 talks about hating every false way because they received understanding from God's precepts. Do you hate sin? Do you know what sin is? In our day and age when it seems like everything is moral do we even know what immorality is? Could we stand up and say certain things are wrong no matter the consequences because we love the Word of God that deeply?

We always love to quote Psalms 119:105 where it talks about the Word being a lamp unto my feet and a light unto my path but what about all those other verses I just went over. In order for the Word to be the lamp for us we need to know the Word.

So, do you know the Word? Have you spent time in your Bible lately?

Everybody wants God to catch them when they have a crisis but when you put other things before your relationship with Him and I'm just as guilty as the rest, sometimes I wonder. There is no doubt God will catch us. But if we had a son or daughter who put no effort into a relationship with us would we catch them when they fall?

Of course, we would catch them. However, it would not have the same closeness of safety because of the lack of a close relationship. It's important to do whatever it takes to build that relationship with God.
******

After church we went out to eat with the Donham's. We had a great time visiting. Bro. Jody Donham looked at me across the table and said, "Sister Susan I need to tell you something God wants you to know. When you learn to accept miracles for others the way you have accepted miracles for yourself is when your ministry will go to a new level."

I felt chill bumps when he said that. Do I know how to do that? No, but I know how to learn. It requires time on my knees and time in the Word of God. This means I will have to pull myself away from things I enjoy doing to learn at the feet of Jesus.

May 6, 2013
Today I have more blood work. Thanks to my wonderful medical history every three months I have the privilege of letting some poor unsuspecting nurse try to get blood from my veins. This is quite the process but thankfully at my doctor's office when I show up they know what to do so usually it's two sticks and they've got it.

Sometimes I'm really blessed and they get a vein the first time. Once you've had a major illness you become a hard stick. It's just something else to make life more interesting. Then tomorrow I have an appointment to see the doctor to get the results.

I spoke tonight at the Fayette County Cancer Support Group in Oak Hill, West Virginia. If you need a volunteer outreach outlet cancer support groups are in need of volunteers and the American Cancer Society is always looking for help.

May 7, 2013
Have you stood on Holy Ground yet this morning?

Morning devotions are so important to the mood of your day. I know even when the kids were little I would always try to squeeze in a few minutes for just me and God. It doesn't have to be a lot but just powerful. Then as you do it more and more you will get up earlier to give more time to spend with Him in the early morning hours before everything gets to going so fast you simply forget the one who gave His all so that you could have all.

Everything turned out great at my doctor's appointment. I don't worry as much as I used to when waiting on those results from the blood work but until I hear the all clear I hold my breath. To someone in remission from cancer bad CEA markers or high liver enzymes usually mean the cancer is no longer in remission. I am so blessed that in my body and blood there is no evidence of cancer. I had one nurse tell me that my blood work should not be as good as it is with everything I have been through.

When God catches us in His arms He takes care of those pesky little problems with our body.

May 8, 2013
This morning I'm headed to Dallas, Texas. It's only for a couple of days. God is so amazing and keeps moving and changing my world. I'm so blessed with so many friends. Thanks to all of you and thank you for all of your prayers. Without prayer there is no way this would be happening. That's the God we serve.

Below is an instant message conversation I had with a friend who needed some help. Her remarks are italicized so you'll know whether it is me or her talking. By the way I don't use anything like this without the consent of the other person.

You have something for a sister who can't sleep because she's struggling with something?

Sure do. It's something God gave me on the airplane. Give me just a minute.

"Trusting in the Lord"
Proverbs 3:5-6, "Trust in the Lord with all thine heart; and lean not unto thine own understanding. In all thy ways acknowledge Him and He shall direct thy paths."

Here's the rest. Hang on for the ride. I'm not sure if this is exactly what you need but God gave it to me for someone and you may be that someone.

You hit it right on the head!!!

These are the thoughts God gave me today on the plane. This is one of the hardest things to do yet one of the most important in your life. Trusting Jesus is all that really matters. Attaining of goals, accolades from peers is not where true happiness lies.

I'm glad I hope the rest of the thoughts God gave me help also. Here we go.

I feel like EVERYONE has direction/purpose and I'm standing in the middle and I don't know/ feel like I fit in?

I understand God gave me something about that today also that may help you.

When you give God credit for the things you think you have provided is where you will find a direction for your life that has been lacking. You see no matter what we think we can do it is nothing compared to what He can and will do for you and your family but it all goes back to trusting Jesus.

When you learn how to trust Him He will order your steps in such a way that you will stand in awe and amazement at how He will pull things together that prior to this you had only dreamed of. I know what you mean by not feeling like you fit in. For years I felt out of place.

I get scared sometimes because I feel we are at a standstill and I DON'T want to go backwards!

Proverbs 37:23-25, "The steps of a good man are ordered by the Lord: and he delighteth in His way. Though he fall he shall not be utterly cast down: for the Lord upholdeth him with his hand. I have been young and am now old; yet have I not seen the righteous forsaken, nor his seed begging bread."

My husband has a calling/ but until that's fulfilled- I feel like I'm in the shadows of everything! Make sense?

I know what you mean about going backwards. That's just a lie from the devil. Consistently move forward. Know God, make sure your god is God (JESUS). Sometimes we get so wrapped up in every day issues, responsibilities that we neglect to take the time to spend with God. Doing so makes other things become god to us. Our God is a jealous God. He wants A-L-L of us.

I understand that also. There is nothing you can do about your husband's calling until he makes up his mind and seeks the counsel to go forward. You are not in the shadows. Your prayers can make the difference and support your husband in a different way. When he sees you change it will encourage him to change.

He was doing so good... Now LIFE has kept him so busy and I get scared. He ran for years and they were not pretty!!!

I know you have a walk with God but God could be calling you to a deeper walk with Him. More prayer, more Bible reading, etc. When you give more time to God that's when those changes will happen. A year and a half ago I decided to make a change.

You just have to start somewhere. Maybe you're awake tonight because God wants to hear your voice.

I'm sitting here with the Bible on my lap- but feel so lost?!
I'm reading- been getting up in the middle of night praying- and today- this spirit of confusion/ doubt/ worry/ fear/ hit me and I've fought it all day and evening!

That spirit is of the devil. You're making him run like a scared rabbit because you've been obeying God and spending time with God. Don't let the devil do that to you! I'm talking to you like I have been one of my close friends. The devil knows how powerful you will be if you are able to get so focused on God that there are no obstructions between you and God. So keep praying. I'm agreeing with you in Jesus name that the spirit the devil has been attacking you with will leave in Jesus name!

Since I've started on this journey sometimes the devil attacks me in much the same way. I'll lay on the floor in travail and put both hands over my mind and plead the blood of Jesus over my mind. I refuse to let the devil have one more day of any type of control over what I do. It's all about God and what He wants!

I heard one man who called people out in Texas in a service I was blessed to be in say these words and I'll never forget them, "If you ever get ahold of the power of God that is within you, then you will be so dangerous for God there will be no stopping you!"

Tonight in church/ oh my!!! When we were praying I put my hand on my forehead and was praying for myself- but I never felt such a resistance!!! I know I'm up against something- so I'm pushing forward- just not sure of myself!

Keep pushing, don't give up! Don't ever give up! The night is always darkest right before the dawn and the fiercest battle right before the victory. Victory is just around the corner. Believe it, act on it and be free from this in Jesus name!

Sorry if I went on but I really feel this and I know exactly where you are when it comes to what you are feeling. I battle this occasionally but I have learned how to fight it and the devil has been shifting tactics on me. He will do whatever is necessary to distract me from my true purpose. We have to learn how to pray for our minds and plead the blood over ourselves.

I sooo will!!! Gods will is my desire!

Speak positive, pray lots, read the Word when it gets really bad and you can't seem to pray. The Word will stop the devil in his tracks. Read the promises of God to him. Remind the devil where he will spend eternity. You won't be there but he will.

I know you will be fine. Don't let the devil hoodwink you into thinking you don't have it what it takes because you do. Sorry I'm really mad at the devil right now so I'm on a roll.

I guess he side tracks me because there are others who are pursuing the same thing- and they are being used/ blessed/ and are going at it head strong!

Too many times we let the devil have a victory that wasn't his to begin with, it was ours all along. As I've ministered recently even to cancer support groups that we've got to get back to the basics. Prayer, fasting, reading the Bible then God will... God just will.

There will always be someone who is doing it better, faster, with more blessings. The Bible says not to compare ourselves. That's where we get into trouble. Don't compare yourself with anyone.

I'm soo glad u were up!! Lol You have been a great help/ blessing!! Thank you!!

We are all on different time frames. I'm glad I was up also. Sorry I got on a roll but I hate this tactic the devil uses on us. It's the same tactic on most everyone and we fall for it, hook, line and sinker. It's high time we put the devil in his place.

Your welcome, love you and good night. I hope I was helpful and not just rambling.....I had to take some medication tonight where they are doing all this dental work and I probably should be in bed but all the pain is finally gone and I just want to enjoy feeling no pain for a little while.. LOL.

I'm glad you got on a roll!!! I got to get used to fighting him/ not letting him beet me down! Like today!!! Need to learn to stand my ground!! And rebuke all doubt/ fear and discouragement!!! Have a great- pain free sleep! Love and appreciate you!!!

I don't know if this is what someone with more experience would have told my friend but it's what I felt God wanted me to share with her. We have to learn to trust ourselves when it comes to what God tells us to share with others.

May 9, 2013
What a great day in Dallas, Texas! It's going to be a great night. You see God is so good He gives us blessings of things He knew we wanted to do but we couldn't figure out how to make it happen. Our God loves us so much!

After we got back to the house I had some time so as I was reading in the book of Proverbs and stumbled across these jewels of wisdom in chapter 15 verse 16. *"Better is little with the fear of the Lord than great treasure and trouble therewith."*

This is so true. I'd rather have little with the fear of the Lord than to have the wealth of this world.

May 10, 2013
I fly home from Dallas this afternoon. I'll lunch here, dinner in Charlotte and a midnight snack in West Virginia. I am so thankful for the nice man that gave me his luggage cart to lug my stuff to the gate at Dallas-Fort Worth International Airport. God knows what we would like and sometimes supplies those needs through total strangers.

Usually flying into Charleston, West Virginia on late flights I get to spend the night in whatever city my connection is through. I was shocked tonight when in Charlotte, North Carolina my flight was not cancelled. Woohoo, I'll sleep in my bed tonight!

May 11, 2013
I've unpacked and tomorrow will repack to head to my mother's for Mother's day. In the morning I will be blessed to see one of the daughters of my heart, Katie Underwood. I love her so and am so excited to see her.

I have a turkey roasting in the oven. The washing machine is churning. I'm writing while I'm waiting on my Katie to get here. Today is a magnificent day in which to worship the one who created all, the one who blessed us with our families, and who gives us each day to do with what we will. Let's make today a good day for the Lord!

While I'm waiting, reading in my Bible and writing I came across Proverbs 16:31-32 *"The hoary head is a crown of glory, if it be found in the way of righteousness. He that is slow to anger is better than the mighty; and he that ruleth his spirit than he that taketh a city."*

I'm going to open up here and let everyone know I think my grey hair just makes me look old. There, I said it. However, my Bible tells me it is a crown of glory. I've had people say that to me but I just can't see it. So I have to reprogram myself and repent. If grey hair is a glory to God why do I dislike it? You see we've been programmed that to look young is beautiful. Grey hair does not look young to me. But as one great woman of God told me, "You've earned every one of those grey hairs and the wisdom that comes with it."

On this journey I'm on with God He keeps shining spotlights on areas I'd rather He left alone but if I'm going to change and really be what He wants me to be I have to change in every area He spotlights. Even when it is something we would consider insignificant because to Him it's not insignificant.

Then the next part of this verse is to be slow to anger. I've not had a problem with that. It takes me a long time to get upset. As my family has told me when I get quiet is when they worry because they know I'm simmering and there will eventually be an explosion. However, in the next part of that verse it says if we rule our spirit we are better than the mighty.

We need to learn how to have self-control. When we learn this we will see changes in our walk with God. Self-control in one area will bleed over into other areas of our lives. Not only will we control our spirit, we will be able to take ourselves to pray, to read the Word. It's so important we understand why we need self-control. When you control your emotions you usually think things through. You also have control of your tongue most of the time. You're not one who gets into trouble easily.

May 12, 2013
It is Mother's Day and I'm blessed to be with my mother and my son. Looking out over the mountains I can understand that scripture in Psalms 121:1 where it says; *"I will lift up mine eyes unto the hills, from whence cometh my help. My help cometh from the Lord, which made heaven and earth."*

My mom, Pam, myself, Sherry, and Sis.Ruby

My Son & I

We're headed to Clarksburg, WV to fellowship with dear friends. My guys are with me and will be with me in church tonight. I'm so blessed!!! I am so enjoying being driven and having my son and my husband with me and carrying the bags. I can't wait until God works it out where my love is with me on the road full time.

So thankful to be home! Even when I'm only home for a couple of days there is nothing like being in your own home. While I am happy to be home ever present with me is the calling of work to do for God. I can't get too comfortable because there is too much to do for our Lord and Savior. I love Him so much!

May 13, 2013
Today was a hard day for us. We had to take our oldest dog to the vet to be put down. Her name is Baby and she has been with our family for about thirteen years. I do realize this is the cycle of life but it still hurts even if it is a pet. She has been a family member and helped comfort me during my battle with pancreatic cancer.

May 14, 2013
I am still remembering Baby. This morning when setting out their food I automatically set out three bowls and then had to correct it with tears running down my face. I know she's in a far better place in no pain but it still hurts. She was always smiling at us.

God is still opening doors. The Pancreatic Cancer Action Network just called me and now we're working together to figure out what I can do to help them. God is so great and greatly to be praised!!! To God be the Glory!!!

Monday afternoon I'll be back in the chair where he told me he would be doing 17 fillings that afternoon. Like I've said before I have this phobia about dentists but my dentist in New Orleans is one of the best and the kindest I've ever met.

Here are a couple of the senior pictures I was able to take of my son before he got tired and said, "ENOUGH!"

May 16, 2013
Proverbs 17:22-23
"Bow down thine ear, and hear the words of the wise, and apply thine heart unto my knowledge. For it is a pleasant thing if thou keep them within thee; they shall withal be fitted in thy lips. That thy trust may be in the Lord, I have made known to thee this day,even to thee. Have I not written to thee excellent things in counsels and knowledge, That I might make thee know the certainty of the words of truth; that thou mightest answer the words of truth to them that send unto thee? Rob not the poor, because he is poor: neither oppress the afflicted in the gate: For the Lord will plead their cause, and spoil the soul of those that spoiled them."

This passage spoke to me in a new way. It made me think that I need to continue to seek the counsel and wisdom of my elders. Most importantly I must go to my knees and into the Word of God to find direction. I need to be certain in my beliefs. I need to know for myself the Jesus I believe in and understand the laws of God for me. So many of us accept everything we are told. We don't have a personal relationship with our God.

The Bible is the mind and thoughts of God. If you never read it how will you know for yourself what is in it. It holds so many secrets and promises in it that God wants to

reveal to each one of us but we have to take time to spend with God reading His Word and praying. It's time for us to give God the two hours and forty minutes we owe him every day in tithing of our time. You say that's extreme. Well, Jesus was extreme for me shouldn't I be extreme for Him?
******

May 17, 2013
Memories!

After taking my son's senior pictures a mother doesn't see a young man. She remembers the day she found out she was expecting a bundle of joy that has turned into this young man. Then in her mind she remembers growing bulky when he was growing inside of her. Then she remembers when they placed him in her arms. The joy and the happiness she felt.

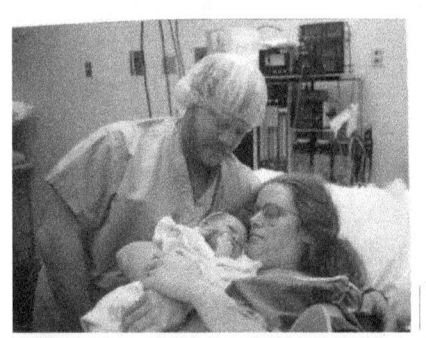

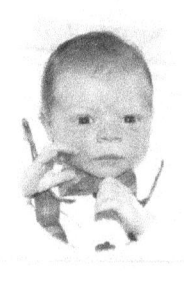

With J.T. moments after his birth.   His newborn picture.

Dedication Feb 1994   Easter 2002   Fall 2003

He was Mr. Personality as a baby, and a child and still is as a young man. It's just hard for a mom to realize her last baby is now a grown man. I'm trying to figure out how to reconcile in my mind the young adult man he has become with my memories. I know he doesn't get why mom is struggling to hang onto her emotions but I see him as this baby boy in my arms. It seems like just yesterday but it's been over nineteen years ago.

May 18, 2013
In watching families interact I'm learning a lot about those who have to figure out how to navigate the waters of split parenting. Some things make you shake your head in bewilderment while others make you grieve for friends who deal with things that God never intended for us to deal with and children that misunderstand motives.
****

So many people get so focused on what might happen they never try. So take a leap if God has told you to do something. The worst that can happen is you fail but the best that can happen is that you will succeed. You'll never know if you don't take that chance with God. So go for it!

May 19, 2013
What an amazing service. God moved in such a mighty way. Pick yourself up, dust yourself off and be persistent. You may be knocked down but you're not knocked out. Stand up and worship!

Remember no matter how you feel about what you're going through, "You are not forgotten".

May 20, 2013
On the road again...just crossed the state line to Louisiana. I have more dental work in New Orleans this afternoon. He said between ten to twenty fillings today so please pray for your friend (thats me) with the dental phobia. LOL

I am so thankful for the medications he gives me to relax me since I'm such a chicken about these things. I'm also very thankful for the prayers. Keep them going up I will be in the chair for two to three hours.

May 21, 2013
Sis. Ladonna Townsend, her daughter, London and I are on the road. We are going to have an awesome time doing some shopping and with me going to the dentist. I can't believe I'm excited to go to the dentist. God is continuing to complete the miracle of my teeth.

May 23, 2013
Of course, me being, the clumsy person that I am had to go and fall down when we were crossing the street. Oh, did it ever hurt…. But I lived. God will keep me humble with my own clumsiness….LOL

May 22, 2013
Today I'm running an errand then a meeting and finally I will be on the road headed towards home stopping in East Tennessee tonight to visit with my cousin Diane Wine getting home sometime tomorrow. Oh, how I will miss being in Jackson but I'm so excited about being home and the doors God is opening for me to work for Him. I love Him so much!

So, whatever is going on in my body forced me to stop and get a room in Athens, Tennessee. I'll continue my trek towards home tomorrow but for now lights out…. Thanking God for a safe journey thus far.

May 23, 2013
Today, I will make it home. I was so tired last night I came in here and went to bed and am just now getting up. Sometimes sleep is truly the best medicine. I'll make

tracks to my cousins in East Tennessee and take a break then drive the rest of the way home today. I can't wait to be home with my guys.

Almost to WV sitting in traffic on the Virginia side of the mountain. So close but so far. Finally, home but I am in cold Fayetteville, West Virginia where it is only 63 degrees....brrrrr. I am missing the warm southern weather.

May 24, 2013
Only in the forties here this morning so when rushing to the doctor I pulled out a lined trench coat to wear. Brrrrr..so cold. I have a headache probably due to fasting for blood work and whatever is going on in my body. In Jesus name it will be simple and simply fixed.

May 25, 2013
So after going to the doctor today being poked and prodded I spent the rest of the day in bed. My fasting blood sugar was normal. Praise God but they went ahead and ran more in depth blood work. I just want to be me again. I know God's got this. I'm in His hands I just have to trust Him to provide my needs because He just simply will. He loves us. In the meantime tonight I'm headed out to see some dear friends children honored at their private school and take pictures. I am so very blessed to serve the King of Kings and the Lord of Lords!

Falling back into the arms of God is also about letting my children go. Our children have to make their own mistakes to grown into the overcomers we want them to be. We cannot protect them from everything. Yes, they will make decisions we won't agree with sometimes but that is when, as parents, we go to our knees and travail for our children. I love my children more than anything and always will no matter where they go or what they do.

Our children have to have a revelation of this gospel for themselves. This is why so many are choosing to not stay with this gospel. They haven't found Jesus for themselves. Every single one of us has to have an encounter with Jesus Christ.

May 26, 2013
On the road again but I'll be home later tonight. Praying everyone has a blessed and safe Memorial Day weekend. Remember those who are grieving and remembering

their loved ones today. Find a place to worship God today! It will be the best thing you've ever done!

May 27, 2013
We are so proud of our son. This picture was taken last May on our back porch. He was in JROTC Army at the time. He has since joined the Air Force and his enlistment date is July 1. I am so thankful for all those who have chosen to join the military to protect our freedoms that I pray continue

What a wonderfully lazy day we have had just being together. Sometimes it's nice to just relax and be....Now to snack again.... I am loving being home with my family.

May 28, 2013
I so enjoy my morning devotion time with God. Some mornings it is long and some mornings God wakes me up with a song and a burden for someone but whatever it is

spending that first bit of time with God in the morning before the busyness of the day takes over is so important. Even if you can only start out with five minutes that five minutes will change your life when you give it to God and focus completely on Him.

It is so hard to believe J.T. graduates Friday from High School and then the Air Force. I think I might need a few boxes of kleenex at his graduation. I will miss him so much!

May 30, 2013
It is a beautiful Thursday. I'm up making blueberry muffins for J.T. as he gets ready to go practice walking for graduation this morning. Then we'll be shampooing the carpets in the house. I'm aching in places I didn't know I could ache but we're only halfway done. Stopping to rest for a little while and making lunch... my semi-homemade spaghetti so thankful for Ragu and Newman's spaghetti sauces...

What an amazing service tonight! I am so awed by the presence of God. He knows.... He just knows and He provides... I pray I'll never cease to be awed by what God does and how God allows me to be a servant to Him. I so love serving Him.

May 31, 2013
Today is graduation day for our baby. We only had two children so when he leaves for the Air Force we will officially be empty nesters. How do I wrap my mind around this?

In my mind he's still a little boy yet he's old enough to graduate from high school and choose to serve His country to protect us. I love Him so and am so proud of Him and excited for the future He is about to embark on! Sometimes it's hard to remember this but no matter what comes our way, God's got this!

I think we need reminded of this almost daily. Life has a way of challenging what we know we heard God say. So remember, He knows the plans He has for us!

He didn't want any senior pictures so the fact I've gotten two sets out of him is amazing. He's never too old to get a kiss from mom in a public place... LOL

June 1-2 2013
A lazy Saturday after graduation. So many emotions but oh, so happy overall. I'm making plans for the future... can't wait... exciting things happening!
So proud of our graduate! J.T. Smith! We've had a great weekend visiting with our daughter and celebrating our son's graduation. It was great to have Leah home if only for a day. They went to my parent's last night to spend some time with them. I know they're having a blast. I'm glad we raised two children who love each other and their grandparents.

June 3-4 2013
I'm on my way to a cancer support group meeting tonight. God is so good to me. Pray for our children they are on their way from their grandparent's home in northern WV to Lexington, KY where our daughter Leah lives. Home from the meeting and just heard from the kids. Everyone will be all safe for tonight in Jesus name.

Sometimes this is so very hard to do but so very important. No matter what is going on in our life we must bless the Lord at all times. God is good all the time and all the time God is good no matter what is going on personally with us.

As my husband continues to battle with his addiction to prescription medication some days I get very frustrated because I want the man back I married. Anyone that is addicted to medications legal or illegal is a very sick person. That is not an excuse for using these drugs irresponsibly. It goes back to never having been taught how to have self-control.

In our country we try to give our children everything. We don't like to say no. No needs to be said. Everyone should know how to be in control of their own lives. People who never learned those lessons will have trouble their entire lives.

Why?

I'll tell you why. The lack of self-control exhibits itself in every part of a person's life. This includes church, work, family life, and everything they do.

June 5-7, 2013
Friday, June 14th I will be participating in the Fayette County, West Virginia Relay for Life. The day after this event I will be on my way to Washington, D.C. where I will be representing the Pancreatic Cancer Action Network by speaking to members of congress on funding for cancer research. Cancer affects one in three people.

We must work while it is day for the night cometh when no man can work (paraphrased KJV John 9:4).Someone reminded me of this just the other night. For some reason someone must need to be reminded tonight. No matter the need, small or great, our God provides!

We should all stand up for what we believe in. It's time we quit letting the liberals walk all over us. We need more people to stand for something instead of falling for everything!

I received my first package from the Pancreatic Cancer Action Network to help start to prepare me for my meetings in Washington, D.C. with Congress about Pancreatic Cancer. You see, our God wants to bless us. Sometimes we have to stretch ourselves to do things for God. It is usually things we, in our minds, could never see ourselves doing but our God knows and our God will lead us each and every step of the way.

June 9, 2013
Below is a facebook post from recent news about the Boy Scouts and Girl Scouts in allowing people who are gay be in leadership of troops. A lot of our churches have troops meeting on their property, however, with this recent ruling should someone we know want to lead a troop that lives a lifestyle our Bible teaches against we will be forced into allowing them to lead impressionable children. You may not see any harm in this but doing so will continue the desensitization of our children into acceptance of these lifestyles.

Just because we love everyone and believe God can save them does not mean we want our children to be influenced by them.

So if my children were the right ages for Boy Scouts and Girl Scouts with all the recent changes I would have to take them out in order for them to not be taught that the things my Bible teaches are sin are ok now. If you're children are involved in these groups you need to research the recent changes, pray and make decisions according to the facts as they are coming out. It looks like we won't have a choice. We will have to make a stand for our beliefs, can you? Do you have enough of God in you to stand for what is right? Do you and your God (if God is your God) have enough of a daily prayer relationship for you to have the power to stand no matter what?

Below is a response I received from a friend of mine with a different viewpoint:
One of the most hurtful labels ever had been "those people." I've always had a sensitivity towards those who are shunned because of how it has been like to be treated that way for any reason. To me there's no love involved.

Try to think of it this way: how does it feel to be treated differently and excluded? Remember when several parents in our community wouldn't support school consolidation, because then we'd be around Those People from Kingwood? Parents in other towns didn't seem that thrilled overall to have Those People from Fellowsville (us) around them. Yet you see what happened after being together and seeing how much the same we all were; lots of priceless friendships made, many of which endure to this day.

Back in the days of our parents and their parents, there were certain groups at different times identified as Those People, to be kept separate and treated with coldness. Many of those same parents and grandparents may very well have been

Those People to someone else.

There's a couple I know on here, thru my friendship with another, that I absolutely admire for their commitment & how much devotion they have for each other. They were recently permitted to be married, and I couldn't be happier for them. Their being together doesn't threaten me; if anything, it's made me reflect on how I wish I had stood beside others in my life as faithfully, and all of the things I can learn from them.

The world's a big place. The more we encounter people different in any way, the more we see one another as individuals, all children of God, valued in His sight.

How does the verse go, that we should be in the world but not of it? If someone doesn't share your beliefs, to me it's a strength and faith in God that calls us to be their neighbors and friends.

I'm afraid that if we all don't follow the greatest commandment - love one another as God loves us - then we may be part of the goats rather than the sheep ... the worst Those People I can imagine.

As always I respect how you feel, of course

The reason I am sharing what I posted and the response is that we need to understand how our family, friends and neighbors feel regarding changes we are seeing morally that sicken us and go against the Bible. However, we, along with our family, friends and neighbors are being desensitized to homosexuality and promiscuous sins.

Below is my response to my friend's response:

I've been treated differently my whole life and was called one of those Pentecostal people. In school as I'm sure many will recall I was teased because of the way I didn't dress and the things I didn't participate in. Now, this is a choice I have made. Should I not have a choice about what I or my family decides to do because of the liberal agenda? This is America where we still have the freedom of religion.

I do agree the world is a big place and that "we should be in the world but not of the world". I love everyone. However, I can love them and hate their sin. When it comes to the decisions made recently by the leaders of the Boy Scouts and Girl Scouts I am so glad my children are no longer small enough for me to have to explain why I would not be allowing them to participate with those groups. You may see me as small minded but I see myself as Bible minded and Christ like.

You see, I don't have to accept the choice others are making for their lives. I don't hate them for those choices, I pray for them. However, the choices they make are not my choices. I should not be required to say it's okay if I don't feel that way. I do agree that we should love everyone and be their neighbors and friends. That doesn't mean we knowingly go along with the choices they have made for their lifestyles that are not Biblical.

The Bible is very clear on what sin is and what it is not. It is not my words but God's. I am not one to hate people but I do hate sin. Yes, I do make mistakes and find myself on my knees asking for forgiveness for my sins. I am not anyone's judge but in "being in this world and not of this world", I have to make sure that I do not go against the Word of God.

This is so much more than agreeing or disagreeing with someone's lifestyle choices. I could go into specifics but that's not necessary. What is necessary is that Christians are informed of what groups are teaching their children so they make informed decisions. That has always been a pet peeve of mine is that people don't check things out thoroughly before making decisions. Therefore, as I see articles I then research before I post to make sure that what is being presented is what has happened.

I am afraid for our country. Most have turned away from God and that scares me. It doesn't scare me for me but for my friends, neighbors and those that have made those lifestyle choices. You see, someday, somewhere, we will all answer to God. Yes, He is a God of mercy and love but there is so much more to Him than that. That's the biggest mistake, we, in this country, have made we have neglected reading our Bible and getting to know God. We have allowed so many other things to become god to us. We have let the media program us so that most now see nothing wrong with things that just ten years ago would have turned our stomachs.

So, I said all that to say this. I am glad we live in America where you and I can have differing opinions while not being afraid of putting our thoughts online for all to see. I respect your opinion and I do love everyone I just refuse to accept everything. I will pray for them but I will not condone their lifestyle choices even for those that are in my own family.
****

I don't know if I responded correctly but having re-read my original post and my response I am comfortable with what I wrote and how I presented it. At this time in America we still have freedom of speech but that right is quickly being eroded away by what is now called "hate" speech. If we have the nerve to believe the Bible we are "extremists" and "combatant".

In thinking about the title to this book, "Falling Back in the Arms of God", I have a feeling that we are going to find out just what that means when we have to stand for what we believe and face legal persecution. Do you and I have what it takes to make that stand? Can we stand like the prophets of old before Kings and declare the words of God? Or will we fold under pressure?

If we stand like the prophets of old we will find our God will catch us when we have nothing but our trust in Him. He will not leave us. The outcomes may not be what we expect but God will be with us through it all.

June 10-13, 2013
I'm up and moving but still weak as a kitten. So glad I'm over this bug. My love has been amazing going and getting me anything and everything I mentioned I might be able to eat. Now that I'm feeling better he's gone to Bob Evans for soup and a salad so I can start feeling better.

The storm is here and has been going on for a few hours now. So far lots and lots of hard rain The wind isn't near us yet and we still have electricity and internet. So thankful to God for the things I still have. Just a couple of miles from us the electricity is out so praying we keep ours. So far no trees down and no debris. Thank you Jesus! I am praying for those I am seeing reporting damage that there are no injuries.

The storm appears to be over. Thank God it didn't become a land hurricane like the one last summer. Our power only blinked off a couple of times.

June 14, 2013
It is time to start packing to head for Washington tomorrow. While I won't participate in Purple Strides tonight I am attending the Fayette County Relay for Life with the American Cancer Society. Monday I will be in a conference with meetings. Tuesday I will be meeting with Congress. So excited to see what I can to do help cancer research funding.

Well, this afternoon I tried on my purple suit because that's what the Pancreatic Cancer Action Network wants everyone to wear (the color Purple) when we meet with Congressmen. I've lost so much weight it just hangs on me but I'll still wear it and just leave the jacket open so they can't tell how much it needs to be taken in. I guess it's time to be skinny again... LOL... or at least not so fluffy.

June 15-18, 2013
We had a nice dinner two blocks from the White House with my friend Michelle. She is so sweet to offer for me to stay with her in her condo. What a lovely home she has.

Today is all about learning what I will be doing tomorrow on Capitol Hill. I'm so excited to do something that will affect change! There is something every one of us can do to help change our world. My question to you is what are you doing?

I'm up and getting ready to head to the Capital. I have five meetings today not counting the session at the hotel that starts at 7 a.m. This will definitely be interesting. Thanking God for this opportunity. When I get home I will post pictures but that will be late tomorrow. I am having such fun catching the subway for my morning commute to downtown Washington D.C. to meet with members of Congress, staff, and The Pancreatic Cancer Action Network.

Two meetings down... four to go and some official photographs. Tonight I will have dinner with Dawn Bolyard and Eilly

June 19-20, 2013
On the road again... I do believe that is my theme song...lol
I had so much fun and feel like much was accomplished while I was in Washington but now I am paying the piper. I am so stiff and sore from all the walking on concrete that I am resting tonight .

When our minds are stayed on Jesus then will we have perfect peace because we trust Him.

Isaiah 26:1-4
In that day shall this song be sung in the land of Judah; We have a strong city; salvation will God appoint for walls and bulwarks.² Open ye the gates, that the righteous nation which keepeth the truth may enter in.³ Thou wilt keep him in perfect

> *peace, whose mind is stayed on thee: because he trusteth in thee.*⁴ *Trust ye in the* Lord *for ever: for in the* Lord Jehovah *is everlasting strength:*

And when we trust in the Lord, in the Lord is everlasting strength. What a wonderful God we serve!

June 21-24, 2013
Next week I will be at my thirtieth class reunion. When did I get old? Wait, I'm not old in my mind only in years... LOL

Here are a couple of facts about pancreatic cancer that everyone should know:

1. Less than 6% of all people diagnosed with pancreatic cancer live five years or more.
2. By the year 2020 Pancreatic Cancer will be the second leading cause of death by cancer.
3. In West Virginia over 1,100 new cases of Pancreatic Cancer will be diagnosed this year.
4. One in three people will be diagnosed with cancer.

So when you see someone battling cancer realize that if it hasn't touched you personally yet more than likely it soon will. Please Be patient, be gentle, and loving to them.

June 28, 2013
Vacation Bible School is a ministry. It is why we do what we do. We want to see others find Jesus and a relationship with Him. This week we have touched 123 children, many of which do not attend the church. The teen class had over twenty visitors overall, that's an additional twenty families touched. Then this night nineteen of the children received the precious gift of the Holy Ghost, evidenced by speaking in other tongues. God just moved in and the kids kept praying and God kept moving. That's the God we serve. They're hungry but where are the laborers? Who will feed them?

Remember this... such wise wonderful words from the book of Proverbs.
   "A person may plan his own journey but the Lord directs his steps." Proverbs 16:9

June 29, 2013
It's been so busy but now I'm up, moving and trying to get motivated. I need to pack, and get ready to drive to my folks. Tonight is my thirtieth class year reunion. Then tomorrow I am ministering. God is good. I am so very blessed.

I've just got a few more things to throw in the suitcase and then I'm on the road again. It's been so nice being home but this is not what God has for me right now. I will be back late Sunday to turn around and leave on Tuesday. It's so exciting to see what God is doing in the lives of people across our great nation!

I'm back at my parent's from my thirtieth class reunion. Wow! Where did the years go. I was not the only one half afraid to go in but what a great time we had. Thanks to all those involved in making this reunion a success.

When I went in I was so surprised that the folks I went to High School stood and clapped as I walked in. We may not know the effect we are having by what we post on social media but this night I found out. One gentleman I went to school with said, "Susan is the class of 1983's bona fide miracle." Then another person spoke up and said, "Thank you for reminding us every day that there is a God on facebook." Then another person said, "I remember you carrying your Bible to school every day. You didn't say anything you just carried it on top of your books like it was a prized possession."

I didn't know how to react I was in shock. I don't think I'm doing anything for God. I really don't. I'm just fumbling along trying to follow God. Some days I feel like I'm making headway and other days I feel like I'm doing more harm than good. Most of us feel that way but if we never make a start we'll never make a difference. It's time we start making a difference!

Our social media pages should reflect our walk with God!

June 30, 2013
Thanking God for WV courtesy patrol. I had a flat on my way home. I don't know what God is getting ready to do but it must be amazing because the devil is pulling out all the stops with everything that has been happening to me.

You should have seen me chasing the spare tire down the hill into a muddy ravine. Now there's a picture for you. Then when I called my husband he couldn't come because our son's car was broke down and he needed to get him from work. Let's just say I was a 'little' frustrated. I actually needed to pray through I was so angry at the situation. After it was over is when I laughed. I wasn't doing much laughing when I was chasing that tire, though….

And then I almost lost my flip flops in the mud... Actually I pulled one foot out and had to reach down in the mud to get the flip flop. Then my hair fell in my face and I reached up to move my hair. Instant mud makeup on my face that I didn't realize was there. Can you imagine?

I am so glad to finally be home.... My God has got this! I can't wait to see what God is getting ready to do.

I'm so excited I just can't wait for her to post this. God is continuing to work amazing miracles.

Sis. Diana Villarreal from Laredo, Texas just posted the following!
We had a healing service in February, Sister Smith preached that Sunday morning. At the end of the service we prayed for about 150 church attendees. We prayed for my cousin from Los Angeles by proxy. She had been diagnosed with uterus cancer in September and was at Stage 4. But, my GOD healed her completely by that week. I called my older cousin telling her that we were going to visit Cindy and she gave me the news, that her sister had gotten a blood work report and the doctor was in awe. Her enzymes in her liver had decreased from a 400 number to an 8. The doctor said it was a miracle !!!! Since then her tumors have shrunk and some have disappeared!!!! Praise The Lord!!!!!

July 1, 2013
I'm amazed! My husband and I got our HAM radio operator license years ago. He was just in here talking to me and had me do a search on my license. I thought they had expired and I'd have to take a test again. They're good until next year. Maybe I need to get back into this with all the travel I do.

So after having a flat tire and chasing the spare down the hill and into the ditch, weeds and beginning of the woods I didn't do anything today. I think I needed a mental health day. My husband even bought dinner and brought it to me. He saw I had meat thawing out and he said you shouldn't cook tonight I'll buy dinner and put the meat back in the freezer.

July 2, 2013
Yes, I'm excited to be going and working for God. However, I'm also torn about leaving my loved ones behind but for now that's how it must be. I'm so blessed to have such a supportive husband when it comes to the things of God. I can't wait until we can travel together. I love him so much!

I did not want to leave to go to Louisiana and on to Texas but I felt in my spirit I had to go. One day I would understand but this day I only knew that I wanted to be with my family.

Something that hasn't been shared except with close friends and family is that the flat I had was when I found out where the car had been walking or sliding across the road had done a number on the tires so they were basically bald. I did not have any money to buy tires. But when God says, Go, you better Go.

One of the tires my husband switched on the car he was unsure of the rotation it needed to go in. If you put a used tire on and have it going the wrong way from front to back instead of back to front it can cause the belt in the tire to break. Hence, a flat tire.

About five hundred miles from home I had another flat but the God I serve had it happen within a half mile of an exit. I was able to limp the car to the garage where I had them put the spare on. They wanted me to get a new tire but that was not in the budget. I barely had enough money for gas and maybe one night in a motel if I needed to stop.

After they put on the tire I felt God impress me to take my Bible out of my briefcase and put it on the seat beside me. As I was driving down the road and the tire would start to make that noise like the belt was breaking I would lay my hand on the Bible. Then I would look up at the sky and say, "God you told me to go, so I'm going. If it was up to me I'd be lying on my couch eating bon bons. You own the cattle on a thousand hillsides. Why don't you sell a few and buy me some tires? I do work for you. Tires are necessary.

Well, God didn't answer that I could hear but I did make it to New Orleans and then on to Alexandria. Sister Haygood knew how bad the tire situation was and had been praying.

I've stopped for the night in Meridian, Mississippi. In the morning I'll head on into New Orleans and then to Tioga, LA for Louisiana camp meeting! I'm exhausted but all is well because God is in control.

This morning in my devotions God knew exactly what I needed and spent some time reminding me of His promises. No matter who we are, what we accomplish, how far we may go sometimes we need reminded of the things of old. When King Hezekiah in the Bible received the letter from the prophet he took it and spread it before God and prayed. He then told the Lord what the enemy had said and asked his God to deliver them. Then the Lord sent the prophet back to King Hezekiah to remind him of all the times God had brought them out, that He knew every time they went in and out. Then the Lord, through the prophet, let King Hezekiah know he would bring them out. God will bring us out. Sometimes we just need reminded. When you spend time with God, He, Himself, will do that for each one of us.

Lastly the Lord thought enough of me to give me this. Today, I know I needed this and I also know we all need to be reminded from time to time of the greatness of our God.

Isaiah 40:28-31
[28] Hast thou not known? hast thou not heard, that the everlasting God, the LORD, the Creator of the ends of the earth, fainteth not, neither is weary? there is no searching of his understanding. [29] He giveth power to the faint; and to them that have no might he increaseth strength. [30] Even the youths shall faint and be weary, and the young men shall utterly fall: [31] But they that wait upon the LORD shall renew their strength; they shall mount up with wings as eagles; they shall run, and not be weary; and they shall walk, and not faint.

I'm here in Marrero, Louisiana waiting for my appointment. I made it to Louisiana Camp Grounds for their 99th camp meeting! It's going to be amazing and awesome

July 4, 2013
Awesome worship this fourth of July. Praying for America to find our way as a country back to our Christian roots.

I was sitting here tonight when The Pentecostal Publishing House representative got up to do their presentation at the end they announced I was here and showcased my book, "Surprised by God with Pancreatic Cancer." I was humbled, shocked and amazed by the wonderfulness of our God. Also can you believe the way I take pictures that I didn't take any pictures. I was so shocked and humbled.

July 5, 2013
I'm up and almost ready to head back to Louisiana Camp Meeting! It's been awesome. It's like I blinked and it's already over. I'm so glad I continued on my journey regardless of the obstacles in my path. I now know why I needed to be here. Sometimes we give up too easily. We have to continue on with God like the old timers. It's time we found our way back to the old paths of true Apostolic doctrine and Apostolic worship. In other words we need to learn how to pray and fast more. It is about spending time on our knees with the King of Kings and the Lord of Lords. Even when we get frustrated because things aren't moving fast enough for us we need to remember it's all in His hands and His time.

So very happy for the unexpected blessing of seeing Bishop & Sis. Tommy Craft. I love them so very much! We got here early to be sure to get seats. I can't wait to see what God will do tonight.

And miracles are happening! I saw a young lady who had been in a wheel chair three years get up tonight and walk and keep on walking. Only time will tell what other miracles happened at Louisiana camp meeting tonight!

July 6, 2013
It's been great to be at Louisiana camp! I love the camp grounds. It had been almost thirty years since I had been here. It still looked and smelled the same. It's amazing the memories that come back when you return somewhere you haven't been in so long. Praying everyone has a safe blessed July 4th weekend!

July 10, 2014
Sometimes we need reminded that He, our God, loves us enough to go before us and makes the crooked paths straight. Trust God in your situation. He will simply take care of the situation.

Isaiah 45:1-8

Thus saith the LORD to his anointed, to Cyrus, whose right hand I have holden, to subdue nations before him; and I will loose the loins of kings, to open before him the two leaved gates; and the gates shall not be shut;[2] I will go before thee, and make the crooked places straight: I will break in pieces the gates of brass, and cut in sunder the bars of iron:[3] And I will give thee the treasures of darkness, and hidden riches of secret places, that thou mayest know that I, the LORD, which call thee by thy name, am the God of Israel.[4] For Jacob my servant's sake, and Israel mine elect, I have even called thee by thy name: I have surnamed thee, though thou hast not known me.[5] I am the LORD, and there is none else, there is no God beside me: I girded thee, though thou hast not known me:[6] That they may know from the rising of the sun, and from the west, that there is none beside me. I am the LORD, and there is none else.[7] I form the light, and create darkness: I make peace, and create evil: I the LORD do all these things.[8] Drop down, ye heavens, from above, and let the skies pour down righteousness: let the earth open, and let them bring forth salvation, and let righteousness spring up together; I the LORD have created it.

July 12, 2013
This morning I was nudged awake by the one who loved me enough to die for my sins so that I could have a relationship with the King of Kings and the Lord of Lords. Not only that but He so graciously gave me a Bible that tells me how He thinks and is full of promises for each one of us. So when I awoke worshipping my saviour about 4:30 a.m. I thanked Him for all of that and for loving me so much to be sure He was the first one I spent time with. Thank you Lord Jesus. I love Him so very much!
Isaiah 54:17
No weapon that is formed against thee shall prosper; and every tongue that shall rise against thee in judgment thou shalt condemn. This is the heritage of the servants of theLORD, and their righteousness is of me, saith the LORD.

Since I'm already in Houston I thought I'd try to get my appointment moved up to August for my annual checkup but they want me to wait until September. It's going to be a long August waiting for that appointment. Once you've gotten bad news you just want the testing over with every year so you can move on and rejoice that yes, the miracle is getting bigger, and yes I'm still in remission. I know God's got this but I just hate waiting... patience is not my strong suit and please don't quote that verse to me in Luke 21:19, *"In your patience possess ye your souls."* You see I never wanted to possess my soul. I want God to possess it. Sorry, just had to rant for a moment. I so want this over for this year.

July 14-16, 2013
Time for prayer! Love to walk in the prayer room at Royalwood! There is nothing like hearing so many people worshiping the most high God, Jesus and travailing for souls. I can't wait to see what God will do!

July 18, 2013
I finally got my copies of the new books. I keep looking at them. I do believe I'm in shock. Dreams do still come true. Not only did God work major miracles in my life but my dreams keep coming true. Each day is a new dream, a new journey. I'm so blessed and thankful to God for all He's done for me!

July 20, 2013
I am so excited. I can't believe I'm privileged to go celebrate a 65th wedding anniversary with some dear friends. Tonight late I'll probably be writing.... I think a long time before I write and then it all comes together with the anointing of God on it.

I had a wonderful phone call with Bishop Craft. I'm so homesick for Jackson tonight but when you know you're exactly where God wants you it is all that matters. Some of us, me especially, would have never known this feeling had God not shaken my world up. I pray God shakes you until you know what it is to be in His perfect will for your life.

We have gotten so comfortable where we are we don't want change but sometimes we need change to find our true purpose and to be everything God wants us to be. I wonder, do you know, what God wants you to be? Have you prayed about it, I mean, really prayed about it. A few hours in a prayer room, just you and God.

A post from my husband early for my birthday!

Happy early birthday Susan. I love you.

Mike
- <u>Susan D Wine Smith</u> *I love you too. Calling now*

July 22, 2013
Praising God for His wonderful amazing blessings to me!!! Last night in church one of the ministers walked up to me and told me God told him to tell me I was getting my miracle and that the obstacles were being removed from my ministry. Today I found out God moved on someone to provide that miracle! Thank you God and thank you to that person for obeying God.

The miracle was that my tires were bald. I had driven from West Virginia to Texas on those tires. God protected me. So, I will be getting tires soon.

July 23, 2013
I am having a busy day so far. Phone calls, marketing, emails..... so much to do. Someday, in Jesus name, I'll have a team who will do this for me. In the meantime I'm the team, LOL, but that's okay. It just requires me to manage my time better.

Please pray for James. He is battling pancreatic cancer. This is urgent! I am at Houston Methodist with the family. There is an important meeting in the morning with the doctors. Thanks for praying. I'm believing God for the miraculous!

July 26, 2013
It's a beautiful day for me to thank God for five years that He has mercifully extended my life. I'm so very blessed. Headed to breakfast with a dear friend who called to wish me a happy birthday!!! God is so good!

I received over 150 Happy Birthday comments! WOW!

Breakfast with Sis. Linda Clark then dinner with Sis. Beverly Haygood at Bubba Gumps.

July 27, 2013
This was part of my morning devotions. In reading Jeremiah where he is prophesying all these horrible things on the house of Israel there is a promise. The promise is this

that if they (we) will seek Him with our whole heart He will be found in them (us). Our country needs to pray.

Jeremiah 29:12-14
[12] Then shall ye call upon me, and ye shall go and pray unto me, and I will hearken unto you. [13] And ye shall seek me, and find me, when ye shall search for me with all your heart. [14] And I will be found of you, saith the LORD: and I will turn away your captivity, and I will gather you from all the nations, and from all the places whither I have driven you, saith the LORD; and I will bring you again into the place whence I caused you to be carried away captive.

Time for church and my first 'official' book signing for the new books this morning at Royalwood! God surely takes care of His children! I'm blessed beyond measure and so thankful this morning

It is time for prayer. Then it will be time for some amazing church! Thanking God for the way He is ordering my steps.

I am resting after an amazing night of church. God came in and glory filled the room! Worship was outstanding! The message from Bro. Macey was just what I needed. Now to rest.... I shouted (danced) before the Lord tonight. I'm getting a little older but when the Spirit gets to moving I forget my age and my ailments. It becomes all about God and the promise I made to Him lying in the hospital one Sunday night that never would a rock cry out in my place and if I ever got well I would NEVER cease to worship and praise the King of Kings and the Lord of Lords!!!

July 29-31, 2013
Write it on my heart dear Lord. I want it to be so much more than words I want the Word to be part of me every day everything I say or do. As God keeps me on the potter's wheel molding me I want to continually be changed so that He can use me. What a promise God has given in Jeremiah that all would know Him.

Jeremiah 39:17-18 Wow! What a passage. After Jeremiah had been rescued from the dungeon and the Chaldean army had burned the city and taken the king that's when the Captain of the guard sent for Jeremiah. Not, only, that, but the Captain of the guard told them to "...*look well to him and do him no harm....*" Jeremiah suffered tremendously for obeying God and preaching judgment but because he put his trust in God he was delivered. I wonder if the same could be said of us?

^{17} But I will deliver thee in that day, saith the LORD: and thou shalt not be given into the hand of the men of whom thou art afraid. ^{18} For I will surely deliver thee, and thou shalt not fall by the sword, but thy life shall be for a prey unto thee: because thou hast put thy trust in me, saith the LORD.

Most people get stopped on their journey because they are afraid of failure. Failure is part of life. If you never fail you have never tried. There will be some failures but get this, THERE WILL BE SUCCESS ALSO! So step out, take a chance, and see where God will take you. As long as your hand is in His, you are grounded in His word and pray nothing is impossible to you!

God lowered the hedge.

Job 1:9-12
"Then Satan answered the Lord, and said, Doth Job fear God for nought? Hast not thou made a hedge about him, and about his house, and about all that he hath on every side? thou hast blessed the work of his hands, and his substance is increased in the land. But put forth thine hand now and touch all that he hath, and he will curse thee to thy face. And the Lord said unto Satan, Behold, all that he hath is in thy power, only upon himself put not forth thine hand. So Satan went forth from the presence of the Lord."

"AND THERE CAME A MESSENGER…"(Job 1:14)

August 5, 2013
What a day this has been!
This morning in my morning devotions part of the scriptures I read was this Lamentations 3:21-26.

"This I recall to my mind, therefore have I hope. It is of the Lord's mercies that we are not consumed, because his compassions fail not. They are new every morning: great is thy faithfulness. The Lord is my portion, saith my soul; therefore will I hope in Him. The Lord is good unto them that seek wait for him, to the soul that seeketh Him. It is good that a man should both hope and quietly wait for the salvation of the Lord."

Waiting on God is so easy to say but so hard to do. Yet we have a promise in this scripture that God is good to those who wait. Also in this same passage it tells us that it is good for us to *"hope and quietly wait for the salvation of the Lord"*. Whatever it is that you're waiting on God to do remember you have hope and a promise.

Then I talked to my husband. He told me that his sleeping medication is no longer working. He has an appointment with the doctor but not for a few days. In the meantime he could not sleep last night so went and bought a bottle of wine. He drank that after taking his sleeping medication. As I tried to reason with him that even though he had no medication for that night medication was still in his system. Adding alcohol to the mix was only going to cause more problems. He sees no harm in doing this.

Before going to Hospice I dropped my car off at the mechanic's shop to get an estimate. I thought I only needed a front end alignment. As I walked into the Hospice house to visit with one of the patients and his family's that I've met and been with through his treatment I found his daughter's picking out songs for his funeral. This man's pancreatic cancer was diagnosed at the same stage as mine. God has so ordered my steps that I have been in Houston, Texas every time something major has happened in his treatment. After this I counseled, visited and prayed with the family.

Walking outside for a few moments I decided I was really missing my daughter. I had texted her earlier in the day but then decided to give her a call at her office. I called her to let her know how much I missed her since I had not spoken to since J.T.'s high school graduation. Usually when I call her office I get her assistant but today she actually answered the phone.

"While he was yet, speaking, there came also another, and said, …"

While talking to her and letting her know I just wanted to tell her I loved you she said, "Oh, mom, I've got something to tell you. Evan and I eloped over the weekend."

As I congratulated her on getting married we continued to talk. During our talk I found out that they had told both sets of grandparents, siblings, and cousins. Then it came out that her husband's family had been there on her wedding day.The only people they seemingly did not tell they were thinking about this were us. While it hurt I was and still am truly happy for my daughter.

It's so hard to believe she is married. Just like with our son I still see her in my eyes as this baby, then toddler, and growing into a beautiful teenager but not a woman who could be married. However, I was her age when we married so I can't say much.

Leah September 6, 1990   Leah's dedication January 1991

"While he was yet speaking, there came also another, and said,..." (Job 1:17)

Later that afternoon the shuttle from the mechanic shop picked me up to take me back to get the car. Upon my arrival there they handed me an estimate for not quite $3,000 to do the repairs on the car. No way do I have that kind of money in the bank. They then told me everything that was wrong with the car. In their explanations to me they made sure I knew that the tires could fall off if some of the things that were wrong were not fixed quickly.

I needed to reread Lamentations 3:20-26 tonight, *"This I recall to my mind, therefore have I hope. It is of the Lord's mercies that we are not consumed, because his compassions fail not. They are new every morning: great is thy faithfulness. The Lord is my portion, saith my soul; therefore will I hope in Him. The Lord is good unto them that seek wait for him, to the soul that seeketh Him. It is good that a man should both hope and quietly wait for the salvation of the Lord."*

Today as I kept getting more and more news I needed to encourage myself in the Lord with what He gave me before I got out of bed this morning. I'm still reading it. Sometimes no matter what comes our way we have to with God's help pick ourselves up with lots of prayer and scripture and trusting in God. As I continued to think on this day I kept remembering my little girl and tried to wrap my mind around the fact that she is now a married woman.

Leah and I 1992   Winter 1993

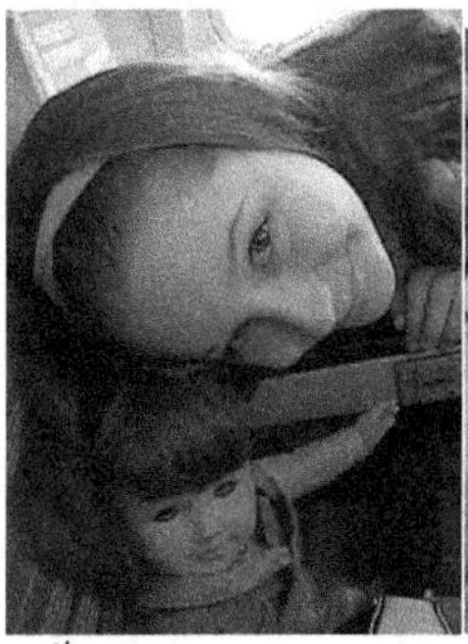

1st Plane ride 2000    Leah singing 1998 Charlotte, NC

Leah Church Camp 2004    Leah 2003 Old Fashioned Sunday

No matter what comes your way you just have to trust in God. Sometimes trusting Him seems impossible for us but it's not. It's then that we fall backwards into the arms of God and He simply catches us.

August 6, 2013
This morning after doing my normal Bible reading I needed something more with all that had happened yesterday in my life. God directed me to John 15:11-16.

"These things have I spoken unto you, that my joy might remain in you, and that your joy might be full. This is my commandment, That ye love one another, as I have loved you. Greater love hath no man than this, that a man lay down his life for his friends. Ye are my friends, if ye do whatsoever I command you. Henceforth I call you not servants; for the servant knoweth not what his lord doeth: but I have called you friends: for all things that I have heard of my Father I have made known unto you. Ye have not chosen me, but I have chosen you, and ordained you that ye should go and bring forth fruit, and that your fruit should remain; that whatsoever ye shall ask of the Father in my name, he may give it you."

If we do what God tells us to do through His Word and prayer we become friends of God. When this happens we have benefits. Oh, I long to be called His friend and not because of the benefits from the relationship. I just want to be His friend, to sit at His feet to worship Him and learn of Him. Yesterday was a day that when driving back all I could say was I believe... I believe.. I believe.. You are the Alpha and the Omega.... You said if we ask anything in your name, anything, you would do it... all of this was said through tears as one thing after another happened but as I fell back into the arms of God I was caught and rested with Him.

Then today I received a few calls and more information about journeys I will soon be taking to faraway lands. No matter what happens to us or how it happens we just have to remember that we are His child and that He's got this!!!! This is so easy to say and so very hard to do. When we don't understand what is going on in our world that is when we learn what trusting God is all about.

August 7, 2013
Tonight I went to church needing something from God. I just needed to know God remembered me. Of course He remembered. He doesn't forget us but sometimes in our humanity we think He does because of our circumstances. We've got to learn to

live above our problems. They exist and we have to take care of them but they do not have to define who we are.

So tonight Bro. Macey ministered directly to me without knowing what was going on in my world. His message was titled, "How long is the night?" He read from Psalms 30:1-5;

"I will extol thee, O Lord; for thou hast lifted me up, and hast not made my foes to rejoice over me. O Lord my God, I cried unto thee, and thou hast healed me. O Lord, thou hast brought up my soul from the grave: thou hast kept me alive, that I should not go down to the pit. Sing unto the Lord, O ye saints of his, and give thanks at the remembrance of His holiness. For His anger endureth but a moment; in his favour is life: weeping may endure for a night, but joy cometh in the morning."

I didn't take too many notes but the few that I did went like this. The one that rules the day rules the night. You do not get to skip the night. When the night comes you endure it and sing praises while enduring.
Then he went to Isaiah 21:11;
"The burden of Dumah. He calleth to me out of Seir, Watchman, what of the night? Watchman, what of the night?"

The last notes I took were when that darkness comes and you don't know how to move forward because it is too uncertain. There are things that normally would not bother us causing us to be afraid. We are in the night but there is light!

In my mind I thought we just have to remember whom we serve. He's the one who is catching us when we learn to fall back into His arms. It's not easy to stand still and fall backwards into someone's arms. That is trust. We have got to learn to put our trust in God. We have to really put our trust in God.

August 17, 2013
Getting up this morning I just wanted to start weeping. I love God so much and I am so thankful to be alive. Today is the memorial/home going service for James. His pancreatic cancer was diagnosed at the same stage as mine, stage I-II and a year later he's gone.

I don't wonder why he's gone because God did the greatest miracle of all. James and his wife were filled with the Holy Ghost and baptized in Jesus name. When we think of great miracles we think of God healing cancer, seeing blind eyes opened, people who can't walk, walking but the greatest miracle is seeing someone filled with the Holy Ghost and being baptized in Jesus name as stated in Acts 2:38. The other is just extra.

My Bible tells me in Matthew 5:45,
"That ye may be the children of your Father which is in heaven: for he maketh his sun to rise on the evil and on the good, and sendeth rain on the just and on the unjust."

We may not understand why some things happen and other things don't but it's not for us to understand. We just have to put our life in God's hands and keep walking with Him. Regardless of the situation we just have to keep on moving forward with God.

This morning I talked to my husband and son. I told them about going to the memorial service this morning and when talking to J.T. I remembered the day we came home and told them I was dying of pancreatic cancer. J.T. looked at me at the wise old age of fourteen and said, "Mommy, God's not going to let you die."

I truly believe I'm still here because of his faith. While battling the disease I don't think I had any faith. I was doing good to put one foot in front of the other. We went from test to test, doctor to doctor, good news, bad news, more good news, worse news until the day we came home and planned my funeral. I have a passion now I didn't have before cancer. That's how I distinguish my life as b.c. (before cancer) and a.c. (after cancer). It simply doesn't matter if people understand why I do what I do these days, it only matters that when I talk to God I obey Him.

No, I'm not going off on some strange doctrine. Yes, I do have elders/pastors in my life who guide me but this passion doesn't give me choices about what I do. I know, people say I do have a choice and they're probably right but in my heart I feel like I'm living on borrowed time. This is time I shouldn't have had and that time has to count for something and not how much money I can make. I want to see lives changed. I want to see people come to God. I want to see people who God called to do something special but they walked away from it decide to go for it.

People are hurting and want what we have but we're not sensitive enough to the Spirit of God most days to help them. I try every day before I touch anything to whisper, I love you Jesus, Thank you for another day and then to listen to hear what He would have me do.

I remember sitting in his home going service as tears dripped down my face onto my lap with abandon. Why? Well, you see I was wondering why I was alive and he was gone. Survivor guilt is a real issue. As I sat there I made a promise to God that my life will count for God.

Driving back to Houston I talked with my husband. He encouraged me to keep on. He reminded me of the many miracles we had seen through the battle we had walked through with my cancer. He reminded me of the people I now help- by counseling, by ministering and by speaking to Congress. It was so hard to drive. The tears just wouldn't stop. Little did I know tears were just starting for me.

August 21, 2013
To be shut in with God! Tonight God had a friend call me with encouraging words. Sometimes the encourager needs encouraged. So then I went looking for this old song I haven't heard sung in years.

August 22, 2013
Habakkuk 3:17-19. Here we can understand the faith Habakkuk had and we should have also. Verse 17 tells it in an easy to understand way. It doesn't matter if the crops are good. It doesn't matter if you have meat. It doesn't matter if you have anything (in their day a herd in the stalls). It just simply doesn't matter what we have or don't have yet Habakkuk said I will rejoice in the Lord. Not only that but he said I will joy in the God of my salvation. Think about it. Can you do that? Could you? Would you? Then the last verse tells us the Lord is our strength!

[17] Although the fig tree shall not blossom, neither shall fruit be in the vines; the labour of the olive shall fail, and the fields shall yield no meat; the flock shall be cut off from the fold, and there shall be no herd in the stalls:
[18] Yet I will rejoice in the LORD, I will joy in the God of my salvation.
[19] The LORD God is my strength, and he will make my feet like hinds' feet, and he will make me to walk upon mine high places. To the chief singer on my stringed instruments.

August 23, 2013
In reading some things I wrote earlier on facebook and notes I have on scriptures God laid on my heart the book, "Falling Back in the Arms of God" seems to be writing itself. I love it when the inspiration flows. Now I just need to finish one of the other four novels I'm writing because "Falling Back in the Arms of God" should not be finished until late fall of this year. There is so much to do, so little time. I'm back to writing late at night when the inspiration seems to flow freely.
In my Bible reading this morning I read Zechariah 4:6, *"Then he answered and spake unto me, saying, This is the word of the LORD unto Zerubbabel, saying, Not by might, nor by power, but by my spirit, saith the LORD of hosts."*

This is something we all must remember it's not by anything we do but by His Spirit!

FYI - Try to see the glass as half full not half empty. Pray for those whose behavior you disagree with instead of being the caretaker. Carrying that load is heavy and not meant for us to carry.

Job 1:6-12
[6] Now there was a day when the sons of God came to present themselves before the LORD, and Satan came also among them.[7] And the LORD said unto Satan, Whence comest thou? Then Satan answered the LORD, and said, From going to and fro in the earth, and from walking up and down in it.[8] And the LORD said unto Satan, Hast thou considered my servant Job, that there is none like him in the earth, a perfect and an upright man, one that feareth God, and escheweth evil?[9] Then Satan answered the LORD, and said, Doth Job fear God for nought?[10] Hast not thou made an hedge about him, and about his house, and about all that he hath on every side? thou hast blessed the work of his hands, and his substance is increased in the land.[11] But put forth thine hand now, and touch all that he hath, and he will curse thee to thy face.[12] And the LORD said unto Satan, Behold, all that he hath is in thy power; only upon himself put not forth thine hand. So Satan went forth from the presence of the LORD.

God Lowered the Hedge!

Come with me on the journey God has taking me on teaching me that when he lowers the hedge I can fall back into his arms and he will catch me. In this book I'm going back in revisiting certain points of time because I have to have closure. To go forward I must go backward and open the wound cleaning out the infection, putting medication in it, so that it will heal without bitterness. Anytime anyone in a family commits suicide whether the coroner calls it accidental or on purpose the family still suffers untold emotional pain.

August 24, 2013

I talked to Mike four times today. While I'm on this journey of traveling and evangelizing which means I have to be away from him he knew I loved him more than life. He also realized that God has to be first. He always encouraged me to follow God.

We did not have the perfect marriage. I know of few that do. We all have struggles and problems. In our case some of our problems were pretty big. In the conversations I had with him I begged him to please not take any more prescription medication. I knew he would not listen.

Yes, he has a medical condition. Herniated disc, ruptured disc, angling spondylolysis of the spine but he has allowed his condition and medication to rule his life. He has been a great father and a great husband. No man is perfect. He is in a lot of pain. Even when someone is in excruciating pain it doesn't give them permission to abuse the medication that they have access to.

Throughout this process I've tried everything I know to do to help him. He's been in rehab three times, detox once, and even arrested once to protect himself from himself. He never harmed us that you could see. Until I started counseling recently I never saw the dysfunction of our family. Looking back now I can see how dysfunctional we were.

This is the hardest thing I have ever had to do other than burying my husband. This book is requiring me to go back and relive the days, weeks and months before and after his death. In order for me to fully heal and root out all the weeds of bitterness that are trying to grow I have to feel this pain again. God has let me know that this book has to be written.

Many people are suffering in silence sitting on our church pews pretending that everything is okay when their lives are completely blown apart. It's time we were honest. I'm not saying we have to confess to everybody what's going on in our world, but, we have to be honest with God about where we are.

Let's go back to my day. The last time I talked to him was about 6 o'clock in the evening I believe. His words were very slurred. He told me I need some more medication because I'm in so much pain. I begged him not to take anything else. I believe I tried to calling back again later that evening but there was no answer.

So I did what I always do I put him in the hands of God and I went to sleep not knowing my love was breathing his last breaths and entering eternity.

Death is Always a Stranger

"While he was yet speaking, there came also, another, and said Thy sons and thy daughters were eating and drinking wine in their eldest brother's hous: And, behold, there came a great wind from the wilderness, and smote the four corners of the house, and it fell upon the young men, and they are dead; and I only am escaped alone to tell thee" (Job 1:18-19)

August 25, 2013

This morning God woke me up with the passage in Zechariah 13:9

And I will bring the third part through the fire, and will refine them as silver is refined, and will try them as gold is tried: they shall call on my name, and I will hear them: I will say, It is my people: and they shall say, The LORD is my God.

As I am reading back on my Facebook post I'm finding the words I penned to encourage others would later encourage me. Here they are:

****

No one wants to walk through the fire but when we do we are refined as silver. When we do this something changes in our relationship with God because we know he heard us. Then we talk about "My God" it's different. There is something in our voice that makes others take notice because we know beyond a shadow of a doubt that He can, He has, and He will.
****

That morning I tried to call Mike three times before I left for church. About a month prior to this God started dealing with me that when I would go in the prayer room at Royalwood before church to stay until time for church to start. Granted those last few minutes I was watching the clock but I felt so impressed by God to stay in the prayer room until the minute church was supposed to start that I obeyed.

Prayer is what makes the difference when tragedy strikes.

I went to church and when church was dismissed I saw that I had four missed calls. Two were from my daughter and two from my son. I looked at Sister Haygood telling her about the missed calls and I was stepping out to return them.

My children rarely call on Sundays because they know how busy I am. Based on that and history with my husband coupled with the fact about three weeks before that God changed the title of this book from "Living the Miracle" to "Falling back into the arms of God" she knew. God let her know what was wrong.

I stepped outside the church and called my daughter. She picked up instantly and said, "Mommy, where are you?" I could hear her crying so I said, "Princess, I have been in church."

You have to understand she was almost 23 years old and had not called me mommy in years. She responded and said, "I told everybody that's where you were."

I then asked, "What do you mean by everybody? Sweetie, what's wrong? Is Evan okay?"

This book is so hard to write. My emotions are still so raw but I've been told that this will help me heal and that this will help others heal as they walk through their valleys. I'm actually talking this book instead of writing it. I don't trust me to write it because my emotions are so uncontrollable. So let's go on with this conversation.

She said, "Evan is okay." I then asked, "Are you okay?"

"Yeah, mom I'm fine."

So then I made a statement I regret to this day, I said, "Sweetie, if nobody is dead whatever is wrong we can fix it."

At this point she started sobbing and asked me exactly where I was in the building. I told her I was standing outside the church leaning up against the wall. She said, "Mommy, I'm not going to tell you what's wrong until you go inside and sit down where there are people."

I said okay and went in the foyer of the church. As I started to sit down I said, "I'm inside and sitting down."

"Mommy, Daddy died this morning."

Time stopped.

I think I screamed. I wanted to pass out. Tears started streaming down my face like someone had turned on a water faucet. I dropped my stuff. I basically collapsed in the chair. You have no control at times like this.

I saw people coming towards me. It was like I was in a fog. Sis. Haygood had gathered together the ministry team and they came to me. One man sat down in front of me putting his hands on top of mine and said, "Sister Smith, what happened?"

I responded, "My husband overdosed."

They started to pray for me quietly as I was still on the phone with my daughter. I found out that my son had found his father that morning and called 911. She did let me know that it looked like he had just gone to sleep and not woken up. When I hung up the phone all I could do was sit there.

The ministry team and many friends gathered around me in that chair travailing for me and my family. I don't know how long we sat there but I really believe that God had me right where he wanted me when I found out so that I would have the support that I needed to get through the minutes, the hours, the days, the weeks, and the months of loneliness to come.

After we finished praying I just sat there. Sister Haygood looked at me and said, "Susie, you need to call Bro. Craft."

I tried calling him but he didn't pick up so then I tried to call Sister Craft. She picked up. She had no idea what I was getting ready to tell her. When I told her Mike died she said, NO, God wouldn't let that happen! We've been praying for him."

With tears streaming down my face now and tears streaming down my face that day I said, "Well, God did." In our conversation it was decided that I would come to Jackson first. I didn't have enough money to fly home. My only option was to drive or so I thought. The wonderful people at Royalwood asked me what I needed. During a time like this you don't have a clue what you need or even what your name is.

Sister Craft and I are very close. She knew I was like her in that the drive to Jackson would be time for me to focus on something other than the crisis and give me time to process the news.

The reason I needed to go to Jackson first was I needed to take care of myself first. I needed my pastor and his wife. I knew upon my arrival in West Virginia that I was stepping into a snake pit and that the strikes were already starting at me once news of his death was out. Whenever you have a family situation that is explosive and many of us have those situations. It is then that you pray for the wisdom of God to know how to step and when to step for yourself and your immediate families protection. In order to be available for the rest of the family we have to fortify ourselves first with God. Many will not understand but in situations like this it simply doesn't matter who understands and who doesn't.

Sister Haygood was my lifesaver this day. As people left she help me get my bearings and pull myself together enough to walk over to her house and start packing. After I packed which probably only took 10 or 15 minutes we loaded the car and she said, "You need to eat."

Food was the last thing I wanted. However, I had not yet had anything to eat and she knew I was getting ready to drive seven hours tonight. I followed her to Saltgrass to eat. On the way there my phone rang. It was one of my friends at Royalwood calling.

When I answered she said that they had heard the news and that they wanted me to fly home. I laughed and told her the zeros in my bank account didn't go the right direction to fly home. She responded by saying, Sis. Smith, you don't understand. I have texted you my American Express information. It is a gold card. It has no credit limit. You are to use it for anything you need."

I couldn't believe it.

Then friends started showing up at the restaurant we were at giving me money to help me through the next few days. I was so humbled by the graciousness of the people who stepped out to help when they didn't really know what to do and I had no idea what to ask for if I would have asked. Some of us don't ask because we have always provided for ourselves and our families.

That is when we need the people of God to be the people of God. Just think what you might want and do that for someone going through a crisis.

Could God really send me people that would be that nice to me?

~~~~~~~~~~~~~~~~~~~~~~~~~~~

Psalm 23 King James Version (KJV)

*The L*ORD *is my shepherd; I shall not want.**2** He maketh me to lie down in green pastures: he leadeth me beside the still waters.**3** He restoreth my soul: he leadeth me in the paths of righteousness for his name's sake.**4** Yea, though I walk through the valley of the shadow of death, I will fear no evil: for thou art with me; thy rod and thy staff they comfort me.**5** Thou preparest a table before me in the presence of mine enemies: thou anointest my head with oil; my cup runneth over. **6** Surely goodness and mercy shall follow me all the days of my life: and I will dwell in the house of the L*ORD *for ever.*

~~~~~~~~~~~~~~~~~~~~~~~~~

This passage of scripture has become something I quote almost every day. It has comforted me. God has held me while I wept.

In writing this section of this book I am going to be going back and forth because my emotions require it. So, let's go back to that day.

Sitting there eating Sister Haygood told me I needed to look at Facebook and make a statement. I was so grateful to have friends that guided me through this day and kept me from making missteps.

Because of this ministry that God has given me whether I want to or not I have become a public person. As such I needed to make a statement. When I opened Facebook and looked at my page I was overwhelmed by all the comments that were showing up. I posted the picture and the following statement:

Our family at J.T.'s high school graduation. My loving husband passed away this morning. Please pray for our children, Joseph , Leah, and Evan.

I just crossed the Mississippi state line. No problem. Other than missing my husband so I used to call every few hours. While my family and I are grieving please know that all things, and I do mean all things work together for the good of those who are called according to His purpose. By the way I'm doing this update with voice recognition software so if some of the words are spelled wrong forgive me. Please lift our family up in your prayers.

As I pulled into Brother and Sister Tommy Craft's driveway I saw a family of deer. They weren't home yet so I just pulled in and sat in the car waiting on them to get home. Once they knew I was there she came immediately.

I never called home again after the initial call telling me what had happened. Mentally I couldn't deal with anything else. When Bro. Craft came in and held me it seemed for a moment that I must be having a nightmare and it was a very crazy nightmare.

As we sat down and started talking about what had happened Debbie and Denny Hahn came in. Bro. Craft wanted to know if I had thought about the service. I explained that Yes, I had and told him I had talked to a couple of pastors in the area and they were willing to be there. He then asked me, "What about me?"

I looked at him, and said, "What about you?"

He replied, "Do you want me to come?"

I then explained to him that I had no access to life insurance. There was no money. All the retirement funds had been spent when I was battling pancreatic cancer. He then looked at me and said, "Did I ask for money?"

I couldn't believe I had a pastor and his wife who not only would rearrange their lives to be available for me but would come over 800 miles to spend a week with me to hold me and my children while we cried. Not only that, but my friends Debbie & Denny Hahn would also come to help me with the service.

That night when it was decided they would come he asked me what I wanted him to do at the service. I told him I wanted him to preach. I said, "I know we will have family that have never heard Acts 2:38 preached and my children are backsliders. I want a church service. I don't want any of them to ever be able to say they didn't hear this message."

After we finished talking Debbie and Denny helped me go online and purchase my plane ticket. I couldn't seem to get it to work. The tears would not stop. It was like I was leaking. I would get control for a few minutes and more tears would come. My emotions were all jumbled up. Nothing made sense.

Could this really be happening to me?

I needed Mike. Why, God, why?
****

All, here's the scripture I posted this morning. I always call Mike when I wake up and then a few times throughout the day. When I read this I had tried to call and there was no answer. God was giving me what I would need for this very long day and devastating news. I still believe what I wrote this morning. While I don't know what the days ahead hold. I do know who holds the days ahead. He will be with our family as we walk this road. So many of you have lifted us up in prayers and I have felt the results of those prayers. Thank you.

Zechariah 13:9 - No one wants to walk through the fire but when we do we are refined as silver. When we do this something changes in our relationship with God because we know He heard us. Then when we talk about "My God" it's different. There's something in our voice that makes others take notice because we know beyond a shadow of a doubt that He can, He has, and He will!

August 26, 2013
As long as I'm in His hands I know, I know everything is going to be alright. I don't change who I trust or how I trust because of circumstances. I fall back into the arms of God and He simply catches me.

As tears rain down my cheeks with a shattered heart tonight one thing does not change this is still my story, this is still my song, Praising my Saviour all the day long. What about you? What's your story? Do you have hope of heaven some day? If not, send me a private message and let me tell you about the one who died for all of us so that we might have life and have it more abundantly.

The next morning I parked my car by the back garage at the Craft's with no clue when I would be back to get it. Then Brother and Sister Craft prayed for me and she took me to the airport.

The easiest way to get home was via Houston believe it or not. But that was okay. While at the airport in Houston Bro. Harper called me. He had known me since I was a small child. When I answered the phone he said, "Smitty, I just heard. How are you? Wait, don't answer that. Sister Starr told me you were numb."

I replied, "Yes, sir. I am."

He then said, "What I'm getting ready to tell you I know you won't take it wrong. I felt this in the Spirit when I heard what had happened. Your shackles are gone. You're free now to do the will of God with no restraints."

He was right. I did not take it wrong. God had drawn Mike to church many times since I started evangelizing and doing book tours. Mike and I had discussed church many times and getting him help for the prescription drug abuse. The last time we had discussed it had just been a couple of weeks before his death. I was begging him to go to church and pray or pray at home but just to pray.

He had told me, "Susie, I can't do this." I'll never forget that conversation. You go over it and over it in your mind. Was there something I could have said differently? Was there something I could have done differently that would have changed the outcome? What had I done wrong? Why couldn't he love me enough to get help with the prescription drugs? Why couldn't he love himself?

No, there was nothing I could do. It was his decision to take the medication even with me begging him not too.

Later I posted the following on facebook:

The viewing for my husband will probably be Thursday evening with the funeral Friday. I will post times tomorrow once all decisions are finalized. I want to thank everyone who is helping us through this.

Mike loved the song Mercy Came Running. I kept trying to sleep but sleep eludes me. God let me remember some of the times we would listen to music together and the Christian songs he loved. They are giving me comfort tonight.He also enjoyed Mercy Said No, I'm not gonna let you go and My Redeemer Lives. We used to stay up late together watching video's like this. I thank God for the comfort He is giving me right now.

When I arrived at the airport I was so thankful to see Mark and Kathy Casto waiting on me. They had a coke waiting for me. I just walked into their arms. I had no idea what I was doing. At times like this you find out who your friends are. They drove me home and we stopped at the house. When I walked in the living room I remember looking out at the porch where he would go to smoke. Something broke inside of me. I fell to the living room floor screaming and crying. Poor Mark and Kathy had to witness my meltdown. It was a meltdown of gigantic proportions. Our dogs came running, Daisy and Brownie, they were my comfort.

I knew everyone would have gathered at my sister-in-laws so I had them to take me there once I pulled myself together. Upon arriving I felt uncomfortable. It was probably me. I was so happy to see my children. Leah, our daughter, had arranged for my mother to come so she was there. We visited for a few minutes and I got the keys to Mike's SUV and drove it home.

That night everyone's emotions were riding high. Things happened and were said that shouldn't have been. When a family is going through something like this everyone has an opinion. Everyone has someone in their family that always has to be right no matter what the cost to the rest of the family.

The only opinions that really matter are the wife and the children's. You can say what you will but those are the closest when the man dies. My children had decided to stay at their aunt's. My mother was with me.

Later that night I continued to listen to music because sleep was so elusive. I wasn't hungry. I didn't want anything but the one thing I couldn't have, my husband.

In my mind I was walking down the halls of memories as I started to work on the slideshow presentation for the memorial service. I remembered I walked down the aisle to James Taylor singing, "You've Got a Friend" when Mike and I got married. This was my husband's favorite song and really spoke of the person he was. Baby I miss you so much tonight!

My love loved to shower the people he loved with love. Those that were part of that group know how much he loved them.

August 27, 2013
Today I went to the funeral home. I took the high road even with our family dynamics and invited any family members that wanted to have a part to come. At first it was me and J.T. Then my sister-in-law came because there were details that needed to be in the obituary about his side of the family that I didn't know.

Because his death was considered suspicious he had to have an autopsy so it would be a few days before the body would be brought back to the funeral home. Even in grief when I shouldn't have been driving somehow I ended up driving seemingly everywhere. Everyone needed something and I had to provide it.

Driving back to our house afterwards I knew I needed some time alone. I needed to pray. There was too much noise in my head. I had too many people wanting me to take care of them and their needs. Dear God, I had needs!!!

Yes, I realize that's selfish but I always take care of everyone else first. In this instant I was drowning with no life preserver or so it felt. God was with me and many people were praying. The ones I needed to step up to the plate were nowhere to be found. They were concerned with how they were dealing with his death. I felt like they thought, who cares what happens to her.

I called Sister Joan Bounds to find out if anything was going on at the church this night. Nothing was. I asked if I could come to the church to pray. She said sure. I called Sis. Marty Angel, Sis. Treasa Dickinson and one other person along with Sis. Joan Bounds.

They met me at the church.

I Worshipped

Job 1:20-22

"Then Job arose, and rent his mantle, and shaved his head, and fell down upon the ground, and worshipped, And said, Naked came I out of my mother's womb, and naked shall I return thither: the Lord gave, and the Lord hath taken away; blessed be the name of the Lord. In all this Job sinned not, nor charged God foolishly."

We went in the sanctuary. Bro. Craft and Bro. Harper had called so I returned their calls. When I got off the phone I went to the altar and knelt right in front of the pulpit. I remember all I could do was cry. Finally, I was able to pray until I was able to pray in the Spirit speaking in tongues, then singing in tongues. Then I got up and I danced all over that church with no music. To people who aren't Apostolic this will sound strange but I needed to worship God. I needed to do this for me as part of the beginning of a very long healing process that continues to this day.

After that I walked and touched every pew praying for those that would come to the service that Friday evening. Afterwards I was able to go home. My mother was there. It's hard to explain. I was glad she was there but I wanted my children and my husband. I couldn't have him but I wanted the children. Emotionally they just couldn't be in the house where he died. I understand that but it didn't help me.

Everyone goes through grief differently. I don't think you will find a right or wrong way to do this. It just comes in waves and unexpectedly. In the beginning it is just one big tornado of constantly erupting emotions.

I would like to say that I was following Jobs example but I wasn't. I just knew within myself that I had to get the voices out of my head and focus on God. I felt like I was losing touch with reality. I needed some God centered time. This was that time for me and the time when I told the devil to get thee behind me. I had to let the devil know that no matter what he would throw at me God would remain first and foremost in my life!

AUGUST 28, 2013
I am blessed beyond measure. I cannot believe the outpouring of love I've seen in the past few days for our family. Thank you all so much for your thoughts and prayers. For those who I haven't called back please know I plan to soon. There is just so much to do getting everything ready for the memorial service for my husband. I'm still exhausted but so thankful I was able to sleep about nine hours last night. The next couple of days are going to be harder than anything I've ever imagine but if I can rest and I'm hoping today be able to eat and the food stay with me I will start to physically feel better.

MY GOD IS FAITHFUL!!!!

Today is a day I am not looking forward to. I am headed to the Funeral Home to view my love before cremation. You're wondering why we're cremating him. Well, his mother had a life insurance policy on him from Gerber Life. He had always told me if something happened to him I would never have to worry about final expenses. With his medical history he had not been eligible for life insurance until he turned 50. However, he was not one that thought ahead. Therefore, he had no life insurance. With my medical history I am ineligible for life insurance until I have been clean ten years. That means no treatment for cancer in ten years.

So, to understand the family dynamics, you need to understand the relationship between myself and his mother. Prior to our marriage they were extremely close so when I married him there was a jealousy of the relationship he and I had. She and I had some issues throughout our marriage that should not have happened.

Therefore, I had no access to the funds to make different choices. Originally he wanted his body to be donated to science because of all of the physical challenges he had. What people need to realize is that when one chooses to take their own life then a body cannot be donated to science.

So, my love's best friend, Kevin came to take me to the mortuary. Leah and J.T. were going to a movie because they had such good memories of their father and them at the movies. I had talked my mother into going with them. Of course, I wanted them to come to the mortuary with me or at least be in the parking lot. My mom, their grandmother, was going to try and get them to be available for me should I need the support.

Before we went to the funeral home Kevin who is like a brother to my Mike and to me took me to pick up a guest book and a few other things I needed for the service. Then as the time approached we went to the mortuary. Walking in was one of the hardest things I've had to do in my lifetime. As we waited for them to come and get us it seemed unreal that this was happening, had happened.

Kevin, what an amazing friend he has been to us, to all of our family. He held my arm as we walked in where they had the shell of the man that was so much more than a husband. With all we had been through he was not just my husband, but my best friend. I would find out later his death was the start of major losses in my life over the next year.

I had no control over my emotions and have no control as I write this today. I don't even notice that I'm crying anymore. I just let the tears rain down my cheeks because God knows my heart and my pain. Until you have lost your soul mate some pains just aren't explainable. I thought cancer was painful but cancer had nothing on this. This pain is deep and there is no drug that makes it go away. You think you've got it licked and a smell, a sound, a noise, a voice, a song takes you back to that pain of the loss of what you once had.

I was able to walk in under my own steam keeping my eyes from looking at him until I got to him. When I touched him he was so cold. He hated to be hot but he hated to be freezing. It's strange the things that go through your mind at a time like this. I've been told to write my feelings because getting the emotions out will help the healing process.

He looked the same. I wanted him to talk to me. I wanted to yell at him to ask him why! Why? Why couldn't he love our children enough to not do this to himself? Why couldn't he love me enough? What had I done wrong? Why couldn't he love himself enough?

We had begged him, pled with him, had him arrested and put in rehab, detox, gone to court? Yet, he couldn't, he just couldn't. Something was broken inside of him that no one could fix other than Jesus. I was reminded of our dreams and plans that now well they were like sand held in my hands that slipped through when I wasn't looking.

Was I mad at God?

Absolutely not!

Why wasn't I? Well, God gave all of us free choice. We are given a set of situations and scenarios but it's up to us what we do. We all make right or wrong decisions. My love made his choice.

Unfortunately for me and our children we have to pay the price for his choice. Our family was already splintered from my battle with pancreatic cancer. It seemed like outside forces were doing everything they could to splinter us even further. I could say a lot about well-meaning people who need to worry about their own problems, and stay out of yours and mine.

Please remember this is my perception of events not anyone else's. I wanted my children with me. I was amazed no-one from his side of the family came except for his brother. As I leaned over his body when his brother came in I felt my legs start to go but Kevin and David held me up. God knew what I needed and provided it.

There was so much I didn't understand about this day. It was just the three of us. As I got a grip I waited until the last possible minute of the time we had been allotted praying that some of his family or our children would show up. If they couldn't come in they would at least be in the parking lot to support me. Yes, I was being selfish. At times like this you don't think rationally. It's really amazing if you can put two thoughts together in any coherent form.

Kevin took me back to the house where I was alone for a while until they came in. I asked the kids if they would help me put together the slide show the next day and they said they would. I was so excited I would have a few hours with my children. They did tell me they were going out on a boat ride the next afternoon but would come later.

August 28, 2013
Tonight is another sleepless night for me. I'm putting the cd's of pictures on my laptop so tomorrow night as a family we can put together a slide show of my love's life. The rocking good times of our Mikie! As I was looking through some photo albums I know I've lost not just my husband, but the love of my life, my soul mate.

He was the yin to my yang. He was always cheering me on telling me to keep going, keep succeeding. Without him I never would have finished college. I have no regrets because we told each other frequently how much we loved each other, how much we loved the support from each other. Yes, we had problems and struggles as all married couples do after twenty four years but we simply loved each other without measure! Oh, how I miss my sunshine!

Psalms 6:6; "....I water my couch with my tears."

My heart is shattered without my love, my other half. Today I will get to go see him to say goodbye before the cremation. As tears run down my cheeks like a river I cannot stop I know all I need to do is lean on Jesus. He is my comforter and even though this is the darkest valley I've been through I know my God works all things together for the good even when I cannot see it. In walking with Jesus it is sometimes like being out on the ocean with no sign of the horizon yet you know it's there. I know my God is with me and on Him I can depend!

I just have to trust Jesus.

I am so exhausted. I am thinking I might be able to get some sleep tonight. I really, really need it. Thank you in advance Jesus for the peaceful rest that I am in need of without tears tonight.

August 29, 2013
We're headed to the church to set everything up for the love of my life. I miss him so....

Everything is ready for my love's final service tomorrow except for the slideshow and program. I don't foresee much sleep tonight. I'm so blessed Bro. & Sis. Tommy Craft, Ed & Alicia Hodge, and Debbie & Denny Hahn are now here with me but much as I love all of them I'd rather my love was still here and alive.

My heartbeat has left.....

In the night my friend Debbie Hahn's husband Denny talked to me about Mike. Everyone was concerned that I wanted to speak at his memorial service. I felt I had to honor the man I had spent over half of my life with. As I cried and we talked over the phone he got me to tell him about Mike and wrote the poem I would read at his memorial service.

Poem about my husband, Mike

My husband was a funny guy from the time he was four,
Ring bearer at his sister's wedding, all you could ask for;
The wedding shower was announced and all that Mike Smith could say
Was, "How can they all get in the same shower at one time?"

My husband had a mind of his own from the time he was young.
He told his sis he was hurt, and she thought he was playing.
So he got in his car and drove himself to the hospital
That day: it turned out, he needed to have surgery!

My husband was a musician who liked to play the trumpet.
He played for his school band and made many memories there.
He played the trumpet when they opened up the New River Gorge Bridge--
It was the world's largest steel, single-span, arch bridge, back then.

My husband was a gentleman from the time I first met him.
Whenever we went out he always opened my car door.
But he didn't show his love by buying me flowers,
Except to announce the births of Leah and J.T.

My husband loved his liter of pop.
That's what he called Leah.
And he sang to Leah before she came into this world.
I was pregnant with Leah, and we would both watch as he sang.
It must have been rhythm and blues as she kicked to the beat.

My husband loved his J.T., the baby that kept us laughing.
He loved rifles, rollercoasters, and fireworks on the beach.
He and J.T. would set off the fireworks and then they would run.
They crashed and burned remote control vehicles at the beach.

My husband loved his sister and her husband ,
And he treated their kids "Chris, Elizabeth, and Adam,"
The same as if they were his own.
The four of us were so close,
If anything happened they would go to the nearest adult.

My husband and I had a Yugo, they had a minivan
Charlie and Sharon would go with Mike's mother, Alice
But all three of their children wanted to go in the Yugo—
We all had such fun, it never seemed to be crowded.

My husband loved his nephew Chris.
They shared Chris's school projects.
One time they built a rocket complete with working lights.
Another time, Chris needed to come home from his school.
So Mike drove all the way to Old Virginney

My husband called Elizabeth the first apple of his eye.
He loved and treated her just like she was his daughter.
Anytime that Elizabeth was in pain Mike was hurting.
There's a rumor that they would play Barbie's together.

My husband loved his nephew Adam, the baby of the bunch.
Mike cried for four hours when Adam went to K-5.
When our kids were little, their kids stayed with our kids a whole lot.
Adam would sleep in our room when he'd come to visit.

My husband taught all five kids how to body surf, no surf board!
No doubt about it – my Mike was a family man!
And that love extended to his two dogs Brownie and Daisy.
So, Mike, you really have seven children missing you now...

My husband, you were the sunshine of my life, and now, you're gone.
But even though I am now alone, I am not lonely!
You have brought me so many precious, wonderful memories –
I don't even know where to begin to thank you...

My husband, my love, you were a true lover, and my best friend.
When we were together, we didn't have to talk.
When we were apart, we could never get enough words to say.
No matter what, you always were my love.

My love, my sunshine, I will always treasure that Irish look
And those twinkling, bed-room blue eyes I fell in love with.
You have been my most excellent partner these twenty-four years:
This West Virginia girl's proud to have been your wife.......

August 29, 2013
I waited for my children to come. They were unavailable. They wanted me to come to their aunt's and watch videos of our family with them.

After going to the church and setting everything up we met the Crafts and Hahns for a bite to eat. I remember Bro. Craft walking up to me and asking how I was. I had purchased these huge dark glasses to hide my eyes. I fell into his arms. He held me as I wept.

Mom was with us. People who haven't experienced this type of loss do not understand the pain. They mean well but the pain, the pain is so great. I was so grateful for all everyone did to help me during this time.

August 30, 2013
The Memorial Service program is complete! Slideshow presentation is about halfway done but I'm actually sleepy so going to try and get a few hours of sleep.

I'm finishing the slide show reflecting upon our life together.... twenty-four of the happiest, scariest, exciting, aggravating, loving years of my life. WOW! What wonderful memories I have! I wish someone had helped me put together the slide show but in a way I'm glad I'm doing this by myself. It's my last gift to the love of my life.

The children went with me to have a mid-afternoon lunch with the Crafts, Hodges and Hahn's. Then I dropped them off at Leah's husband's mothers. They were to get dressed and come for the service.

My friend, Treasa Dickinson, was waiting at the church to do my hair. She knew my love loved when I wore it down. She helped me get dressed. John Gross took care of the slide show for us. Others were manning guest books and looking at the photographs I had placed on the walls in the church foyer.

Even almost fifteen months later it still doesn't seem real. I've talked to other widows, some who have remarried and have full lives, and they tell me some days even years later it still doesn't seem real.

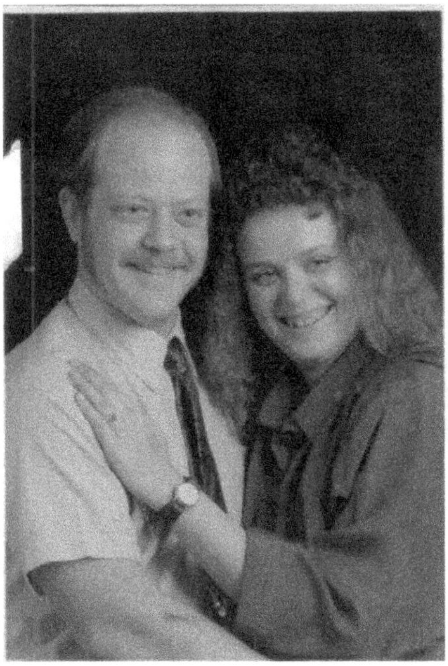
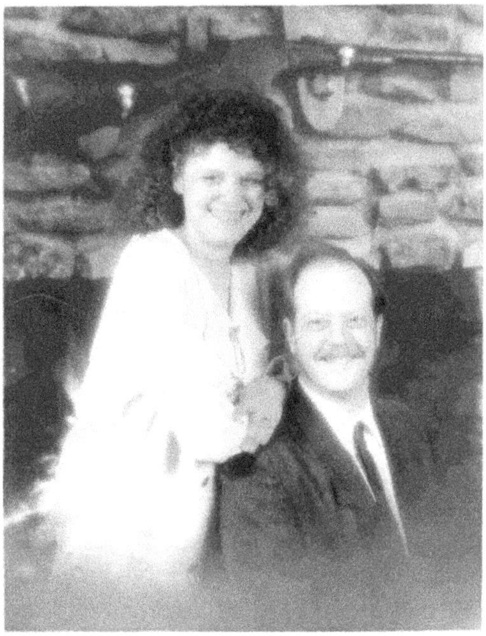
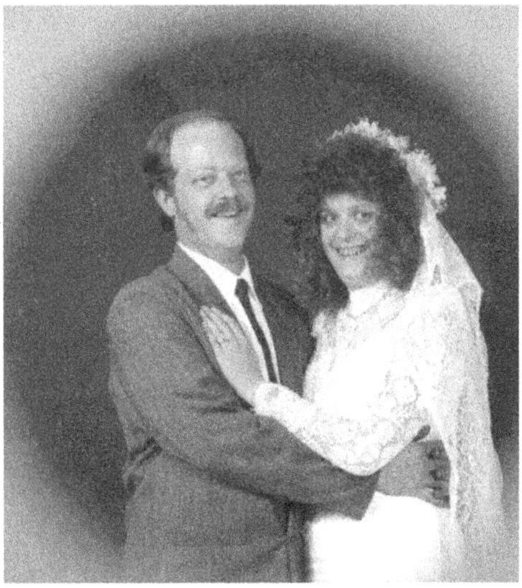

Still in love after 25 years.

When it was time to start my children were not there. My niece and nephews surrounded me. Finally my children came in and we started. We gave all in the family and close friends an opportunity to tell something they remembered about him.

I know this is going to sound crazy but I dressed for him. He loved when I was dressed up with my hair down. I know he couldn't see me but to me it was one of my last gifts to him to show him my love.

During the memorial service I worshipped God while songs were being sung. I know family members did not understand it but my comfort was in feeling God's arms wrapped tightly around me.

The church had prepared a dinner that was amazing for our family and friends. I never expected everything to be so nice. I have been blessed with so many wonderful friends and church family. Truly my church family from around the United States stepped up to the plate when my husband died and loved me and our family. They are still loving us.

At times like this family can be so insensitive. A family member came up to me at the end of the dinner and asked me point blank how much money I had been given since he died. I think the look on my face said it all and then I said, "Now is not the time or place for that discussion." Actually, never was the time or place. While my husband relied on his family for a lot as his wife I did not. Somehow, they had missed that important point.

At times like this it's important to bite your tongue and just get through it. Now as I'm looking back and details are coming back to me of things that happened I'm amazed I held my tongue in certain situations and in others amazed that I said some of the things I did.

The Holy Ghost will give you the strength to take the high road and be the better person when all you would like to do is get down in the mud and start slinging it back. Sometimes we override the Holy Ghost. That is when we need to pray that God will control our tongue and our spirit. We cannot allow ourselves to stoop to their level.

What people don't realize is that when a husband or wife dies the suffering does not stop the week after the funeral, or the month after, or a year after. There is always a hole where that person used to be. No matter how you move on in your life that hole is never filled. It can be ignored to a degree but at some point the grief will have to be dealt with.

I could never thank everyone who came and helped at the church with everything enough. It was amazing and wonderful. Now reality hits but with God I will be fine in Jesus name.

August 31, 2013
I need to thank everyone from Glen Ferris Apostolic Church who worked to make my love's final service such a memorable one. I also need to thank Bro. Tommy & Sis. Diane Craft, Denny and Debbie Hahn, Ed & Alicia Hodge for stopping their lives this holiday weekend to come be with me. I am heading out to say goodbye to them and then try to start a life without my sunshine. Please,, when you pray, remember myself and our children as we walk this new walk.

Today, I allowed my friends to minister to me. They'll never know how much they helped me by being here. I love them so much. I thought they would be rushing off but everyone seemed to have time to be with us.

My friends took this day and ministered to my soul. It started out with breakfast with my mom (Pat Wine), Bro. & Sis. Craft , Denny & Debbie Barraza Hahn, Ed & Alicia Hodge then lunch. Lastly we had an impromptu worship service at Bro. & Sis. Lloyd Hart's church in Beckley, West Virginia. Thank you all.

This evening I went to my sister-in-law's house for dinner with my children and the rest of my husband's family. Our daughter was supposed to come but was unable to. I'll never forget sitting at the table realizing it would probably be the last time we would all be together because of the family situation but I was drinking in my niece and nephews faces.

I loved those three as my own children. Knowing I probably won't see them again was tearing me apart. Not only had I lost my husband but I was losing the rest of my family except for my children.

After dinner my brother-in-law wanted to know about Bro. Craft. So I told him of his wonderful ministry. Then he wanted to know how my evangelism was financed. I told him it was called, "Living by faith and that it is not for the faint of heart. It is getting in the car when you're not sure if you have enough money for gas to head to the next place. Somehow God provides."

Then he asked this question, "How do you make miracles happen?"

I responded, "I don't. I just raise people's faith by telling them of the miracles in my life. I'm just the vessel God uses to raise faith to a level where He will meet it and meet their needs."

I will never forget what he said next, "Susie, don't ever stop doing what you're doing."

Then my husband's sister said, "You've walked the walk before us all these years. Now, you're talking the talk."

I could have been paid no higher compliment by anyone in this world. These are people that have seen me at my worst and they were saying words like that to me.

You never know who is watching or when they are watching. Consistency is the key to witnessing to those closest to us. The ones that see us when we blow our stack or when we don't act like the Christian we should be acting like. They watch and they know what we are and how we live. Be careful what you do, say and how you act for you don't know who you might be leading to Christ or leading away from Christ.

September 1, 2013
I got up early Sunday morning to start the two hour drive to meet Dad so Mom will be able to go home. My daughter arranged for Mom to come to the funeral and be with me this week. However, Mom needed a way home. She was very worried about how she would get home most of the week. It seemed to be best that I take her and meet Dad about an hour from their home.

I'm going down memory lane after dropping my mom off. I knew for myself I needed to be in church this morning. So I am at the church where my love and I went when we were dating and where he was baptized in Jesus name in 1988. Also this was the last church we were in a church service together.

I almost didn't go in the church in Clarksburg, West Virginia. It was not because of anyone or anything in the church but because of me. When I pulled in the parking lot waves of fresh grief overwhelmed me. There are so many memories at this particular place. Thankfully I had texted Sister Cheri Sandy. She knew I was outside and came out to walk in with me. Walking in, knowing that was the last church we had been in together and the first church when we were dating was almost too much for me emotionally.

Thank God for such wonderful people as Bro. & Sis. Joseph. During the service he had everyone to come and pray for me. I will never forget how they reached out to me with so much love. I was able to just sit there as the memories flooded my soul and the tears streamed down my face. I didn't know I could cry rivers of tears until my love died.
Tears seem to be a part of me now.

After church I went to Buckhannon to visit with the Moorings. Bro. Mooring was one of the ministers for the service for Mike. These folks are family to me..My friends from around the nation have truly all been there for me during this time. Some were available on the phone and others by allowing me to drop in and to just be in their presence understanding the tears that I could not stop.

September 2, 2013
I've cleaned out the Expedition of all the pictures we had taken to the church. Now I am on my way to go pick J.T. up and find something to eat. I really have no appetite still so please pray for me that I can eat something and it will stay with me. God is good all the time, and all the time my God is GOOD!

I can't say it will never rain if you follow Jesus. But I can say that if you keep your eyes on Him, He will cover you when the storms hit.

Regardless of this curve ball I've been thrown I want all to know I am well and more importantly, IT IS WELL WITH MY SOUL!"

Tis so sweet to trust in Jesus! Sometimes trusting in Jesus is all we have, when that happens we learn how to fall back into His arms and He simply catches us.

Throughout this most recent valley I've taken many times to take myself away with God to pray and worship Him. In every valley, through every circumstance, God is still God and I never lost my hope or my praise! I may have been sucker punched and had to catch my breath as the punches have come. I have fallen to my knees while being seemingly kicked with new blows but always with my hands raised never ever losing my praise!

Please notice that above I did not say I felt like praising or I felt God. Praising God when you don't feel it, when you don't want to do it is the most important time for you to do it!

Thank you, Shanna Dobson for messaging the song, "You Are God" to me. Since I got the news of my love's passing I have listened to this several times. Y'all have ministered to me. God has sent me so many angels in the form of my friends to minister to me and remind me of the basics. Sometimes when we walk by faith and our world is shaken to such a degree everything we touch shakes including us. We can shake as long as our foundation is sure and we know in whom to trust and we continue to pray and worship.

When you can worship through a crisis and dance before your God even though your world is crushed I believe the devil and other folks just don't understand. Then we can look up and let the devil know he should have never bothered us. If he thinks I was doing everything I could do before this happened once I get everything done that has to be done I will do everything to help everyone find God and a relationship with Him. I intend to be the devil's worst nightmare in Jesus name!

September 3, 2013
Someone messaged me Psalms 32:7-12 to comfort me during this time. I don't know how many times I have read this particular passage but it gives me comfort. I know that I know God is my hiding place in this storm I find myself in.

"7 Thou art my hiding place; thou shalt preserve me from trouble; thou shalt compass me about with songs of deliverance. Selah. 8 I will instruct thee and teach thee in the way which thou shalt go: I will guide thee with mine eye. 9 Be ye not as the horse, or as the mule, which have no understanding: whose mouth must be held in with bit and bridle, lest they come near unto thee. 10 Many sorrows shall be to the wicked: but he that trusteth in the LORD, mercy shall compass him about. 11 Be glad in the LORD, and rejoice, ye righteous: and shout for joy, all ye that are upright in heart."

When it rains in lives, strong people go to their knees. Since last Sunday when I received a phone call that my husband had suddenly passed away it was to prayer I immediately went. All week while making plans and grieving it's been to prayer I've gone. Our strength is in prayer.

When you know not what to do simply pray.

I've had a busy morning. I finally found our wills so a trip to the courthouse, then errands and now to go pick J.T. up from work. For some reason I am wanting a hot dog with french fries.....and maybe a vanilla shake when I should be eating sandwiches but for something to finally sound good. Who knows I may just come straight back here without picking up hot dogs. My brain still isn't functioning on all cylinders yet but I was also on the phone cancelling stuff and making calls.... busy... busy. Hopefully, tomorrow I can rest.

Upon finding the wills I knew with our volatile family situation I needed to get his to the courthouse immediately and have it filed. I did not want it to be lost. Grief affects everyone differently. Some people are so wrapped up in money, position, and power that they can't handle it when they know they have lost the ultimate power with something or someone they thought they had control over.

September 4, 2013
So we're up early this morning. I started laundry, making phone calls and paying bills but no heart to get dressed yet. Eventually, yes, I realize this is probably TMI but trying to figure out this new world I've found myself in. Learning how to navigate it is crucial to moving forward.

Regardless of what happens in my life I am B-L-E-S-S-E-D!!! I had twenty-four of the most amazing, loving, aggravating, accomplished, and so on years with a man that treated me like I was his princess and I treated him like a prince (well most of the time we did, we did have our moments, LOL). I can never thank God enough for all the blessings we had in our twenty-four years together but I do miss him with every breath I breathe and every syllable I utter.

This morning I heard a knock on my door. When I went to answer it a man unrelated to me in any way but the man currently living with my husband's mother was at the door. He had been sent over to my home to tell me that she would not be leaving until the bill at the funeral home for her son was paid. He then said, I need to know exactly how much money you have and what you're planning to do about the bill. I looked at him, took a deep breath, and politely said, "I'm not worrying about it. I have more important things to worry about like feeding my family and keeping the lights on." I then shut the door.

Needless to say that was not the answer he wanted. However, that was the answer he received and I shut the door locking it. Next I went to Lowe's and bought new locks for the house. My husband's mother has an apartment attached to my house with a separate entrance. When she is there in the past I would park my car behind the house and go out the back door to avoid problems. When we were first married she intimidated me but as I got older I just didn't have the time to put into the problems that seemingly arose from that relationship. I had more important things to deal with.

When we have the Word written upon our heart then when trouble and adversity barrel into our lives we have encouragement within ourselves. We know that we know that it will be okay because God is with us. It does not matter what you're going through; death, divorce, cancer, job loss, financial crisis, family issues know that Gods got this. Just fall back into His arms and let the God of Glory catch you! He will! Just trust Him. I know of what I say.

Proverbs 3:1-7
1 My son, forget not my law; but let thine heart keep my commandments:² For length of days, and long life, and peace, shall they add to thee.³ Let not mercy and truth forsake thee: bind them about thy neck; write them upon the table of thine heart:⁴ So shalt thou find favour and good understanding in the sight of God and man.⁵ Trust in the LORD with all thine heart; and lean not unto thine own understanding.⁶ In all thy ways acknowledge him, and he shall direct thy paths.⁷ Be not wise in thine own eyes: fear the LORD, and depart from evil.

So very true. We are all in His hands!

I so wish I could hug my love today but he is in my dreams.

Memories keep coming at me. It's probably because I'm alone most of the time now. He so enjoyed going to the beach. Myrtle Beach was his favorite place. What fun we had. Usually we were there two times a year at the minimum some years 3-4 times. Other than West Virginia the beach and vacations with our children were his favorite places. He loved our children more than anything else.

My love loved our children more than anything else.

He was always helping others, and making our children's dreams come true.

Oh, how I miss my love!

The Stripping!

"³ And the L‍ord said unto Satan, Hast thou considered my servant Job, that there is none like him in the earth, a perfect and an upright man, one that feareth God, and escheweth evil? and still he holdeth fast his integrity, although thou movedst me against him, to destroy him without cause.⁴ And Satan answered the L‍ord, and said, Skin for skin, yea, all that a man hath will he give for his life.⁵ But put forth thine hand now, and touch his bone and his flesh, and he will curse thee to thy face.⁶ And the L‍ord said unto Satan, Behold, he is in thine hand; but save his life."

September 5, 2013

When going through a crisis in life I've seen many who think it's a weakness to seek professional help to deal with your grief. I, on the other hand, think it's a bigger weakness not to seek professional counseling along with the counsel of your pastor and elders. Prayer, to me, is the most important ingredient as life continues and we have to continue one day at a time and some days one step at a time. .

Before going to the counselor I was taking J.T. to drop him off at his friend's home and we decided to stop and check with the State Police about my husband's guns. J.T. waited in the Expedition while I went in. Going in I didn't think anything when they said the Sargent wants to see you. He took me back to a room and sat down.

Then he started interrogating me. I was questioned for three hours as a suspect in my husband's murder. First of all, it wasn't murder. I found out that they considered it suspicious and had not closed the case and would not close the case until they received the official coroner's report. That could take six weeks. When I told him I wasn't even in the state the officer took the tactic of you must have been separated and wanted him dead. So who did you have crush the pills and put them in him? I was shocked. I sat there and said, "I live by faith. I have no money. Check our bank accounts."

I then told him my husband and I talked every day four to seven times a day and sometimes more. He then admitted they had pulled my cell phone records and my husbands. They also saw that I had talked to him several times the day he died and the next day I had tried to call three times before I was notified he was dead.

They were determined I was guilty until I explained where I was and how many people had seen me. Not to mention I had gas receipts and plane tickets. Needless to say when I walked out of there I had found out the guns had been given to my husband's mother.

After that I realized we have a lot of people probably sitting in prison that are innocent along with a lot of guilty people. Therefore, I now have a compassion for them I've never had before. That officer let me know that had I been home I would have been arrested and prosecuted on circumstantial evidence. I could very well be in prison for a murder that wasn't a murder.

Going to the session at the counselor was necessary for me. Even though I have a college education and minored in Sociology, Psychology, and now I counsel with others I had no idea how to help myself through this. Upon my arrival at the counselor they handed me a form to fill out. When I got to marital status I lost it. I couldn't control the tears. Married, Single, widowed? What a question for me to answer when I was still reeling from the fact my husband had died just a little more than a week earlier.

I could never say thank you enough to all those that have ministered to me this week and continue to do so. I was listening to old song, "Leave it there." This song reminded me to take my burdens to God and leave them at His feet.

There's just something about the older worship songs. Oh, how I love Him. Oh, how I adore Him... My all in all. He truly is my all in all whether on the mountain top or grieving in the valley He remains all in all!

I've had a good day. It's had its moments but overall I am blessed. Last night I went to church and tonight I again went. Some may not understand this but my greatest strength comes from worshiping the Lord of Lords and the King of Kings regardless of my circumstances. When I'm in the Word of God learning of Him and spending time in His presence is how I'm getting through each day. God is my very best friend.

September 6, 2013
Today is my daughter's 23rd birthday. I don't think any of us did anything for her. We are all too wrapped up in our grief. Did you know grief can become a blanket? You can start to enjoy your misery.

That is why in the middle of a crisis/disaster in our lives it is sometimes hard to remember that the battle is not ours but Gods. When we remember this is when the battle becomes smaller. Keeping our eyes on Jesus is what makes the difference.

II Chronicles 20:15 *And he said, Hearken ye, all Judah, and ye inhabitants of Jerusalem, and thou king Jehoshaphat, Thus saith the* LORD *unto you, Be not afraid nor dismayed by reason of this great multitude; for the battle is not yours, but God's.*

I just talked to my friend Debbie from Mississippi. They are so sweet calling me every day along with a few others to check on me. Any who, they told me at the Mississippi Lady's Conference they made a big to do about the book God inspired me to write, "Surprised by God with Pancreatic Cancer" and talked about the ministry God has opened to me. Thank God for His many wonderful blessings even when walking through the valley of loss.

September 8, 2013
I just beat J.T. in a game of scrabble. I think it's the first time we've played until we each only had two letters and could do nothing with them. Love our son. I'm going to miss him while he's at his sister's in Kentucky but I know he needs this. It's going to be a l-o-n-g- two weeks without him running in and out of the house.

I love being with my Leah and J.T. They are and always have been the loves of my life. We enjoyed lunch at Pita Pit. I couldn't believe our discussion today.

They think I should get married again. Really? Why?

Then I find out my husband's mother has been talking to them. She has put them up to asking me to change the deed to the house putting it in their name and walk away. When I refused they told me that they had been told I would refuse because I would see it as a paycheck. Really?

For twenty-four years I supported my husband financially, physically, and spiritually. When I couldn't provide certain big ticket toys he wanted he would let her know and she would make it happen for him. Did I sometimes get a side benefit from this? Yes.

Did most of our arguments stem from me wanting him to wait until we could afford to do some things on our own? Yes. Seemingly they remember things differently and think I didn't do anything all these years with him being sick. What they have to remember is my perception is my reality while I have to remember that their perception of events is also their reality. I just hate how facts are being twisted to influence my children against me. I know one day they will remember all the times Mommy was at work taking care of them.

Today I talked to Leah about bringing her dolls and old fashioned dresses for her to have. As I followed them to the interstate and headed towards Fayetteville while they headed to Kentucky a feeling of desolation, of aloneness as they went one way and I went the other....

Tears once again rained down my cheeks with abandon until I could almost not see to drive. I didn't know that tears could run like a raging river until I started through this crisis. Heartache and heartbreak are the most painful diseases one can suffer.

This is a new life for me. Yes, I was traveling before but my love was always on the phone. He was always supporting me. Now, well, now it's me and Jesus.

Two weeks ago today my family's world started rocking and while it hasn't stopped the shaking is not so bad now. We had a major earthquake and now we're in the aftershocks which I'm told will last quite a while. I'm so grateful for those very close friends who have been texting me scriptures.

The one today really spoke to me, Proverbs 3:5, *"Trust in the LORD with all thine heart; and lean not unto thine own understanding."*

When going through something like this that there is no real understanding of why, that's when you learn how to trust, really trust God, no holds barred. This is a whole new level of faith, one that I really would have rather not experienced. Now that I have I don't quite know how to explain what God is doing to me through this but He is changing me yet again. I am still very blessed!

The verse God gave me two weeks ago when I was driving from Houston to Jackson. We must all remember that, *"ALL THINGS"* not just the good things but even the bad things, *"...work together for the good"*.

Some things should never change regardless of your circumstances. When it's time for church you should make yourself get dressed and go. God will meet you there. For me that is what I'm doing. I love God but even though the last thing I feel like doing right now is getting dressed and going anywhere it's Sunday night. It is time for church! Let's worship God and thank Him for His many, many abundant never-ending blessings on us!

So tired but excited about some things God may be working out. Most of the time we just plod along not knowing what the next right step is and then God just plops it in our lap. We look at the solution with wonderment. Then always pray before making a decision. So I'm at the prayer step but I'm still excited thinking about what this means if it works out. I know I've piqued your interest but I can't really share anything else right now. Just pray. There is so much to do, so many decisions to make but my God has got this. I am continuing to trust Him to show me His will.

September 9, 2013
This morning in my devotions I have been reading in Matthew 1 where it talks about the angel appearing to Joseph about the situation where Mary had been found with child of the Holy Ghost. What really stood out to me was verse 24 where, Joseph did as the angel of the Lord had bidden him. I wonder how many of us would have simply obeyed. Most of us, myself included would have needed a list of why we should obey and would have waited until someone else confirmed it to be sure we were in the will of God. Isn't it time my generation quit generating excuses to not obey God?

In my Bible it tells me in I Samuel 15:22, "...*Behold, to obey is better than sacrifice,...*". So the next time God whispers into your world simply listen and obey. God will not tell you to do anything that will go against his Word. That next voice you hear that tells you that wasn't God, check it. Think about it and think about what Joseph did.

Sometimes we need to be reminded this is spiritual warfare and we are in battle. This is not for the faint of heart. In order to be prepared it requires daily devotions, daily prayer, daily Bible reading. In order to fight you must know your weapons so you can fight with strategy and be successful. I want to be a mighty soldier in the army of the Lord. I do not just want to be a soldier or someone that stands back while others are in the heat of the battle

Missing my love so much today who liked to wear what hair he had a little long, loved ball caps, guns, driving fast, fixing the stuff I invariably broke, and so on. One thing we both loved was going for long drives on roads that weren't roads and sometimes the four wheel drive would get hung up. I miss you baby!

When walking through a valley you should seek messages that will minister to you in the midst of the valley. So this morning God has been leading me to specific messages that are speaking to my world. If you need encouraged this is a good message to listen to, but don't just listen, let it minister to you and change you like "Testing our Faith" as preached by Bro. Lee Stoneking.

It is a busy day but regardless of how busy I am first thing on the to do list is spending time with the Lord of Lords and the King of Kings. Then it's been clipping coupons, working on the Thank you cards, and now to take a break and walk the dogs. I love my Brownie and Daisy. Each day they cheer me up especially now that J.T. is gone for a few weeks. I love my kids and so glad they are close to each other.

I'm so blessed. Last night I wrote until about 11 p.m. and now I'm making Chef-Boy-Ar-Dee Pizza for myself and our two puppies. Every time I would come home from a trip that would be one of the first things I would want so Mike and I would have a 'party'. Then this afternoon counseling and then I'm headed to Huntington, WV to be with the ALC Ladies tonight. God is doing G-R-E-A-T things. I will praise Him no matter what!

September 10, 2013
My love was most comfortable in raggedy old t shirts and jeans. Three years ago we went to the Petrified Forest in New Mexico. It was one of my bucket list trips. He really enjoyed it. If we had known we would have made him a bucket list and went to all the places he wanted to go. I miss him so but I was so blessed to be his wife.

It is time to get ready to leave for counseling and then head to Huntington to be with the Harper's tonight. It's going to be awesome!!! I walked the dogs and am I ever out of shape. I'm so glad for the sixty pounds I've lost but need to lose some more. Hopefully walking will take it off. Have a great blessed day everyone. Please know that I am indeed blessed of God!

September 11, 2013
No matter what we should give thanks to the Lord. When trouble comes as it does to all we have to remember on whom we believe and take our needs to Him. He is still God no matter how dark, lonely, and forgotten we may feel. All we need to remember is that He is close to the broken hearted and cry to Him. He will be everything we need!

Psalms 107:1-9 *"O give thanks unto the L*ORD*, for he is good: for his mercy endureth for ever.² Let the redeemed of the L*ORD *say so, whom he hath redeemed from the hand of the enemy;³ And gathered them out of the lands, from the east, and from the west, from the north, and from the south.⁴ They wandered in the wilderness in a solitary way; they found no city to dwell in.⁵ Hungry and thirsty, their soul fainted in them. ⁶ Then they cried unto the L*ORD *in their trouble, and he delivered them out of their distresses.⁷ And he led them forth by the right way, that they might go to a city of habitation. ⁸ Oh that men would praise the L*ORD *for his goodness, and for his wonderful works to the children of men! ⁹ For he satisfieth the longing soul, and filleth the hungry soul with goodness."*

As my tears flow down my cheeks today I am reminded of how much my love loved me. When I was so sick he took care of me never once complaining about the constant care I needed. We were so looking forward to our 'golden' years traveling working for God. When I reach for his hand and it's not there my breath catches and the tears begin to flow without me even realizing. I miss his twinkling blue eyes, the way he would throw his head back in laughter when he got a good joke, and the many times he would just come sit by me so we could just soak up being together. Love your loved ones today fore no-one knows what tomorrow holds.

Just saw this on facebook. Another person enjoyed the book I wrote, "The Blood". I guess it's time to quit feeling sorry for myself and start writing on those other novels.

It's time for church. As I travel through this grief process I am a person who has always been an overachiever yet now I find myself wanting to curl up in a ball & let everything pass on by. I can't do that. I have to move forward. God has given me a mission. All the things that have happened to me will somehow help me help more people. We should all take the things that have happened to us and somehow find a way to bring glory to God. After all, it's about showing others who Jesus is. If we get locked up in our own needs we'll never accomplish anything for Him. So I guess I said all that to say I'm giving myself a swift kick and making me go, making me continue all the while spending private time grieving but in the meantime trying to find someone to help, someone that needs love and prayer whose needs are greater than mine at this time.

On the next page are a few comments from Facebook I felt led by God to leave in this book for you to understand who I am:

Dawn Sigley
God made our earthly bodies to bare more than we think we can stand. But he has you in his arms at this very moment. When My son went to be with the Lord I was profoundly aware of his presence with me and the time that we shared just me and my Lord. Healing, Breathing, Grieving is where I drew my strength to get by minute by minute. I have always admired your faith, even in high school you carried your Bible. Thinking of you....

Regina Horne
You are a true Christian, Susan. Praying for you.

Aurelia N John Hopkins
The Lord Jesus has much confidence in you to allow you to go through such great trials. Even though that statement brings you no comfort it is true that HE trusts you and knows that you are a "Vessel of Honor"

My reply to their kind words:
Thanks, everyone. I'll make it because I know on whom I depend, His name is Jesus! @ Dawn Sigley, I had forgotten about carrying my Bible to school until you mentioned it. I do remember now. What wonderful memories I have. Thanks for reminding me.

Memories keep coming. I was recalling how after Mike had surgery for possible colon cancer he was in the hospital for two weeks. Before he had the surgery we had prayed. They did four colonoscopies on the table and couldn't find the polyps/cancer. They still took 18 inches of his colon out. Three days in ICU and two weeks in the hospital then he went home to recover. Colon cancer did not take his life.

He is so missed. I keep expecting to hear his voice but I never will except on our videos. Wishing he was with me tonight but I know God has this!

Matthew 15:22-28; I wonder how I would have reacted when going to Jesus in such desperation for my child to hear him say I didn't come for you but for the special people(the children of Israel). Isn't that how we see it some of the time. God won't do it for us because we're nobody but this woman didn't quit. She was desperate! She reminded him even the dogs get the crumbs. All she wanted was a crumb from the Master's table. Because of that persistent faith her daughter was made whole.

We have access to the banquet yet we don't have all we need. Some days all I ask for are the crumbs when the King of Kings and the Lord of Glory is saying come and get what you need from the table. You and I don't have to accept crumbs we have access to everything. I needed reminded this morning of that access. So if you're sick or in need just remember who you serve. He's waiting for you.

Just because things have changed radically in your life and mine does not mean it's over. It's time for a new beginning with God.
A fall rainstorm and I've had a few friends tell me I should stay in tonight so I'm beginning to think maybe it's okay for me to be still, curled up with our doggies remembering our life together. I'm just afraid if I start to stay in I'll forget to go out. That is a problem for people who are grieving. Then I'll become someone I don't recognize but then again I don't recognize myself anyway so no great loss.

I'm getting off facebook to think, pray and do some writing. That's the hardest part to write about everything that's happened the past two and a half weeks. Don't get me wrong there's been so much love poured out on our family but the reality of the situation is what is hard to deal with.

I know I'm falling back into God's arms and He's simply catching me, holding me and loving me. I know my friends are right. Sooner or later I'll have to be still long enough to deal with the emotions of grief. Even the grief counselor reminded me that Jesus took himself away.

Sometimes though we as humans would rather avoid than deal with the emotions inside of us but if we don't deal with them they will haunt us in the future. I definitely don't want that. I only plan to travel this road once with Jesus as my pilot. So pray for me as I take some time away.... I'll probably be back on here much later tonight but for now I'm off. Blessings to all of you! Love your families!

September 12
Since my love left this world God has so ordered my steps to be in church or in prayer with friends a portion of each day. God knows how much I miss my love but also how much I love God. Soon it will be all systems Go for my ministry and book writing but while I'm here in this place it's about me learning how to trust God in a whole new way, just falling back and letting the Lord of Glory catch me, hold me and minister to me.

Malachi 3:6 - He never ever changes. No matter what is going on God is still God. I need to rest in that promise. Watch and see how God will comfort you and me.

Malachi 3:6
"For I am the LORD, I change not;..."

I'm not sure what the right or wrong thing to do is regarding grieving and what I share but I'm going to share what I feel God wants me to share about this valley I'm walking through. While it is a valley and today has been a hard day in all things I will give thanks fore I know Jesus is carrying me through this valley. Today when I was distraught God sent a friend to call me and another friend showed up at my door. You see that's how God works. He had already sent me comfort before I needed it. So no matter what journey you're on rest in the promise that God will meet your need. He just will!

September 13, 2013
Today I listened to songs and let them minister to me as I read facebook and took comfort in those that were praying for me and my children. Some days the grief is just so overwhelming yet I know who holds my hand and who is leading me beside still waters.

September 14, 2013
This morning started out with me not wanting to do anything be anywhere but a few phone calls later I pushed myself to get up and dressed. Lunch with a dear friend and then home where exhaustion claimed me and I slept all evening. I am very blessed of God indeed. I pray that I never cease to thank Him for all of His many blessings on my family and myself.

I took great comfort in words like the ones following from my dear friend, Sis. Aurelia Hopkins.

I have continued to pray for you Sis. Susie and so did LT on Thursday night! You're not alone even though you might feel alone. You are in may people's thoughts and prayers!

My reply to Sis. Hopkins and the many that had commented letting me know I was covered in prayer. Thanks all. @. Aurelia N John Hopkins You can always read me. Yes it is a lonely road but I know I'm covered in prayer. Tonight I'm praying God gives me strength to start going through 24 years of a two story houseful of memories and things only keeping the necessary items. Memories are constantly with me.

Cocal Cola Museum Atlanta, Georgia 1999.
My love's favorite vacation spot, Myrtle Beach, SC. It doesn't seem real. I am missing him. He wasn't just my husband but my best friend.

I really should go to sleep but I've been watching Bro. Macey preach at Royalwood.cc online since our two dogs woke me up needing to go out and now I'm wide awake. Hopefully soon I'll wind down and head to bed in the meantime I've heard some fabulous anointed preaching!!! Just what I needed!

The doggies are begging to go to bed... Lol. They're not happy when I stay up past eleven p.m. It is like they have an internal clock that says all should be asleep by a certain time. All you can see in the pic is little Brownie. Daisy had jumped up on me (miniature black lab) begging for bed.

Both dogs were begging for bed so I reckon I should put them out of their misery and go to sleep. Now she's trying to talk to me. It is pitiful but I love them. They are so much company.

As I was playing a game God started talking to me about strategy for spiritual warfare. We strategize when we play games, lead staffs, and/or plan for the future of a company. God was telling me basically about how I try to make things to complex when the answer is very simple and straight forward from Him. My generation has relied too much on what we could accomplish and not focused on the spiritual. We haven't given God credit for the everyday miracles in our lives.

Sometimes we need to realize that a flat tire(any delay) could be saving us from an accident or delaying us so that we can meet someone who needs something from God and we are to be the vessel. If we are too upset and don't try to see how these delays could be used to glorify God we might find we are missing some of our biggest blessings. So, I said all that to say when trials and valleys come our way as they oft times will look for how you can bless someone and bring glory to the King of Kings and the Lord of Lords.

My Bible is my roadmap. That's why I highlight and underline certain passages to remember that God loves me to speak to me and give me a clearer understanding. Here, Jesus was hungry. He came by a tree that bore no figs. That could be us never accomplishing anything for him. He looked at the tree and said, "Let no fruit grow...". The tree withered and died. All we need is faith. With faith we can ask anything in prayer if we believe and we will simply receive. What if, instead of always using this passage about our needs we turned it around and asked God to lead us to hungry hurting souls? What type of revival could we have then. It is time to Get it Out as Sis. Vesta Mangun would say.

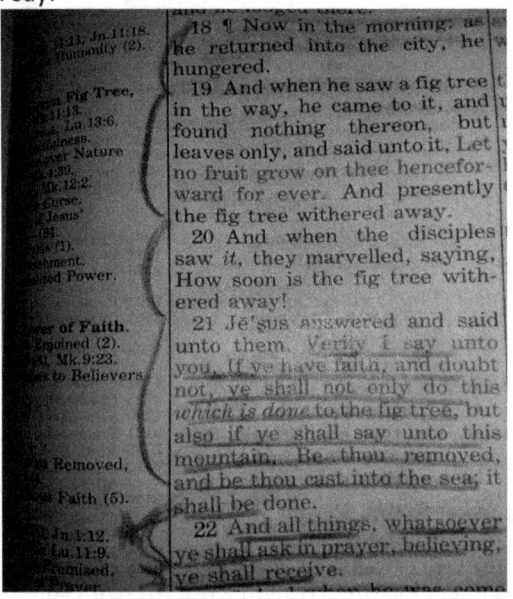

As the kids will remember ("adopted" and biological) The Big Purple as they called our huge van took us to many church camps and on many vacations. We would fill it up as full as we could get it. My love so enjoyed taxing us around in "The Big Purple". Lots of fun, laughs, interesting smells, etc... I'll never understand why they called it the big purple since it was a blue stretch van. LOL. Kids are so funny.

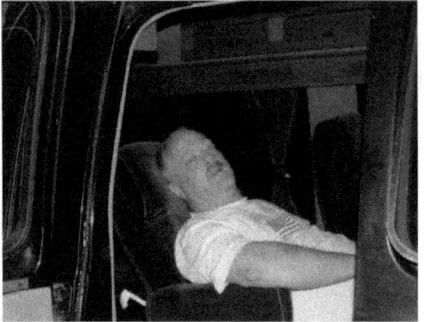

My love loved the water, whether out on a boat, lakefront, beachfront or any other way. We so enjoyed having fun together with our children and friends. Every shirt my husband owned eventually had a stain because he was always fixing things for everyone. I could never get him to remember to change shirts before diving under the hood of something, wiring something, or pulling his tools out to work on something electrical or electronic. He could fix anything. —

For those that are calling every day to make sure I'm eating, I'm making oatmeal and bacon for me and the doggies this morning. I will eat at least a small bowl with a piece of two of bacon. While I don't have an appetite I am making sure to eat at least once or twice a day. I am drinking a lot of water so don't go worrying I'll get dehydrated. I love y'all and appreciate the fact you love me enough to check on me. What would we do without our church family/friends? I never want to find out.

What a lovely afternoon and evening I have had with Randy and Lois Pitsenbarger, and D.J. and Cindy Pitsenbarger. The food was amazing and the company was even better. Thanks for including me and for the eggs! I feel refreshed for the first time in three weeks. I know it's going to be a long road but with friends who lift you up it won't be nearly as dreary. Again, Thank you all!

September 15, 2013
Late last night or early this morning around 2 or 3 a.m. I was talking to my friends Debbie & Denny Hahn. They were asking me what I was going to do today. I told them I didn't know if I could go to church but I know it's time for church and I am reminded this morning of Hebrews 10:25 where it says, *"Not forsaking the assembling of ourselves together, as the manner of some is; but exhorting one another: and so much the more, as ye see the day approaching."*

So no matter what we are going through when it's time for church, it's simply time for church and time for us to get ready to go worship God. No matter what we always have something to worship Him for. He died for us, He gave His life that we might have life and have it more abundantly. The sky is blue, or it is raining so the grass and plants will grow, even in the midst of a great valley we have so many things to thank Him for. So I'm off to church to worship God and you should be also. Have a great blessed Sunday!

My love enjoyed Bridge Day. It's always held the third Saturday in October. In High School when the New River Gorge Bridge opened he played the trumpet in his high school band. It's been three weeks today since you left us. They say my grief will get easier with time but so far it seems to get worse. I miss you so!

We don't live by feelings and it's a good thing. If we did when bad things happened we'd just stop, go in our homes, and never come out again. Instead we have to brush ourselves off, grieve, pick ourselves up and continue on. There's too much to be done for God to stop.

So tonight I'm getting ready to head for church. I need to commune with God. Yes, I can commune with Him in my home but there's something about being with the saints of the most High God. So find a church, worship God!

September 16, 2013
Wow! What a Word God gave me this morning. This portion of scripture is so powerful for those of us who are suffering one way o another. My God is the God of all comfort. So while I've been grieving and alone when I felt like someone was holding me my God was.

Reading and hearing that He is your comfort is one thing but experiencing that comfort for yourself is something supernatural. I am so blessed and privileged to have a relationship with God that supersedes anything man can try to explain. Thank you Lord Jesus for being my comforter and continuing to comfort me. Praise God from whom all blessings flow.

I Corinthians 1:4-7, *⁴ Who comforteth us in all our tribulation, that we may be able to comfort them which are in any trouble, by the comfort wherewith we ourselves are comforted of God. ⁵ For as the sufferings of Christ abound in us, so our consolation also aboundeth by Christ. ⁶ And whether we be afflicted, it is for your consolation and salvation, which is effectual in the enduring of the same sufferings which we also suffer: or whether we be comforted, it is for your consolation and salvation. ⁷ And our hope of you is stedfast, knowing, that as ye are partakers of the sufferings, so shall ye be also of the consolation.*

While I am still grieving today is the day I have to start moving forward one step at a time. This will not be easy but I will do it and the memories of the one I have loved and will always love will comfort me during those times when grief overtakes me.

September 16, 2013
So it is time to get busy and work on laundry. I hate it but I have to get started going through our stuff. Until you have to go through it and figure out what to keep you don't realize how much you have accumulated. In the middle of that I have a novel I need to finish writing and my friends seem to think I should eat so I'm laying out some hamburger to cook something later. I still don't have an appetite but I am eating a little something each day.

As I was walking Brownie Daisy howled at the injustice of being left behind. Her walk is next. Walking the dogs has been a lifesaver but they are both so busy I can only walk them one at a time.

And now walking Daisy.

I think I'm going to fix something to eat. A hamburger and mac & cheese. I realize it's not a balanced meal. Hey, I'm eating. I have started going through our stuff so it's comfort food and a reward. Also today I'm feeling somewhat normal and that's so under-rated.

September 16, 2013
I just got off the phone with my Uncle J.C. who just celebrated his 99th birthday last week. He apologized to me for not calling when my love passed away a few weeks ago. I love my Uncle J.C. He and my Aunt Jean were missionaries to Africa at one time. When we talk it's like our hearts commune about the things of God. Unfortunately, I'm not a very good niece and I don't call often but I did promise to do better. It was so good to hear him sounding so lively. I pray if the Lord tarries and I live to be his age I am able to be as active and in control of my faculties as he is.

Some days I just managed to get through. There wasn't much to say as life was being lived in a blur. Until you're in the middle of this process you really have no clue that some days you do good to remember to breathe through the tears let alone do anything else.

September 17, 2013

When going through the grief process I feel all alone. However, I know, that I know that I am not alone. Just because we feel all alone and in seeking God, like Job we feel that we can't find God He is there. Once we are tried we shall come forth as gold. If we stay ourselves in Jesus regardless of what we are going through and keep one mind to the things of God nothing will be able to turn us from our walk with God. We have to realize as it says in Job 23:17, *"Because I was not cut off from the darkness, neither hath he covered the darkness from my face."* Sometimes we have to face the darkness to not only appreciate the light but be able to help others when they are faced with these valleys in their life. So, no matter what you're going through realize Jesus will bring you out just trust Him.

Today is a busy day with many things to do but first of all I spent some time with God in morning devotions and now I've put trying to get warm at the top of that list. It's so cold here (46 degrees) this morning. I feel like an ice block... brrr.

It's been a busy day but somehow I squeezed in a lunch with my friend Treasa at Logans. I so needed that. I still managed to do laundry, sort, go to grief counseling, go to the cleaners, walk the dogs and some writing. Multitasking is my name these days. So much to do but it will all get done in Jesus name.

Here is a picture of me with my love after church eating out with friends. We had so much fun with our church family in Charlotte, NC. Miss my love so much! Wish he was here so we could pop down to Charlotte for a weekend! By the way that's one of my infamous wigs I wore during chemo.

Think about the words to the song... On the other side of broken... Jesus dries my tears... As the tears roll down my cheeks today I am praying and hoping that someday I will be on the other side of broken.

Don't wait until the battle's over... SHOUT NOW!!!!

That's hard to do but oh, so important. My worship even when I'm alone has to be even more so. I have to worship God when in the depths of despair and despondency.

Tonight I needed reminded what God has done for me. You don't know like I know what God has done for me so when I worship just understand I have a lot to be thankful for therefore my worship is something between my God and I. It's special and unique.

I didn't know it was possible to miss someone more instead of less. Time, I've been told, makes the grief easier to bear.

2006 Eating Christmas Dinner. Missing my love more with each passing day.

September 18, 2013
I need motivation today. I even bought a bag of little sugar donuts and milk for me but I can see them from where I'm at but no appetite. I will get up and eat some then I'll have a sugar rush so hopefully will be able to sort through more of our stuff today and continue writing.
Until you've walked the road of the grief of your spouse you really don't fully understand that type of grief. Over the past 3 1/2 weeks I've been rocked to sleep in the presence and arms of God most nights and when it has been too much for me to bear God has simply caught me and held me.

The God I serve walks every road with us and when we don't think He's there is when He is actually carrying us. I am so very blessed to know a God who is always there, always with me, no matter what. Just think He will be there for you, no matter what. God is all comfort. He comforts me so one day I can comfort others in any trouble showing them the comfort God is showing me.

At this time I had no clue but the weight was falling off of me daily because when I would eat it was very little. After a person dies and everyone leaves is when the grief stricken loved ones need people to stop by, encourage them, and see that they eat. It's not about buying the food it's about the eating. You have no appetite and seemingly no will to live.

Now I'm heating up my leftover lunch from yesterday. I'm eating so little that one lunch from Logan's has made meals for me for three days. Then since Brownie kept me up and down all night I'm thinking a nap before church might be in order.... LOL. J.T. comes home Friday evening... I'm so excited!!!

This afternoon I was having a conversation with God in my kitchen about some needs. I was basically telling God I needed Him now not tomorrow. Sometimes I forget who I'm talking to because He's my best friend and sticks closer to me than anyone else. He hears my every cry.

Anyway, this afternoon my best friend, God, supplied my needs. When things get hairy as they sometimes do when you live by faith you just simply stand on His promises. Then watch God do what He does best, provide your needs. I know I'm not the only one with needs but now as a widow without my love there to bolster me I am a finding a new level of trust with God. I miss my love but I love falling back and letting God catch me. Now it is time to go worship the King of Kings and the Lord of Lords!

Psalm 37:25, "I have been young, and now am old; yet have I not seen the righteous forsaken, nor his seed begging bread."

September 18, 2013
I am so hoping I can sleep tonight. I have been sleeping well but last night one of the dogs kept waking me up to go out. So I'm exhausted tonight. I really need sleep

tonight if I'm going to be in a room full of teenagers tomorrow night. LOL. It will be fun and I would say exactly what I need. I can't wait to see what God will do for everyone at Esther Conference. I'm so blessed to get to enjoy part of it.

It's been an amazingly interesting day filled with revelations I knew were probably coming but still stunned me. However, I know in whom I believe and as Sister Haygood reminded me of what I'd written in the novel the blood, angels are standing round about me with flaming swords of protection. I can't go into details but know that your prayers are keeping me going and know, that I know, that God's got this!

This is nothing for Him! He is my provider! He is my best friend! He is the most precious gift I've ever been given. Jesus, I love you regardless of situations, circumstances or anything else, I just love you!

How much do you love God?

September 20, 2013
Today before going to Esther Conference I am picking J.T. up in Huntington and letting him have the Expedition so he will have wheels and I will ride home with my friend Treasa. In the car on the ride to the hotel J.T. and I were talking. He was letting me know he doesn't believe in God anymore. He loves me he just doesn't believe there is a God.

Since my husband died every day has been a new blow from somewhere unexpected. As I reel from one punch another one comes at me but with each punch God provides another miracle for me. I'm trying to be sensitive and recognize the miracles. It's hard when you're in the middle of the crisis.

Today as I arrived at the hotel and went to the room my phone rang and it was my nephew, Wesley Gallaugher, who is like another son to me. He said, "I just felt you needed me." Little did he know how much he was needed. Before the phone rang I found a corner in the hotel near the elevator and curled up beside my suitcase letting the tears flow until I almost couldn't breathe. Thank God for dark sunglasses.

Walking into the room my friend, Treasa knew something was wrong so she had the kids to leave me alone while I answered my phone. His loving words brought me comfort after the conversation with my son. Please don't get mad at my son. We are all grieving. During grief things are said that perhaps should never be said but if that is the way someone feels it needs to be told. The pain of grief is unbearable and made doubly so when hurting people hurt people. However, that is what people do. They usually strike out at the ones they love the most.

On the next page is a picture from Esther Conference that night as we are going to church of the Chaperones: Alyssa Kincaid, Nancy Dorsey, Treasa Dickinson-Dickinson, myself in the middle, Edna Myers Kincaid, Melanie Armstrong, and photo bombed by Sister Teresa Wallbrown. Sister Wallbrown brings life to every party!

September 20, 2013
Mark 1:35
"And in the morning, rising up a great while before day, he went out, and departed into a solitary place, and there prayed."

How long has it been since you were in a solitary place for prayer?
Sometimes when life throws us curve balls that we can't understand we neglect the one who can help us curve successfully and don't spend the necessary time in prayer. Perhaps we need to follow the example of Jesus taking Himself away to a solitary place to pray.
With all that is going on in my valley right now I know I need much prayer and I'm spiritually in a solitary place. When I spend time in prayer during a valley experience is when I learn so much more about my God and how close He is. I just want to serve Him, no matter what.

Can you say that?

Memories continue to overcome me. Here in 2004 on one of our many education trips. This one to northern Pennsylvania where we toured Penn Caves. We had a great time! Missing my morning, mid morning, afternoon, early evening and bedtime chats with the love of my life.—

Love this young lady below who made me feel so special this weekend. I thank God for everyone that came to me and let me know they are praying for me. Thank you so much!

This young lady's mother wrote on my facebook: She has talked so much about you, and I'm so happy to have had her with somebody that is such a positive inspiration-- no matter the storm, you stand firm and strong.. I love you .

I feel so small looking back on the words this young lady's mother wrote above I realize how misplaced those words were. I was barely standing. It was all an act. I was going off by myself and sitting down curling up to weep where no one could see me.

My response to those words at the time were I love you too Lola! You are so sweet. I had such a good time with her and all of the young ladies that went. She was always checking on me when my grief would overwhelm me. It's like she had a sixth sense and knew when I needed a hug or a word. You have raised a very sweet sensitive daughter.

Just when I don't think my heart can be broken a new way, guess what. It happens. You'd think by now the devil would get a clue. No matter how many times my heart is ripped out of my chest and stomped on, I will serve God. I will be the devil's worst nightmare. God will bring this all around for His glory. I will trust in my God because He is simply my God. He's all I have now and to Him I give my all.
WV Esther Conference has been amazing and life changing! —

September 21, 2013
So thankful I was at Esther Conference tonight with the young people from all over West Virginia but especially Glen Ferris Young ladies! God knew where I needed to be and the comfort I would need. I'm so thankful for my church family that has loved me. Y'all are the greatest!

I cannot quit thinking about everything that has happened in the almost one month of my husband passing from this life. However, I put my trust in God and as verses five and six say of Psalms 130, *"I wait for the Lord, my soul doth wait, and in His word do I hope. My soul waiteth for the Lord more than they that watch for the morning: I say, more than they that watch for the morning."*. Last night when my tears wouldn't stop the songs at the talent show for the Esther Conference truly ministered to me but that's the way God does things. You see He does all things well. And now with tears threatening I am simply waiting on God more than they that watch for the morning.

The song, "Take me to the King", ministers to me every time I listen to it. With this new road I'm traveling I find myself spending more and more time with God letting the devil know that my worship will not change unless it gets deeper, more intense but never less. No matter what comes our way, whether we feel worship or not, we need to worship God and pray continually. No matter how many times someone rips our heart out and shreds it Jesus can put it back together again as we worship Him and thank Him for our blessings. No matter what we're going through worship is the key that unlocks the door for our miracle.

No truer statement than that the more I seek you, the more I find you when referring to God. I just want to sit at His feet, lay back against Him and breathe, knowing that He is catching me when life overwhelms me. Oh, how I love and worship my God! No matter my situation or circumstance... Here I am to worship.... my worship is not dependent on my mountain top or valley... it's dependent on the walk with God I've built through the years.

September 22, 2013
I needed reminded that nothing is too hard for God! God just is the I AM!

It's time to get ready for church to worship the King of Kings and the Lord of Lords. This morning in my devotions God brought to mind the following:

This is the testimony I NEVER want and I strive to do the opposite of the following words found II Timothy 4:10, *"For Demas hath forsaken me, having loved this present world...."*

What do you love more than God? Think about it. Just when you think you're doing all you can do is there something else standing in the way between you and God? It's time we cast everything aside that hinders us as it says in Hebrews 12:1, *"Wherefore seeing we also are compassed about with so great a cloud of witnesses, let us lay aside every weight and the sin which doth so easily beset us, and let us run with patience the race that is set before us."*

I am ready for more church today. There is nothing more powerful than Sunday night Apostolic Church!

Do you see what I am doing as I am going through the grief process? It is rare I am staying away from church. As a matter of fact I am finding more reasons to go to more services because I know in my depressed grief stricken state it is in the house of God where I will find my strength.

September 23, 2013
So exhausted but finally home. What a great service at Huntington, Now I need to share what God has dealt with me about all afternoon and until now. Matthew 8:21-22, *"And another of his disciples said unto him, Lord suffer me first to go and bury my*

father. But Jesus said unto him, Follow me; and let the dead bury their dead."

God has dealt with me all day about my grief and the toll it is taking on my body. The weight loss, fatigue, and depression of which my God wants to deliver me from. God gave me that verse and I thought, really? Are you crazy, God? But that's how we are. When God started dealing with me about it today as I was driving from Buckhannon to Huntington I heard God tell me it's time to quit grieving and look towards the future.

This doesn't mean I won't grieve or have bad moments for a very long time. It just means my focus has got to be on other things not on what I've lost. While I will always miss the love of my life I know God is getting ready to do something so wonderful and great. I can't wait to see it but in the meantime I need to be moving forward with plans to give more to God than I ever have before.

My worship has once again changed. Before this my worship was deep but now it's like it has moved to a new level. I so love having the privilege to worship the King of Kings and the Lord of Lords!

After church this night I was privileged to go out to eat with Fred and Lisa Ray where we caught up with each other's lives and the road the ministry is taking us down that God has given us. Even in grief I know I am not just called by God but chosen to do something special for Him.

So today has been quite the day with an interesting twist. These twists and turns that are coming my way are not changing the way I worship or believe that God will take care of me. If anything because of these twists and turns I will worship more and I will believe God will take care of me even more so. The God I serve is ever present in time of troubles and trials. Before you wonder what's going on suffice it to say I know that I know that my God has got this! That's really all that matters.

September 24, 2013
This morning after reading I decided to flip through my Bible and find something more for me today and I came across Deuteronomy 1:28-33; *"Where can we go up? Our brethren have discouraged our hearts, saying, "The people are greater and taller than we; the cities are great and fortified up to heaven; moreover we have seen the*

sons of the Anakim there. 29 "Then I said to you, 'Do not be terrified, or afraid of them. 30 The Lord your God, who goes before you, He will fight for you, according to all He did for you in Egypt before your eyes, 31 and in the wilderness where you saw how the Lord your God carried you, as a man carries his son, in all the way that you went until you came to this place.' 32 Yet, for all that, you did not believe the Lord your God, 33 who went in the way before you to search out a place for you to pitch your tents, to show you the way you should go, in the fire by night and in the cloud by day."

Isn't this passage of scripture just like us? We tell God why we can't. Our enemies are bigger than us. They have more weapons. And, the devil is there. (I'm using Anakim as a symbol of the devil.) So what if he is there.

Then they are reminded that the Lord our God goes before them. Aren't we like that with everything we've been through when another crisis or trial enters our life we think we can't make it and someone or God has to remind us of what He has done in our lives before. So what if we're discouraged in our hearts, God still goes before us. Why do we not believe God? When will we get it? Really get it? This walk with God is not for the faint of heart, however, we have a God who goes before us. He clears our path and provides our needs. All we have to do is follow Him with our whole hearts.

So today no matter what you're going through remember He goes before you. It simply does not matter what your enemies are throwing up in your face God is simply going before you. Trust in Him and see what He will do for you.

September 24, 2014
I'm making J.T. and I a roast and potatoes today with corn when he gets home from work. So for those that are wandering I am eating. However, it is usually one to two meals a day with a snack thrown in. I have no appetite. I think my stomach has shrunk. After we eat it will be time for me to go to counseling. So far today I have been on the phone most of the day but all is well. I really need to write but have been avoiding it because of the emotions involved. I probably will write tonight but for now I think I should walk the dogs.... LOL. I know they are waiting wondering why I haven't yet.

Just when I think I'm finally getting my feet under me along comes another shock. Regardless I have never seen the righteous forsaken nor His seed begging bread.

Please pray I need another miracle. I know God has got this. I know that I know. I will worship and praise the King of Kings and the Lord of Lords.

Here are the details of the shock I received today.
I received a letter in the mail from my homeowner's insurance company stating that it had been cancelled. My husband's mother paid this as she has a husband's mother suite attached to the home and this was originally her home but had been given to my husband. In life and in our grief we have had challenges. This was unexpected to put it mildly. I had planned to have a yard sale and get rid of some things but now I have not been given a choice I must have a yard sale to raise money for homeowner's insurance.

First, because my name is not on the deed I had to find an insurer. Let's just say today has been a day of unnecessary challenges. When the devil can't get you one way he will try another. The best you can do is keep on going, keep on worshipping, keep on praying! Never stop, no matter what!

Tomorrow will be one month since my husband died. It seems so hard to believe I've spent this evening taking pictures out of frames and unloading tables for a sale. Life definitely has taken more twists the last few days than I ever thought possible. Twenty-Four and a half years of marriage relegated to some boxes and furniture. All of a sudden a home that we lived in and loved each other in is now just a house.

Tomorrow going through our things is what my focus will be. Even in this I will worship and praise my God because while I may not know His plan I do know that He is in control so I will just continue to trust Him.

A comment from Melissa Harris It is said that death not only takes loved ones but takes the life out of the sentimental parts of our reality... Nothing can take the love through memories of the lives we share with loved ones ... Not even death. Praying for you and I know God will continue to be your strength and put your life in order. God has big things for you, Sis Susan!! God is a comfort in grief and will become our joy through sorrow ... The Joy of The Lord is Our Strength!! God Bless YOU!!

September 25, 2013
I know what you're doing, and it's not going to work!!
This is battle!!

Micah 7:8~Rejoice not against me, O mine enemy: when I fall, I shall arise; when I sit in darkness, the LORD shall be a light unto me." What's next? I'm ready now!

So today has been quite the day and the week has been quite the week. Did I say plenty without saying anything? So today has been spent taking pictures off the walls and out of frames, boxing things up, cleaning things out. Well, tomorrow should the weather cooperate I will be having a yard sale. There will be clothes, furniture, shoes, tons of Christmas Decorations, Christmas Trees, Christmas houses, books, computer desks, stuffed animals, a 5250 watt generator, TV's, Cb's, etc., and miscellaneous household items. I also have two nice Ham Radio base models that will not be part of the sale but must be sold. All must go!

That was my facebook post to start to raise the money for the homeowner's insurance. Yes, there were people I could have called in Mississippi and Texas who would have sent money but I wasn't raised that way. I was raised to take care of myself so I didn't feel I had a choice but to start taking the pictures off the walls. I found out the nice thing about having a large home is that you have an abundance of stuff.

Later that day a friend from Texas asked if anyone was helping me. My response to her was me, myself and I. A friend was to come help the next day but that day I was alone. What most don't realize is I didn't just lose my husband I lost my entire family in one fell swoop. Oh, my children were alive but thanks to issues with their father's family a wedge was being driven between us.

Some friends of my sons were also trying to drive a wedge between us by making him believe you didn't need insurance and the only reason I was selling our stuff was because I just wanted the money. I was doing well to feed us let alone take care of other expenses that were cropping up. I found our utility bills had not been paid while I had been gone. The utilities were being shut off unless I came up with hundreds of dollars to pay them. These were the bills my husband had always taken care of. I had no clue what else would happen or what I would find as I began to clean out our home.

When this friend continued to ask me about getting someone to help this is how I responded. It makes me smile today because I know how angry I was this day. Unfortunately everyone works so it's hard. Many have offered but kids and family make it difficult. I didn't mind being alone today. I was amazed at what I managed to lift and move by myself. You know, the madder you get the more energy you get. LOL

As I was cleaning I was finding under beds liquor bottles. My husband when he would run out of medicine had been known to drink a fifth of vodka. Evidently he was drinking much more than a fifth of Vodka. I found bottles under beds and in closets. I couldn't believe I was the one having to bag that mess up and touch it. I have never drank alcohol or indulged in drugs yet I was cleaning it up. I know I sound bitter but I was mad. I was mad that he couldn't love himself enough to get help. Forget loving me or his children.

He couldn't love himself!

Let's just say God and I had a lot to talk about as I cleaned, cried, prayed, and shouted at the injustice of it all.

Someone recently asked me how did I miss all of that. He was good at hiding it. Under our beds was clean and he had pushed bags full of empty liquor bottles up under the beds. A closet in the room he spent most of his time in that he smoked in was full of liquor bottles. Needless to say, with asthma as severe as mine I left that room alone. The man I married was a clean man but in the last few months prior to his death he had changed to someone I no longer recognized.

September 26, 2013
No matter what, no matter where, no matter how, God has my life in His hands and joy comes in the morning! Right now I can't even fathom the word joy much less feel it but someday, someday I will again feel joy! Therefore, I know that I can make it with the help of God!

When you feel like this music and reading your Bible can be your best source of comfort. Some nights I would just lay in bed and hold my Bible while tears rained down my cheeks. All I wanted was someone to hold me while I cried. I had the best person, I had Jesus holding me.
All I can say is that I must be really close to God the way my heart feels. LOL. I must maintain a sense of humor regardless of the situation I'm in.

My God has got this. He knows my every need before I even know I'm in need. It seems every time I turn around it's another surprise but all is well with my soul! You see the God I serve is amazing, wonderful, all powerful and owns the cattle on a thousand hillsides. I will ever love and trust Him! My circumstances don't determine the way I serve, worship, or praise my God! So no matter what you're going through know that you know that God is walking with you holding you up when you can't hold yourself up

It's time to put my garment of praise on. So that's what I'm doing. I'll probably be late but I am definitely going to church tonight to worship God. When I get back I will be continuing to get things ready for the sale in the morning. Please pray for me for strength to get it all done.

I am missing my pastor, Bishop and Sis. Tommy Craft today. I thank God for them. Through all that has happened they have been by my side or on the phone encouraging me, praying with me. I am blessed beyond measure with them in my life.

I so enjoyed my chat just now with Sis. Wanda Hammer. I love my Texas friends. Now to get back to sorting out our movies and home video's so I don't accidentally sell something that's priceless to me. Also listening to youtube video's of uplifting Christian music while I finish this task. I think I'm in shock that I'm doing all of this already but it's okay and I'm okay.

This is how I've been feeling.... Lead me Lord, I'll simply follow you...
I reckon it's time for a nap before the sale starts in a few hours. I continued to listen to music as I realized just what was happening and that I had no control over it. For someone who has always been in charge the loss of control is devastating.

Today was about packing up the dreams I had for our lives. I am blessed that many people came to the yard sale and purchased items but as I was watching them go through things I couldn't quit singing this song especially the first verse. God basically wanted me to know that the dreams now will be new dreams yet as a human being it's hard to let go of the old dreams. I trust Jesus always and forever.

I want to thank Kevin Price and Paul Ratliff for helping me today. They rode to my rescue. They were the best friends of my love and treat me like a sister. I'll never forget all their help! Thank you both so very, very much!!!

I know with the latest crisis, what the devil meant for my bad has been turned around into a blessing. To find out I had no homeowners insurance via a letter was devastating. Today not only is my home insured but it is insured for over $60,000 more than it was.

Also I found out when the estate is settled they want to reassess again and possibly double the homeowners. God is taking care of me in ways I cannot even begin to fathom. Then what I needed to accomplish everything God gave me more than enough so I was able to order more books to have when I minister.

People watch us in our adversity. When we know whom we serve and act accordingly God blesses us. I'm so happy God meant it for my good! Now I must really go to sleep I ache in places I had forgotten I could ache and I'm so tired I'm rambling. I pray blessings on all my friends so much more than you can contain!

September 27, 2013
Psalms 55 spoke to me this morning. As I am walking this road of unbearable grief and turmoil with so many twists and turns every day.

"16 As for me, I will call upon God; and the LORD shall save me.
17 Evening, and morning, and at noon, will I pray, and cry aloud: and he shall hear my voice. 18 He hath delivered my soul in peace from the battle that was against me: for there were many with me. 19 God shall hear, and afflict them, even he that abideth of old. Selah. Because they have no changes, therefore they fear not God. 20 He hath put forth his hands against such as be at peace with him: he hath broken his covenant. 21 The words of his mouth were smoother than butter, but war was in his heart: his words were softer than oil, yet were they drawn swords. 22 Cast thy burden upon the LORD, and he shall sustain thee: he shall never suffer the righteous to be moved."

Regardless I will continue to call upon the name of the Lord. In walking this path I am even now more aware of how close the coming of the Lord is. Each day as I am slapped in the face with the reality of more problems and finding that folks think I am using God as a crutch and to hide behind.

I wonder how they get through each day without God to talk to or guide them. You know I know God hears my cry. I pray continually and God gives me peace no one can understand. When I cast my burdens on Him He simply is there providing what I need every day. When I need strength He provides and I need strength. You see the last few words of this passage says, "*...he shall never suffer the righteous to be move.*" I'm human and I make but I strive to do what is right so this is a promise I have from God that I will never be moved. Therefore I will continue to pray my way through this horrible dark valley because my God will sustain me.

I'm trying so hard to be normal when all I want to do is sit and weep. So today I have spent time weeping talking to God about everything that is going on and the misconceptions many have about the situation and problems that have unfolded.

My grief counselor told me to limit my time weeping. I am weeping another loss today one I cannot discuss but one that hurts almost as much as my love.
What Sis. Beverly Haygood reminded me of was all of the prayers that are being raised on my behalf and that even if I feel all alone I am not. I have angels

surrounding me to lift me up. Others have called and I will be forever grateful for their counsel and obedience to God somehow knowing I needed them today. That is the God I serve He provides for our needs and lifts us up.

I'm in need of prayer! So much has happened and continues to happen. Somehow by the grace of God I will make it in Jesus name. I don't think my heart can take much more but I'm so blessed to have Jesus holding my hand through this stormy turbulent time in my life.

A comment from Sis. Aurelia Hopkins: *"When thou passest through the waters, I will be with thee ; and through the rivers, they shall not overflow thee; when thou walkest through the fire, thou shalt not be burned; neither shall flame kindle upon thee"*.
Isaiah 43:2
His Promises are True! Hold on! In Jesus Name!

A comment from LaWanda Tullos Weidman A setback is just a setup for a comeback.

A comment from Melissa Harris I'm praying God touches everything & I stand amazed at your love & faithfulness to God - most would give up but you know your strength & help is in The Lord!! God Bless you in a special way, Sis Susan!!

No-one knew what had happened. I found this message sent to me privately on Facebook from a friend of my son's:

9/26, 11:37pm
I just wanted to say that I feel you've handled things terribly with recent situations. You've not been there for your children, or your husband, when they needed you. I do apologize for being so rude and so blunt, but I love your children and feel that the absence of you (or your neglect) has really hurt them. I realize I do not know all the information, but I know enough and I have seen plenty to know that you do not represent your Lord like you say you do. Your actions speak much greater and those actions are those of greed and self-pity (or selfishness) and many more things that very clearly contradict your religion, or rather what you pretend to be. I see through your facade and it's been painful to watch. I think someone needed to tell you what I know a lot of people think. I know your children love you because you are their mother, but you've hurt them more than I think you realize, unless you simply just do not care. Of course, none of this is from the mouths of your children, but I have little

to no respect of you. I wish you a great life, ma'am. However, you have a dirty soul and that saddens me. I feel sorry for you, I do... because there is much more to life than money, there is much more to life than simply who you are alone. I am also very offended that you use God as your cop-out. It's a bit disturbing really. Again, I want to apologize for sending such a rude message, but I felt you should know. Because obviously people see your facade and believe it. I am happy to see you've been taking things so lightly and that you haven't allowed yourself to be too hurt. Unfortunately, not everyone has. I hope that you really can find truth of the Lord and one day maybe really work in His name, rather than your own. I am sorry for your recent loss, as well. I send much love to your family and always will... but I will never find respect for you in my heart. There is no need for a response to this, as I feel this shouldn't offend you providing my feelings and information are all false. If you do feel offended, you may want to re-evaluate how you handle things, because you are hurting people you claim you care for. And again, please realize life is more than money. Have a lovely night and sleep well. I would also like to just reiterate that none of this is from your children, nor does anyone know I've sent this message. Therefore, there is no need to penalize anyone. Good bye.

My response as below:
Everyone has a right to their opinion but until you take a walk in the shoes a person is wearing you have no idea what or who is causing them to make the decisions they are making. You are right that this did not require a response. My homeowners insurance was canceled by a family member and the way I found out was via the mail. Should something have happened to the house while we were uninsured we would have been homeless. There is no money no matter what others may seem to think. Normal everyday bills like water and electricity had not been paid. Ever since Mike decided to go down the road of prescription drug abuse we have been on a rollercoaster ride most have no clue about. Arrests, court appearances, drug rehab, and detox are very ugly things. When I left a year ago it was with high hopes he would wake up and pursue help. I begged JT to come with me. I love my family dearly but there comes a time you have to choose tough love as a last resort. Thanks to the sale yesterday I was able to pay for insurance. I am not going shopping or traveling with that money. When I travel now it is because friends are inviting me. Even the grief counselor when looking at the facts not my perception of those facts tells me I have to move forward. Moving forward simply means I have to clean up the messes left behind by Mike and other family members. Right now it doesn't matter what I do or don't do my children will see it as wrong. That is their perception and they have a

right to that. Someday with maturity and time they will see I was backed into a corner and in order to survive had to make certain decisions. I just hope and pray they never find themselves in a similar situation with family and extended family who wish to judge but never helped and actually some tried to stop me from trying to get help for a loved one who was sick. Prescription drug abuse is a huge issue in this country and needs addressed. My husband applauded and encouraged me from home to go to help others and to tell his story so it would help others. No one will know the depth of the love we have for each other nor the loss I feel every day. I now have to find a way to live without him when in December plans had been made for us to be on the road together. Now, however, because of a decision he made I have to make hard decisions no one should ever have to make. You may think I'm hiding behind a facade when in reality I don't understand how folks who don't have a strong walk with the Lord make it through any day much less the past month I have gone through. My faith gets me up in the morning and no matter how many problems come my way I go to my knees and talk to my God. He gives me strength and guidance to make the decisions I must make. When you don't understand why or what someone is doing you should pray about it. I don't know you that well and know you don't know the situation like you think you do so I want you to know I harbor no hard feelings toward you and I will be praying for you. By the way if I was all about greed I would have taken the six figure job I was offered a year ago. This is about so much more than money. Take care and know I'm praying.

I had J.T. to read this and then he told me he was moving out. This had been planned and the same people he was moving in with one of the sisters had written the above to me. They wanted him to move out without telling me. This came from the parents of the friends. People sometimes just blow me out of the water how little consideration they have for others. Any time I am dealing with someone's children I always remember the parents. I always reiterate to the children that they must talk to their parents. That is what everyone should do.

That afternoon when he told me what he was doing it floored me. I did not act like a mother but as someone who was hurting and couldn't take anything else. I lay down on the floor in our family room and cried like a baby. I couldn't control the tears. No, my son should not have had to stay with me just because I was alone.

He was an adult and as such could make his own decisions. That did not mean that his decisions would not affect me emotionally with all we had been through. I told him I needed to leave. I couldn't be there when he moved out. We were good. We hugged and said we'd stay in touch but as a mother I knew it would never be the same again. As I left the house I could hardly see to drive. I got about fifteen minutes from the house and had to pull over for a while because I was crying so hard I could hardly breathe. I was trying to get to Huntington, WV where I wanted to audit the Purpose Institute class that Bro. Harper was teaching that night.

I thanked God I had purchased big dark, really dark, sunglasses. These sunglasses hid my face very effectively. I walked in late to the church with the dark glasses on and he was teaching from I Timothy 5 about widows that should marry. This is not what I wanted to hear. But Bro. Harper was able to get me to laugh which was a rarity and something I needed that night.

Then when I went to leave on top of everything else I have lost my phone.... just another bit of drama added to an already dramatic day. It really didn't phase me, I know it will either turn up or I will get another one.

Afterwards I went to a friend's house where they provided me an oasis from my problems and begged me to spend the night. Thank you, Bro. & Sis. Starr, for being my oasis in the middle of the storms of my life.
At their house I got on the scales.... Great news... I've now lost a total of sixty pounds since May!!! Most of that loss was since August 25th.

September 28, 2013
This morning in my devotions God gave me a message from the book of Job regarding the attack on my character. This passage of scripture is after his friends had been attacking his character.

Before I quote the passage of scripture I want to remind everyone that it's easy to be an armchair quarterback. When you're on the outside of the game looking in you have wonderful ideas about what to do but you can't see or encounter all the problems or obstacles in the path of the quarterback.

Back to the passage God gave me Job 38:1-3; *"Then the Lord answered Job out of the whirlwind, and said, Who is this that darkeneth counsel by words without knowledge? Gird up now thy loins like a man; for I will demand of thee, and answer thou me."*

What this said to me was who was that talking to you? What do they know? They know nothing about your situation. For lack of better words the next part was like God telling me it was time to put my big girl clothes on and only worry about answering to Him. So many times people try to distract us.

They don't realize it but they are being used by the devil to try to distract us in a time when our focus needs to be on God. Thank you, Bro. & Sis. Ray for calling yesterday to remind me to keep my focus. I was distracted for a bit then I remembered I serve the God of Glory! He's got this! I trust in Jesus! He will bring me out of the miry clay.

A comment from Bro. & Sis. Fred Ray. If we all could realize, if we are living for God, the way we should be, we are going to be attacked from every angle. Sometimes, from the ones who are the closest to our hearts. The devil is an idiot, but he knows where to hit for the greatest effect/reaction from us. What we do with those attacks is what counts. Are we going to tuck our tails and hang our heads and run or are we going to realize the authority and power we have thru God Almighty that allows us to tower over the powers and principalities that are coming at us. Remember.....this is a war!! Put on that armor of God! LR

A comment from Leslie Esquibel. The devil's favorite weapons are discouragement and hurt from friends/brethren when nothing else works to stop us. Every time you come to my mind, I pray for you, Susie and I know that there are many others lifting you up in prayer. *"But I have prayed for you, that your faith fail not; and when you have returned, strengthen your brethren."* Luke 22:32

Then I received a message from the mother of the young adult that had sent the original facebook private message to me: She took it as a slap in the face what I had posted about the devil using people. I'm sorry but if we allow it the devil can use us to hurt people and injure them emotionally effectively stopping others from following God and/or the will of God for their lives. That is why it is so necessary we be careful and prayerful with our words and actions.

I thank God I was in a safe place when I received this second more hurtful message. I was held and prayed for before I headed home.

Praising God and so thankful my phone has been found!!! Thank you to the folks who are part of Purpose Institute in Huntington, WV who kept looking! Now I am going to lunch before heading home to continue going through our stuff. Please continue to lift me up in your prayers. Today will be the first time to go home to an empty house. Well, our two dogs will be there. I am not looking forward to this but I know God will give me strength. In the meantime lunch with dear friends who I know are holding me up in prayer as are many others.

September 29, 2013
Here is a repost of mine from January with a comment from my deceased husband. Sometimes the dead communicate better than the living. In case anyone of you out there has any doubts about how Mike Smith felt about my travels here are his own words unedited contained under this post in the comments section.

I'm just thinking about something someone said to me. On facebook all I post most of the time is about the following:

1. God
2. Being close to God
3. The travel

What I typically don't mention is the flip side of that coin which is being away from my family, missing them, the tears, and the loneliness that comes with doing this. I know some don't understand what or why I am doing this but my husband, son, God and I do. My love and I are communicating daily and can't wait for the day he will travel with me at least part-time and hopefully full-time. Time is scheduled to be home with them but it is always too short and goes too fast.

We both know God is in this and we want to be in His will for our lives. God is doing a work in my family that I can't wait to tell everyone about but right now I am unable to say anything about that. Please just remember us in your prayers that God continues to make it possible for my love and I to be in God's will.

Every day my first call is to my love for our morning talk and then we talk off and on all day. So you see we still love each other and want only what's best for each other. My husband supports me without fail 150% and has always done so. I am blessed beyond measure with such a man and love him so much!

A comment from Mike Smith Susie, I believe in what you are doing is for God and support you 1010%.
January 26 at 10:12am · Unlike · 4

Another comment from Mike Smith Even though I love and miss you.
January 26 at 10:12am · Unlike · 2

Susan D Wine Smith I love and miss you too sweetie!
September 29 at 12:44am · Like · 1

Tonight I'm missing my husband so very much. We were soul mates, the best of friends, and each other's staunchest supporters. I'm wishing he were here so he could sit some people straight. For those of you that knew him knew he would in no uncertain terms. He always told me I was too nice, LOL. I miss my defender

It's time to head to the house of the Lord and simply Praise Him any and every way that we can. No matter what is going on in our life or what vicious attacks are thrown at us from the enemy camp we simply need to worship the King of Kings and Lord of Lords! He is worthy of ALL our praise! King David taught us to worship regardless. So today put on your garment of praise and see the salvation of the Lord!

It's been a great afternoon! I am having lunch with my handsome son. Now I'm home and going to walk the dogs. Then I'm going to start cleaning up the outside of the house.... and then tonight church!
Oh, yes, I must pack for General Conference. Thanks so much to church family who are blessing me to be able to go and take care of the business side of the books and work on getting the international part of this ministry rolling. God knows I need a break and has supplied a dear friend of mine and my husband's best friend to take care of the dogs while I'm gone. Love all of you so much! —.

Back in church! Love praising God! Surprise visits from two dear friends. They will never know how much they cheered me up. I am so very blessed! God knows what we need before we ask and He simply provides!

Home after an amazing service in Oak Hill, WV where Bro. Greg Hurley preached, "There's a Miracle at the Door". Now, I'm packing listening to the washer and dryer running so grateful I only have to drive to Huntington tomorrow and then I can sit back and relax while I'm on my way to St. Louis.

September 30, 2013
I just checked the weather in St. Louis and thank God it's supposed to be in the 80's most days until Friday when it rains and the temp starts dropping... brrr.... then it will be cold. Not looking forward to that. But I will enjoy the rest of the week's weather. I am so blessed to be able to go but I have so much to do while I am there. Hopefully I can finish packing soon so I can get some shut eye.

It's time to get moving, finish packing, get dressed, do dishes, walk the dogs, shower, dress again, go be interviewed by a local paper for a possible profile (please pray God orders my steps and my words). Today remember Mark 10:27 where, *"And Jesus looking upon them saith, With men it is impossible, but not with God: for with God all things are possible."* I know y'all probably get sick of hearing it but I should be dead yet God keeps working miracles in my life. I must thank and praise Him every single day regardless of what I am currently going through. I am so humbled by the God I serve and so unworthy to be His servant. I pray I always bring honor to Him and souls into the kingdom of heaven. I just want to work for Him!

I'll be with these three this afternoon!!! Almost a whole week, we will have a great time together. These three gorgeous ladies are the nieces of my heart and they know it! I will also be with Bro. & Sis. Randy Tenney, and Bro. William Mooring who is like a Father to me.

Almost ready to leave. Sending more information to the newspaper and two magazines for possible articles. God is great and greatly to be praised! I have no clue where it's going but if you don't step out you never accomplish anything... so take a risk... do something for God and watch what He does!!

Finally having some fun watching Bro. Randy Tenney thinking he knows what he's doing and Bro William Mooring supervising but I don't think Randy's listening.

Well, this morning I accomplished more than I even had on my list because I had left some things off but somehow someway I got it all done. Thank you Jesus. When walking the dogs I fell down and now have a nice black and blue bruise in a circular pattern above my right eye and my phone screen splintered. I am so glad it still works. I really don't want to get a new phone right now so God really took care of me.

Daisy was chasing another dog and when she realized I wasn't pulling on the leash anymore she came back to me with a look that said oops, I'm in trouble now and started licking me. How could I stay mad at her? She was so cute.

October 1, 2013
I am so enjoying not having to drive. The company is great as long as Bro. Randy Tenney sticks to driving so Ann, the girls and I can visit. It is so rare I don't have to drive that this is a real treat.
They took me to Skeeter Mountain..... Lol. So thankful for such wonderful friends who are taking care of me.

We're here!!! Hallelujah!!! A lot of people feel like God isn't necessary anymore. I pray they wake up before it's too late.

I am almost ready to go to the first service for General Conference 2013 United Pentecostal Church International in St. Louis. I can't wait to see what God will do tonight! It's going to be awesome and wonderful! The presence of God is so refreshing!

October 2, 2013 –
The ladies in my room were already asleep when I got back so I'm sitting in the bathroom uploading the pictures. Thank God they went fast but tomorrow is a full day so tomorrow night might be different. Tired or not, I reckon I should go to bed. I have a breakfast meeting in the morning. I will enjoy it. I'm missing my wild friends tonight.... Love y'all. These folks are real nice they just go to bed early... emphasis on early... that's before 1 or 2 a.m. LOL. Oh, well, 7:30 a.m. comes early. Praying I can go to sleep quickly...

We don't know when Jesus is coming back to earth again. It scares me when I see some who have always put the things of God first changing so radically and going in a direction that contradicts the Word of God. But then I look at those who remain and who strive to be closer to God then I am excited. God is going to do a quick work. I do not want to be sleeping but found working for His kingdom accomplishing all that He blesses me to. I long to continually be molded in His hands a humble and willing servant. Let's see how Mark 13:35-37 puts it.

"[35] Watch ye therefore: for ye know not when the master of the house cometh, at even, or at midnight, or at the cockcrowing, or in the morning:[36] Lest coming suddenly he find you sleeping. [37] And what I say unto you I say unto all, Watch."

I am working on my Article for Reflections Magazine this morning. It's time to get moving for the Lady Ministers and Minister Wives breakfast. In the meantime God woke me up early and I was able to write the article for one of the UPCI national magazines. I can't wait to see what happens with that. God is opening more doors. I just pray that I stay in His perfect will.

General Conference Thursday night actually I believe this was very early Friday morning about 1 a.m. Can you tell we had been laughing about something and having a great time. They keep trying to take me back to Mississippi this weekend. I told them two weeks..... or so and I'll come back for a week. I can't wait. I miss Mississippi and all the folks there!

October 3, 2013
Loving being at General Conference but this is so hard for me. I miss my love so very much. I will get through this. I will survive in Jesus name because I know God is carrying me. I trust in God!

October 4, 2013
I am almost ready to head to the morning sessions then a noon meeting and youth service and lastly lunch with Wes Gallaugher and Steven Russell both of whom are like sons to me but I so miss my Joseph Smith. My daughter would have loved the excitement of being here also. Someday Lord wiling my family will be here with me but being here is a lot of work so while I miss them I know next weekend I will be with both of my children for a little while. I am so happy to see old friends also. I have run into so very many and God is blessing me with my friends who have been praying for me and loving me. I'll never forget the many kindnesses the Lord has brought my way. Thank y'all so very much!

This morning I went to a seminar on dealing with grief by Bro. Dan Seagraves. As he taught I sat there with tears rolling down my cheeks wondering if I will ever be happy again or at least not so sad. I'm trying to look forward but all I see when I look forward is a life filled with loneliness. Yes, Jesus is with me. I get that but it's hard to explain there is no-one to share the excitement with, no-one to share the sadness or joys with, the frustrations of life with. For over half my life I didn't even have to think about it I knew my husband understood me and cherished me.

I was so very blessed to spend time Friday night after General Conference being advised by Sister Wendell, one of the matriarchs of Pentecost and former missionary to Africa. God is ordering my steps in such a supernatural way. I could never say enough good about God!

October 5, 2013
In the Grief Seminar I went to yesterday this was one of the scriptures that really helped me. Basically no matter what we are going through we have a promise in this scripture that it simply does not matter what we are going through NOTHING can harm us. Oh, we might get knocked around a bit but we are OVERCOMERS!

Isaiah 43:2
² When thou passest through the waters, I will be with thee; and through the rivers, they shall not overflow thee: when thou walkest through the fire, thou shalt not be burned; neither shall the flame kindle upon thee.

So exhausted but finally back in the room and I am packed. I am setting an alarm for the first one of us who has to be up at 3:15 a.m. to catch a very early flight. Then I am leaving at 7 a.m. or think I am. I'll find out in the morning but I'll get up and be showered, dressed and ready to roll by 7 a.m. It's been awesome. I can hardly believe the week is over... now to trek back to West Virginia.... but we'll have fun with the kids!

We are in Illinois almost to Indiana and then we will be in Kentucky. Randy is starving me! I don't eat much these days so this is TORTURE! LOL! Then he is driving and taking pictures of me sleeping and posts them on Facebook. Ann would have nothing to do with it. Thank God for good friends.

October 6, 2013
When I cry to God He simply answers me and strengthens me. Even though I am walking through the darkest valley in my life with trouble all around me I know my God will revive me and take care of my enemies. I know, I know even in the valley of such unbearable grief that my God loves me so much He's got this. So remember no matter what you are going through we serve a God that loves us enough to have died for our sins. Why do we let things (positions, houses, cars, etc.) stand between us and God when in the end we can't take it with us. I'm not just talking about doing things anymore I'm stepping out and doing what God has asked me to do. Why aren't you? Nothing matters except what we do for Jesus!

Psalm 138:3 , "³ In the day when I cried thou answeredst me, and strengthenedst me with strength in my soul."

Psalm 138:7-8 "⁷ Though I walk in the midst of trouble, thou wilt revive me: thou shalt stretch forth thine hand against the wrath of mine enemies, and thy right hand shall save me. ⁸ The LORD will perfect that which concerneth me: thy mercy, O LORD, endureth for ever: forsake not the works of thine own hands."

This morning Sis Starr's alarm scared me into a new life I knew God wanted me up because He had dropped a thought in my mind. So I spent some time reading and learning at His feet where I found in I Peter 3:12-13 a passage that ministered directly to me.

1 Peter 3:12-13, [12] For the eyes of the Lord are over the righteous, and his ears are open unto their prayers: but the face of the Lord is against them that do evil. [13] And who is he that will harm you, if ye be followers of that which is good?

I've heard it through the years but never did it speak to me as it did this morning. It was like God Himself was telling me don't think it's strange that you are going through this right now but you should be rejoicing and joyful. My grief is raw and fresh yet God has filled me to the brim and overflowing with joy in the closest relationship I have had with Him.

While the tears flow less frequently now they still flow yet I have a comfort few have. The comfort I have is the one true comforter who wraps His arms around me and holds me close to His heart when my heart has broken seemingly beyond repair. Jesus I simply love you and worship you regardless!

This is so easy to say, but, oh, so hard to do.

When we truly get our lives centered on Jesus sin truly isn't an option. It becomes all about pleasing Jesus. After all, He gave His all for us, how can we give anything less?

I find my comfort in music glorifying the King of Kings & the Lord of Lords and on my knees alone in the midnight hours when it's just me and God. He is catching me when it's just too much for me to bear. I simply fall back into His arms. I am headed to prayer then church. There is power when you are on your knees. No one knows how much power you have when you pray. God simply meets you and me. So I'm going to go pray more before church.

What a great service tonight at Apostolic Life Cathedral! God really moved throughout the whole service. It was just what I needed. Right before heading to the church to pray God swept in the living room and I had a little talk with Jesus. There's absolutely nothing like the sweet presence of God. There is no amount of money, prestige, or power that can compare to the power of God. The fellowship I've had and how God is providing my needs is so miraculous I am humbled before God and so thankful, so very thankful.

October 7, 2013
On the road again.... I am headed to the house in Fayetteville.
The puppies are so excited I am with them. I'm making chicken with noodles for dinner. They keep coming over to me because they can smell it... LOL. They are like two toddlers continually begging whether for attention, treats or food.

One of these days my heart won't be so broken....in the meantime I will worship God and express joy because I know soon I will feel real joy again.

October 8, 2013
During this time in my life I spent a lot of time walking the dogs, crying and praying. It was a form of therapy for me. The dogs understood my loss because we were all grieving together

Last night I was sitting on my sofa looking into my foyer where boxes of books are stacked. Somehow God has provided all of my needs including being able to order more books. I am so humbled by the wonderfulness of the God I serve to provide.

I am on the phone on hold.... I hate being on hold... but it's a necessary part of life in order to get some things solved. There are still issues but God is working them all out. I am so very blessed to be able to serve such a wonderful amazing God.

Almost ready to leave for tonight.... on the road again... my theme song. I'll be back tomorrow. I'm headed to Huntington tonight to minister to the ladies at Apostolic Life Cathedral on Staunton Street. This will be the first time since my love died. Please say a prayer for me. I can think of no place I'd rather be doing this except for Jackson or Royalwood. A few months ago my love went with me to Morgantown, West Virginia when I ministered at Hope Church.

What is going to be hard is the chats we had before I spoke and the chats after. Now I will chat with the very best friend ever, Jesus. It's time now for me to start doing what God wants while I continue to finish closing things up in West Virginia.

A Comment from Sis. Aurelia Hopkins After great Breaking... greatness will follow. The Broken discover what is truly Important in Life! Fulfill your Calling... what you've been Broken to Do... That HE may be glorified in the lives of many people in shining through you!~ Sis. H

A comment from Lisa Ray, God and you did a good job... I love preaching but I also love when God uses someone to speak of life experiences and how God brought them thru! Great way to build peoples faith. We all have a story we need and should tell. What He does for one He will do for everyone. He is a great, big, wonderful God!! Love you!

October 9, 2013
If people in any of our children's lives and those young people God has brought into our lives are pointing them away from God I ask that the Lord remove those people from their lives.

I love this old song, Keeping your mind stayed on Jesus will bring you perfect peace. If you're under attack spiritually realize you might want to start focusing on Jesus. He will relieve your worries. There is just something about the peace He gives us. It defies explanation. When walking through this huge valley I'm in when I begin to feel overwhelmed I sit down and pick up my Bible or hit my knees. You know what Jesus is right there to wrap His arms of comfort around me. He catches me when I fall back because my strength has left. That is when I become strong because He gives me of His strength. So when things/situations overwhelm you remember He's got this and you in the palms of His hands. Have a blessed Wednesday!

Isaiah: 26:1. In that day shall this song be sung in the land of Judah; We have a strong city; salvation will God appoint for walls and bulwarks.² Open ye the gates, that the righteous nation which keepeth the truth may enter in.³ Thou wilt keep him in perfect peace, whose mind is stayed on thee: because he trusteth in thee.⁴ Trust ye in the LORD for ever: for in the LORD JEHOVAH is everlasting strength:

Jesus is providing all my needs....ALL!!!

Visiting friends where I used to work right before I became ill with pancreatic cancer. Now I am on my way to Beckley to have lunch with a dear friend. While I'm so blessed with so many friends who are encouraging me and helping me I long to hear the one voice I will never hear again or feel his arms around me. My God is walking this road with me carrying me. I'm still so very blessed!

I can hear Bro. Murrell Ewing singing I know you're gonna make it... You're gonna make it! You've got what it takes... To win!!!

On the interstate I noticed my brakes were not appearing to work as they should. Then I noticed smoke. Lo and behold my Expedition had caught fire and burnt through the brake line on the driver's side. Not only that but I was doing 70 miles per hour on the turnpike when this occurred.

The brakes had failed so in order to slow down I shifted down until my speed slowed enough to use the emergency brake to stop. The devil really doesn't want me to continue but God was in total control. God has allowed the hedge to be lowered and harm to come to me but the devil has not been allowed to take my life. Thank you, Jesus!

I managed to get off and called a tow truck once I got parked. I found a mechanic near the house and had it towed there. The tow truck driver that came was Apostolic. Now that is God. I was having a little bit of an, "Oh, my God moment when he showed up."
The miracle in this is that God protected me. I could have had a wreck on those curvy roads going that fast or the flames from the car could have caused something else to catch fire causing an explosion. God keeps giving me miracles as the devil tries to give me obstacles. The obstacles are just opportunities for miracles!

I am trying to be normal. I keep walking Brownie and praying. Regardless I will worship the King of Kings and Lord of Lords. He is worthy!! He alone is worthy of all praise and adoration!!!!
Trying to stay encouraged as the tears continue to roll down my cheeks I marvel at the beauty of God's handiwork. What an awesome amazing God we serve to surround us with so much beauty! Oh, how I love Jesus!

Worshipping God when the world continues to collapse is where you find your strength! — at Solid Rock Worship Center

October 10, 2013
While I was sleeping God impressed these scriptures on my mind, Matthew 12:22-23; and Matthew 13:12-16.

Matthew 12:22-23, "²² Then was brought unto him one possessed with a devil, blind, and dumb: and he healed him, insomuch that the blind and dumb both spake and saw.²³ And all the people were amazed, and said, Is not this the son of David?"

For verses 22-23 I believe God wanted to remind me that with everything that is happening in my world right now I could go back to work living a life of luxury. However, it would choke me and I would not be the fruitful minister I have been called and chosen to be.

I believe He also wanted me to know that by continuing down this road with Him I would see many come to Him. I'm so humbled God thinks of me and will even allow me to have a little part in doing something for Him. I love Jesus so very much!

Matthew 13:12-16, "¹² For whosoever hath, to him shall be given, and he shall have more abundance: but whosoever hath not, from him shall be taken away even that he hath. ¹³ Therefore speak I to them in parables: because they seeing see not; and hearing they hear not, neither do they understand.¹⁴ And in them is fulfilled the prophecy of Esaias, which saith, By hearing ye shall hear, and shall not understand; and seeing ye shall see, and shall not perceive:[15] For this people's heart is waxed gross, and their ears are dull of hearing, and their eyes they have closed; lest at any time they should see with their eyes and hear with their ears, and should understand with their heart, and should be converted, and I should heal them.[16] But blessed are your eyes, for they see: and your ears, for they hear."

In this last part of the passage I woke up knowing God wanted me to read was also to remind me to share out of my abundance with others. Right now I don't feel that I have anything to share but that is precisely when we do.

Give and it shall be given. I don't give to others for what I can be given but simply because it's the right thing to do. Lastly, the big thing I think God wanted me to know with the latest crisis was when it happened I immediately knew God would take care of me.

Yes I was scared and yes I trembled but ultimately I knew He was in control and somehow it would work out. I, literally, have no one but Jesus these days so I fall back into His arms and let Him solve my problems.

I am not so heavenly minded I'm no earthly good. Today solving this and coming up with money for repairs is what I am doing. While I don't want to have another sale I have no choice. I believe we have to do everything we can.

I know God will bless my efforts. I trust Him. I stand upon His Word. His promises are true. So no matter what you're going through know that your God has got this!!!

I was privileged to hear this message at Louisiana camp meeting this summer. It, along with situations in my life and my walk with God, and have revolutionized my thinking. I no longer look at things, houses and cars like I used to.

They will not matter when we die. The only things that will matter is what we have done for Christ. Please listen to this message on youtube by Bro. Anthony Mangun, "The Fashion of This World". Let it change you.

After the latest debacle today this song has ministered to me amazingly. God knows our needs. My angels are guarding me with flaming swords. Someday the devil will get the message but in the meantime I fall back into Gods arms letting him catch me remembering all the time that God's got great things in store for me!

October 11, 2013
I'm having another yard sale. Hopefully after this one I will only have one more. Cleaning out a house is so emotionally draining not to mention the hard work. I'm so blessed my love's two best friends are so willing to help me get things ready. We will hopefully start at 8 or 8:30 and close up around 3 pm or so.

Sitting here watching people go through our stuff. Twenty-four and a half years soon all that will be left are memories, pictures and videos. Once this is all past I will be completely broken before God. There will be no doubt when I sing Jesus at the center of it all. I keep singing this song. It is keeping me together right now. When you pray I ask you to please remember me that I continue to feel the loving arms of my God wrapped around me.

My wonderful helpers. My love's two best friends. I could never thank them enough for all their help. Everyone needs friends like this! .

Kevin Price and Paul Ratliff
My two angels God sent to help

Now, at my lowest, somehow I will encourage myself in the Lord. The trick to this is in the Lord. I cannot encourage myself but Jesus will. I have wondered how people could do this when one crisis after another would roll in and now I do. I truly understand Psalms 23 and the book of Job in a way I wish I didn't. So now I need to encourage myself by worshipping Jesus, praying, and studying His Word. To worship Him it helps me to listen to music and praise Him with hands lifted high when it is just me and Jesus. Then I pray and lastly I spend time learning at His feet by delving deeply into the Word of God and letting Him speak to me through the Word. It is amazing what you learn in the breaking process if you just let God work on you from all angles. Oh, how I love Him! How I adore Him. My breath, my sunshine, my all in all! The great creator became my savior!!!!

Just simply worshipping Him because of who He is! Regardless of situations, circumstances, where we are or who sees us worshipping Him. When I worship my God in private is the treasure box I want to fill full.

October 12, 2013
Tonight has been wonderful. While I've talked with a few of my nearest and dearest friends most of this evening early morning hours has been spent with Jesus studying for tomorrow evening when I will be ministering at Lupe Creek Baptist Church right outside of Oak Hill, West Virginia at a Fellowship Meeting starting at 6 pm. I absolutely cannot wait to see what God will do! It is going to be awesome because God will be with us!
Luke 5:1-7. Last night I fell asleep listening to Bro. Stoneking preaching. Then this morning I start spending time with my Lord and He gives me this morsel. The thought God gave me was on this wise, launch out into the deep.

Luke 5:1-7, "And it came to pass, that, as the people pressed upon him to hear the word of God, he stood by the lake of Gennesaret,[2] And saw two ships standing by the lake: but the fishermen were gone out of them, and were washing their nets.[3] And he entered into one of the ships, which was Simon's, and prayed him that he would thrust out a little from the land. And he sat down, and taught the people out of the ship.[4] Now when he had left speaking, he said unto Simon, Launch out into the deep, and let down your nets for a draught.[5] And Simon answering said unto him, Master, we have toiled all the night, and have taken nothing: nevertheless at thy word I will let down the net.[6] And when they had this done, they inclosed a great multitude of fishes: and their net brake.[7] And they beckoned unto their partners, which were in the other ship, that they should come and help them. And they came, and filled both the ships, so that they began to sink."

For so long, we, (most especially me) let things, careers, home, families keep us from following the wondrous call of God and being obedient to Him. Now I find myself in a unique spot where the children are adults, my husband has passed away yet I have a house and other things I could let stand in the way of following the call to a life of sacrifice.

I have been given the opportunity to give God all. Now when I sing I surrender all it means something so different to me. I am going to obey because I love Him and I want to see a great harvest of souls for the kingdom of God. I know it will cost me more than I've already paid but no sacrifice is too great for God! I want to see the nets so full and overflowing more and more have to help.

Has God chosen you to do something special? What's holding you back? It's time to put God first, really first and obey Him.

I've seen God do miracles. Actually I am one of those miracles. My God specializes in things thought impossible!
I am waiting to get the Expedition back. I hate waiting. Regardless tonight I will be at Loup Creek Baptist Church ministering and sharing my testimony. The many miracles God has done in my life defies explanation but that's the God I serve

I just made plane reservations to Jackson, Mississippi. I'll get to be 'home' for a week or so. How I've missed Mississippi. I will be changing planes in Houston and know of one dear friend I will get to see. I'm so excited. Monday I will be shipping books to Jackson. I just can hardly wait to get there!

October 13, 2013
It's a great day to worship God!!! Singing my theme song these days.... on the road again! Picking my J.T. up and headed to Huntington for Sunday school then to Lexington, Kentucky to see Leah and Evan for a short few hour visit. I love my children and am so blessed to spend part of this day with them storing up memories for the lonely days ahead. I'm so very wonderfully blessed to serve Jesus!

CHURCH--NO BETTER PLACE TO BE!!! — at Apostolic Life Cathedral.

I just finished a late lunch in Lexington, Kentucky with my Leah and J.T. As I sit here in the parking lot grief has overwhelmed me today. It is rough.

I thought I knew what pain consisted of but until you've felt this all other pain pales in comparison. Regardless, I know in whom I trust. Jesus is with me and on Him I depend. I will never cease to thank and praise Him for all the blessings I've been given. Even with all the issues of grief and family drama I can still say I am blessed and highly favored of God. My walk with Him is not dependent on circumstances. I will still trust Jesus, love and serve Him!

I didn't say a whole lot but the folks, rather extended church family, at Apostolic Life Cathedral loved me, held me while I cried and encouraged me. I'll never forget their many kindnesses to me. Bro.& Sis. Harper are so lovely one of a kind folks.

Wow! What a hot time Jesus and I had in the prayer room!!! When going through anything prayer should be a consistent part of your life. When that has been established it doesn't matter what happens you automatically start praying. You don't even have to think about it.

October 14, 2013
On the road again... leaving Huntington, WV to drive back to Fayetteville, WV. Countdown has begun... five days and a few hours until I fly back to Jackson, Mississippi!!! I can't wait. I'll be bringing home my car and enjoying my church family there.

October 15, 2013
While grieving God has given me something every day from His Word to counsel me. This morning it was Ecclesiastes 7:1-5.

A good name is better than precious ointment; and the day of death than the day of one's birth.[2] It is better to go to the house of mourning, than to go to the house of feasting: for that is the end of all men; and the living will lay it to his heart.[3] Sorrow is better than laughter: for by the sadness of the countenance the heart is made better.[4] The heart of the wise is in the house of mourning; but the heart of fools is in the house of mirth.[5] It is better to hear the rebuke of the wise, than for a man to hear the song of fools.

No one wants to understand that it is better to go to the house of mourning or that sorrow is better than laughter or that it is better to be rebuked (corrected) than to hear the song of fools. I think this morning God wanted me to know I'm right where He wants me.

I may not like it and may wish the pain would go away but through the pain I am learning to put more trust in Him than I ever have before. Today, no matter what you're going through, always trust Jesus. He knows what's best for us even if it hurts.

Throughout my days I tried to stay normal as you can see from the post below however underlying all of this was the grief that just would not go away.

I have a wonderfully busy day today. I've already done three loads of laundry, now I'm getting ready to walk the dogs, write, then later lunch with friends, a trip to Jo Ann Fabrics for buttons, grief counseling, and lastly pondering the thought God woke me up with for a series of books. I hope I never get over the goodness and majesticness of the God I serve. He loves each and every one of us so much!

These dear friends helped me so much by making sure I got out and did not become a hermit. One time I went a week without getting dressed or bathing. This was unheard of for me before grief. Grief changes you completely.

I have been so genuinely surprised by the friends that have reached out to me as I travel this valley of grief. Thank you all so very much! My church family from across America has stepped in to help me in so many ways. I am truly blessed to have all of you in my life. Again, thank you!

October 16, 2013
We all know the story of The disciples being afraid when Jesus came to them walking on the water. However I saw something this morning I had not noticed before in Mark 6:51-52,

"And He went up unto them in the ship; and the wind ceased: and they were sore amazed in themselves beyond measure, and wondered. For they considered not the miracle of the loaves: for their heart was hardened."

Isn't that just like us? We've seen God do the impossible over and over again. Yet when we have a need or are going through a deep trial we don't consider what God has already done. We let our hearts grow hard. I can hear you saying No I don't. Sit there a minute and really think about it.

These were the disciples. They walked with Him and talked with Him. They saw the miracles with their own eyes yet had trouble believing for themselves for a miracle.

In this valley I'm in I could let it swallow me whole. Some days I do but then I encourage myself in the Lord. I remember when we planned my funeral. But I remember hearing the words, You might have six months to live. Get your affairs in order.

My God performed the impossible with me. He will do it again! I only have to trust Him. So no matter what you are going through remember Jesus specializes in things thought impossible by men. Think spiritually not humanly.

He will do it again!!!

Today is going to be a hard day for me. What I'm doing I should not be doing alone. God knows and I won't be alone He is with me. Friends have offered to help but there are some things that family should be present for. Tomorrow friends are coming to help but for today I am going through the rooms we used the most deciding what to pack up, what to sell, and what will be thrown away. I'm cleaning out this house that is no longer a home for me.

As I was going through the house I found where my husband who had the addiction problem to prescription medication had stashed alcohol bottles everywhere. I, who, had only had one sip of alcohol in my life was cleaning up messes and touching things I'd never thought I would touch in my worst nightmares. Sometimes our nightmares come to life.

When they do, pray. Trust God. Keep on putting one foot in front of the other and if you find yourself getting too discouraged call one of the people in your life who can encourage you and go to their knees warring for your soul and your mind. God has blessed me with many people in my life who have literally when they see my number pop up on their phones stopped what they were doing to be available for me. That is a miracle in my eyes.

I am blessed beyond measure with a loving God who is once again wrapping His arms around me to comfort me. Do not feel sorry for me or pity me. Through all of these trials my relationship with the King of Kings and the Lord of glory has deepened to such a level I stand back in humbleness and awe at how He is taking care of me. Even the dogs are grieving. She is begging for a walk shedding tears so I'm going to put on my tennis shoes and take them for a walk

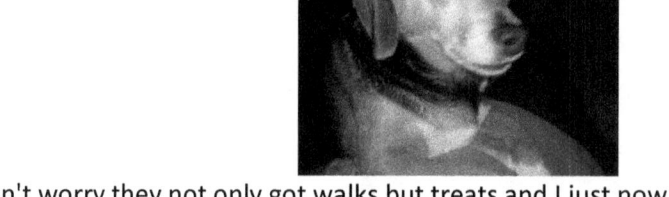

Don't worry they not only got walks but treats and I just now brought them back a McDonald's hamburger.each. just the 99 cent ones. They are too spoiled.

I finished with our family room. Now I'm getting ready to start on the kitchen. The china is stacked on the counter.I'm wrapping it to give to my daughter and she's to share with her brother once he gets a home of his own.

I'm getting rid of all of it only keeping two bowls, two plates and a very few things. This has been quite the journey. Things (stuff) no longer mean what it once did.

The only things that will last are what we do for Christ. I now have an understanding of those words that I never had before.

October 17, 2013
I've had an extremely busy day and put this off until last hoping it would resolve itself. Sometimes decisions have to be made in the best interest of the whole family (extended family included). While I have made this decision I could not gave made it

until a dear friend uttered those words we really don't want to hear in regards to our own situation, "What would Jesus do?"

Even if Jesus was hit and slapped he would keep turning the other cheek. I feel completely beaten up but what I'm about to do is the right thing. Today when making decisions think on those words, "What would Jesus do?" You won't go wrong.

This afternoon instead of calling Bishop James Kilgore who I knew when I posed the question to him would automatically say, "Have you prayed about it?" Then his next question would be, "What would Jesus do?" Therefore I did not call him. I called another friend who was raised in the same church, Sister Aurelia Hopkins. Really? I should have known better... LOL. But it was the words I needed to hear when I put to her the question.

My husband's ashes have not been buried yet due to family issues. I was putting it off. I was avoiding family problems. So, today, I decided it was time to finish this. I, personally, wanted to take the ashes to the top of the mountain he loved and scatter them.

Originally my husband wanted to be donated to science. Any time there is a suicide that is no longer an option whether it is accidental suicide or on purpose. When I called Sister Hopkins and explained my dilemma. She asked me to be quiet. I'll never forget her next words, "Sister Susie, I know this will be hard but do not say anything until I am finished. So I listened. At the end she asked me, "What would Jesus do?" Then she said, "I think you need to go pray."

I replied, "No, I don't need to pray."

Her reply was, "What?!"

I said, "I know what Jesus would do. He would let them kick him, slap him one more time. It's not about me. It's about healing this family."

She then said, "So what are you going to do."

I told her I would text my sister-in-law which is what I did. I received a text that afternoon requesting that I agree to sign a document stating that his ashes would be buried in the family plot. I did forward this to my pastor and a friend who was an attorney. I wanted to make sure I wasn't missing something. Then they wanted me to agree to let the ashes stay at her home instead of the funeral home. I would not agree with that. I wanted them to be in a neutral place.

I called Sister Lois Pitsenbarger to go with me this afternoon when I signed the agreement at the funeral home. In the agreement it also stated that upon receipt of my husband's ashes I would be required to ride with my sister-in-law to the graveyard which is two miles from the funeral home.

The funeral home advised me not to sign the agreement. In the agreement it used my full name as on facebook which is not my legal name. I had researched the legalities of such a document and knew that by signing in red ink and by printing my name the document could be questioned in a court of law should the need arise. I agreed to bury the ashes on November 7th. I wanted it near his birthday which was November 6th and to give our children and other family enough time to make arrangements to be available.

Time for C-H-U-R-C-H!!! In my mind that means it is time to worship the KING OF KINGS & the LORD OF GLORY!!!

I have been so blessed with so many that have given me rides while the cars have been broke down, brought me food, and took me to eat that I could never say thank you enough.

I am so tired. While cleaning today I decided to rearrange the family area. When I am cleaning anger is a great motivator. I moved the couch from one side of the room to the other. Then I did the same thing with the recliner. Now my body is aching all over. Someday I will learn...lol. (I Got MAD!!!)

October 17, 2013
II Peter 2:4-8. I tried to get away from this passage this morning. It is not what I normally post. I try to be uplifting but God kept drawing me back to it. We've all heard messages preached about hanging out with the wrong crowd and how it will affect us. Well, here it is spelled out for us.
2 Peter 2:4-8, "[4] *For if God spared not the angels that sinned, but cast them down to hell, and delivered them into chains of darkness, to be reserved unto judgment;[5] And*

spared not the old world, but saved Noah the eighth person, a preacher of righteousness, bringing in the flood upon the world of the ungodly;[6] And turning the cities of Sodom and Gomorrha into ashes condemned them with an overthrow, making them an ensample unto those that after should live ungodly;[7] And delivered just Lot, vexed with the filthy conversation of the wicked:[8] (For that righteous man dwelling among them, in seeing and hearing, vexed his righteous soul from day to day with their unlawful deeds;)"

To be vexed is to be frustrated. Our soul gets frustrated when exposed to filthy conversation. It does affect us. Sometimes it leads us to sin. I hear folks justifying everything they're doing saying they're living by grace. Yes, we are all living by grace but that does not give us a right to do those things the Word of God tells us are sin.

I don't know about you but when I'm in those situations where conversation drifts down a road it shouldn't that's when we need to walk away or let them know in a kind diplomatic way that we can't participate in that conversation.

We are to be in the world but not of the world. In bringing others to Christ that is no excuse to justify listening and/or participating in those types of conversations. As my life has changed so has my consecration.

I was so shallow until the past few years when God started changing me. I consider myself a normal everyday person God is drawing closer. The closer I get to Him the more things I find I don't need or can't do because I don't want my mind fogged up with the garbage of this world. Think about it and apply it to yourself and your walk with God.
Taking a break from cleaning and purging...

Thanking God for the calvary in the form of Joyce McCann and Treasa Dickinson coming to help me. Love you both so much!

I'm exhausted. I knew I lived in a large home but I have way too much stuff. As I purge, give away, and throw away old broken things the stuff seems to multiply. . This is all still so very emotional. I don't know how I'd cope without all the friends that are here physically and those who are praying. Please don't stop praying for me. I could never thank you enough for your prayers.

Getting ready for church! Going to church and just being is the one thing that has kept me going since my love died. When I'm in church worshipping God it is like I feel His arms being wrapped around me holding me. There is no comfort like the comfort of God. Therefore I try to be in church as much as possible.

If I know of a church in the area having service of some type no matter how I feel I get dressed and make myself go. If we would all do that I think we would find our problems would grow smaller not larger.

I am home from a great service. I try to stay busy so I won't think about things. All that does is push the inevitable back. Anyway I'm headed to bed soon praying I can go to sleep without thinking. I so need to be in Jackson! Thank God in less than 40 hours I will be there. God knows what I need and He will take care of me.

October 18, 2013
This morning after my night of grief God inspired me to read over half of the book of Job. What I found made me realize it is okay to have the feelings I do as long as I remember Job 19:25-27.

Job 19:25-27, "[25] For I know that my redeemer liveth, and that he shall stand at the latter day upon the earth:[26] And though after my skin worms destroy this body, yet in my flesh shall I see God:[27] Whom I shall see for myself, and mine eyes shall behold, and not another; though my reins be consumed within me."

No matter what happens, no matter when things may happen, no matter who may come against me I know my redeemer lives. After all these trials have passed I know I shall see God. I will see Him for myself!

Through all of the things that have happened my God is more real to me than ever before. I can still say as it says in Job 13:15, *"Though he slay me, yet will I trust in Him:..."*

Walking Brownie this morning with a leash jerry rigged from one of the kids old karate belts. Somehow in the purging yesterday God only knows where the real leash is. Fall in West Virginia...cold...brrr... fall. I can't wait to be warm.

Have I ever mentioned I hate cleaning. I hate cleaning!!! If my rich uncle ever gets out of the poor house I will hire the cleaning done...lol Any way two closets completely done and now working on the Master Bedroom closet.

When I get back from Mississippi I will have to tackle the other half of the house. Actually we are probably only a third if the way done. I do believe this house is getting bigger. We have stuff everywhere.
I'm so thankful for Lois Pitsenbarger who has been there for me in so many different ways. Love all of my church family from everywhere. I've never felt so loved by all of you. I'm so blessed with friends.

I am taking a break. I walked the dogs again so probably walked a mile and a half and we cleaned like mad women! LOL. Soon I'll get cleaned up for dinner with Treasa and Danny. They called and will be picking me up in a little bit. Then we will come back and do some more. After that I will pack to catch my plane in the morning.
Tomorrow I'll be in Houston, Texas and Jackson, Mississippi. I can't wait to get my hugs in Houston and be in Jackson in my home church. I so need this trip!

This has been the never ending day...I just finished packing. I pray my suitcase is not over fifty pounds otherwise I will be redistributing the weight. All the work that has been done is paying off. I can't wait to start my journey tomorrow.

OCTOBER 19, 2013
Thank God for Facebook. On my way to Houston this was arranged on Facebook.

LaWanda Tullos Weidman What time will you be in Houston?
October 19 at 9:02am via mobile · Like
Susan D Wine Smith 2:40 on United from Dulles International Washington D.C. My connection is at 4:46 to Jackson. I'll be at Intercontinental.
October 19 at 9:04am via mobile · Like · 1
Susan D Wine Smith Sis. Haygood is meeting me there for a brief visit. I just talked to her. She's supposed to call you.

Plesse pray on a puddle jumper plane. They seated us to distribute weight more evenly on the plane... lol.

Thanking God for friends watching facebook that began to pray. For some reason God wants to test me every time I turn around or so it seems to me.

Thanking God the flight was uneventful, just a little turbulence so it wasn't bad. I did wonder however at the beginning if we would make it to Dulles.

Landed!!! Now for the challenge 45 minutes or so until my connection to Houston. Of course the connection is on the other side of the airport. The next flight is three hours so hoping to find a snack before boarding the next flight — at Washington Dulles International Airport.

Thank God for shuttle busses to go from one side of the runway to the other...lol. let the race begin! Boarding my next flight in twenty minutes.

I found a snack...Starbucks. A bottle of water and a slice of banana nut bread. No time for anything else.

I'm boarded...what a jaunt with carrying my books with me. Now I'm ready for a long nap...three hours until I land I. HOUSTON!!! So excited to see Sister Beverly Haygood if only for a brief visit then the last connection for today into Jackson.

A comment from LaWanda Tullos Weidman I'm coming to see you too - yay!!
Susan D Wine Smith Yea!! My arms are full. Can you or Beverly bring something simple to eat. I had to travel with my books so no arms...lol. I pitied the people I had to climb over to get in my seat...lol. it is hilarious.A cheap burger from Whataburger is fine with fries. I'm eating very little but making sure I get something or even just a piece of fruit.

I love the Houston George Bush Intercontinental Airport. It is so easy to get around in. I had a great visit with both, Sister Lawanda Weideman and Sister Beverly Haygood, my friends. I still had more than enough time to get to the gate and fix my hair. Now I'm waiting to board. Thank you both for my Whataburger and the luggage cart. Y'all are awesome!

LaWanda Tullos Weidman It was great to see you. love u
Susan D Wine Smith It was great to see both of you! What a treat from God!

I have just landed. So very excited! — at Airport Jackson International.
Tonight I'm headed to a reunion party at Bro. Tommy & Sis. Diane Crafts home to remember the first Sister Mary Craft.

> A comment from Billie Chisholm Savoie Wonderful memories I have of each one! We had a blast! My only regret (or one of them) was that my daughter could not be there and get to better know all these wonderful people! My other regret was that everyone could not be there! Thanks, Susan, for documenting all these smiles!

Of course, I'm the one in the pictures with the camera. Love my Bishop and Sister Craft like parents.

October 20, 2013
I was so blessed to get to the party just as it started in Jackson remembering Sister Mary Craft. Now it is time for bed and tomorrow a book signing at FPC of Jackson. I so love being with my church family. I've been treated wonderfully and cheered up immeasurably.

We need to remember that the fear of God is the beginning of wisdom. Some fears are unhealthy but this fear will keep us close to God.

Job 28:"^{27} *Then did he see it, and declare it; he prepared it, yea, and searched it out.* ^{28} *And unto man he said, Behold, the fear of the* LORD, *that is wisdom; and to depart from evil is understanding.*"

Yesterday while flying God impressed me to read and reread the book of Job. This morning when I woke up I felt impressed to share this passage. We have all, at one point or another sought the brass ring.

Wisdom is the ultimate brass ring. Here in Job it talks of the value of wisdom and lets us know that it is hid from the eyes of all the living.

Job 28:13-28, "^{13} *Man knoweth not the price thereof; neither is it found in the land of the living.* ^{14} *The depth saith, It is not in me: and the sea saith, It is not with me.* ^{15} *It cannot be gotten for gold, neither shall silver be weighed for the price thereof.* ^{16} *It cannot be valued with the gold of Ophir, with the precious onyx, or the sapphire.* ^{17} *The gold and the crystal cannot equal it: and the exchange of it shall not be for jewels of fine gold.* ^{18} *No mention shall be made of coral, or of pearls: for the price of wisdom is above rubies.* ^{19} *The topaz of Ethiopia shall not equal it, neither shall* *it be valued with pure gold.²⁰ Whence then cometh wisdom? and where is the place of understanding?²¹ Seeing it is hid from the eyes of all living, and kept close from the fowls of the air.²² Destruction and death say, We have heard the fame thereof with our ears.²³ God understandeth the way thereof, and he knoweth the place thereof.²⁴ For he looketh to the ends of the earth, and seeth under the whole heaven;²⁵ To make the weight for the winds; and he weigheth the waters by measure.²⁶ When he made a decree for the rain, and a way for the lightning of the thunder:²⁷ Then did he see it, and declare it; he prepared it, yea, and searched it out.²⁸ And unto man he said, Behold, the fear of the L*ORD*, that is wisdom; and to depart from evil is understanding".*

We read in verse 13 that man does not understand the price of wisdom. Verse 23 lets us know God understands the way thereof and knows the place.

Lastly in Verse 28 where we read the fear of the Lord is the beginning of wisdom we also read to depart from evil is understanding. In our generation where things that God hates are being pushed in our face as normal and justified by men we must stand for what is right no matter the cost.

When we do this the last few words in this chapter tell us, *"and to depart from evil is understanding"*. We must, in love, depart from evil. As I've heard and said myself many times, "If you don't stand for something you'll fall for anything". That doesn't mean hate sinners. We must love them but hate their sin. As we should our own, for all have sinned and fallen short of the glory of God.

Most of us need more kneeology and less criticism of others. When we spend time with Him issues become clearer. We need to pray for a burden to pray for the lost. Then we can simply stand back and see the salvation of the Lord.

After a morning talk with God now its time to head for church and get set up for the book signing!!! I am loving being home in Jackson, Mississippi!

I love Sister Craft's Sunday School Class. This morning they were telling their love story. Can you see the love between them? It's beautiful!

October 21, 2013
Job 3:11-17, "¹¹ Why died I not from the womb? why did I not give up the ghost when I came out of the belly?¹² Why did the knees prevent me? or why the breasts that I should suck?¹³ For now should I have lain still and been quiet, I should have slept: then had I been at rest,¹⁴ With kings and counsellors of the earth, which build desolate places for themselves;¹⁵ Or with princes that had gold, who filled their houses with silver:¹⁶ Or as an hidden untimely birth I had not been; as infants which never saw light.¹⁷ There the wicked cease from troubling; and there the weary be at rest."

However, reality has now set in. My love will never hold me again. I will never hear that voice or see those twinkling blue eyes again or be comforted in those arms that would hold me until the storm passed over. So as reality has set in I am finding I am more than human.
I wonder why I'm here when I had the death sentence of pancreatic cancer. I am not about to do anything stupid but we all have to realize its normal to have questions when things like this happen. Grief has its own timetable. I do go to God in prayer. I grieve and my God holds me.

Job 3:18-26 As Job said the thing I feared the most is now reality. My safety net is gone. I'm paraphrasing.

¹⁸ There the prisoners rest together; they hear not the voice of the oppressor.¹⁹ The small and great are there; and the servant is free from his master.[20] *Wherefore is light given to him that is in misery, and life unto the bitter in soul;*[21] *Which long for death, but it cometh not; and dig for it more than for hid treasures;*[22] *Which rejoice exceedingly, and are glad, when they can find the grave?*[23] *Why is light given to a man whose way is hid, and whom God hath hedged in?*[24] *For my sighing cometh before I eat, and my roarings are poured out like the waters.*[25] *For the thing which I greatly feared is come upon me, and that which I was afraid of is come unto me.*[26] *I was not in safety, neither had I rest, neither was I quiet; yet trouble came.*

When you lose the one with whom you built your life you not only lose your arm, your comfort, your love but you lose your life. Yes, ,you are still alive. However, the one person you've lived with, loved, laughed, and bore his children is now gone suddenly and without warning.

Then while you're reeling from that blow you receive one blow after another. People don't understand why you do the things you do but neither did they understand Job. God, however, understood Job. He heard Jobs cries and defended him.

Something people don't understand about grief is that it has its own timetable. When waves of grief hit you have no control. For someone like me who is almost always in control this is scary. It is like you can't breathe, your chest hurts, you can't control the tears or the heartbreaking anguish.

It is not that you don't trust God or love Him. I still do. I don't know what it's like not to have God in my life. I couldn't imagine how anyone could go through grief like this without God. I worship God and pray but now with this new road there is a new fervency in my prayer life. Regardless, God is still God. I still believe He knows what's best for me!

Some comments on this picture:
Fred Lisa Ray Ummm.....not much color in that.... try some green beans and carrots....
Diane Wine What kind of vegetables?
Susan D Wine Smith Comfort vegetables! LOL
Diane Wine Mac&Cheese and mashed potatoes?
Joyce Mccann looks like mine. lol
Ronda Dalton Mac and cheese yum, works for me...
Elizabeth Vaughn Let me guess! Macaroni and Cheese and Dumplings!
Susan D Wine Smith You got it Liz but you've been with me when I've ordered it before...lol For some reason since I got to Jackson everyone wants to see me eat...lol. y'all seem to think I'm too skinny....
David Kevin Price They're trying to fatten you up it appears.
Susan D Wine Smith Yes they are!
Aurelia N John Hopkins ALL I SEE is starches! Did you say Vegetable Plate! I'm headed to Cracker Barrel! :)) ~ Sis. H
Susan D Wine Smith I call those comfort vegetables! LOL Enjoy Cracker Barrel. Eat my kind of veggies.

October 22, 2014
It's a beautiful day in New Orleans! It is 71 degrees now to be 75 today. I'm going to enjoy this day. Then I will be back next week for another day visit. I love New Orleans!

In New Orleans on our way to... guess where... time to eat the one thing New Orleans is known all over the world for... my mouth is watering just thinking about it..

Time for beignets — at Cafe Du Monde.
We are bringing some home for the Bishop

I've had a wonderful morning prepping for more writing tomorrow. Now it's time to take a break and head out to meet up with Deb Lockwood for lunch and fellowship. They just keep wanting me to eat... LOL!

I'm so glad I'm in Mississippi where it's warm and not snowing.... Well, it's chilly but still in the sixties right now. It's almost time to head to the church. I'm so privileged to be living for God. He's been so good to me! No matter what comes my way, and plenty has, I can still say I am blessed! I can also say it is well with my soul!

October 24, 2013
It's hard to believe it will be two month's tomorrow since you left this world. I love and miss you so much baby!

No matter what is going on in our world God is always worthy of praise. In the darkest of nights, the deepest valley or high on the mountaintop He's so worthy of all of our praise!

One of the secret's to the joy of the Lord is never losing our praise. When I didn't know how or if I could my hands still went up to worship the King of Kings and the Lord of Lords. Keep worshiping Him. Keep praising no matter what!!!

OCTOBER 25, 2013
Habakkuk 3:17-19 "[17] Although the fig tree shall not blossom, neither shall fruit be in the vines; the labour of the olive shall fail, and the fields shall yield no meat; the flock shall be cut off from the fold, and there shall be no herd in the stalls: [18] Yet I will rejoice in the LORD, I will joy in the God of my salvation. [19] The LORD God is my strength, and he will make my feet like hinds' feet, and he will make me to walk upon mine high places. To the chief singer on my stringed instruments."

Regardless of what comes my way, even if I have nothing yet I will rejoice in the Lord. This morning on the two month anniversary of my love's death I am learning more and more each day that, "The Lord God is my strength. .." I know that one day soon, "...He will make my feet like hinds' feet, and He will make me walk upon mine high places..."

Waiting for that to happen is so very hard on me. We want things to happen when we want them to happen. We forget Gods timing is not our timing neither are His ways our ways. Our thinking needs revolutionized to think like our God.

When that happens to us the valley will still be long, hard and dark. However, we will have a different attitude about the valley. I'm sure that there will still be days when we will wonder if it is over yet.

However, hopefully most days we will be trying to find out how this valley we are walking through will help us help someone else. Showing others who Jesus is, is what it is all about no matter our situation or circumstance.

Today remember no matter our personal situation it's about being Jesus to others. It will change how you act and think.

Just because I'm in a valley don't count me out. As friends have told me I'm in the valley where I'm being molded, I'm growing. Most growth is done in the valley. That's where we learn to trust Him in ways we never fathomed before.

I had people to see tonight and things to do but I felt I needed to be alone. Grief sometimes overwhelms you. You have to step back, take a breath, spend some time alone. Spend some time remembering and talking to God. I'm so blessed no matter how beaten up I may be. I could never thank God enough for all He has done for me

October 25, 2014
Wow, what changes a few months makes in a family. No matter what I am blessed beyond measure! We miss you my love but somehow, someway we keep putting one foot in front of the other. We only wish you were still with us.

We must leave our comfort zone... Let God challenge you....

OCTOBER 26, 2013
II Chronicles 15:7-15 is where God directed me this morning. In my valley God is reminding me to be strong and to keep renewing my altar.

2 Chronicles 15:7-15, "⁷ Be ye strong therefore, and let not your hands be weak: for your work shall be rewarded. ⁸ And when Asa heard these words, and the prophecy of Oded the prophet, he took courage, and put away the abominable idols out of all the land of Judah and Benjamin, and out of the cities which he had taken from mount Ephraim, and renewed the altar of the LORD, that was before the porch of the LORD.⁹ And he gathered all Judah and Benjamin, and the strangers with them out of Ephraim and Manasseh, and out of Simeon: for they fell to him out of Israel in abundance, when they saw that the LORD his God was with him.¹⁰ So they gathered themselves together at Jerusalem in the third month, in the fifteenth year of the reign of Asa.¹¹ And they offered unto the LORD the same time, of the spoil which they had brought, seven hundred oxen and seven thousand sheep.¹² And they entered into a covenant to seek the LORD God of their fathers with all their heart and with all their soul;¹³ That whosoever would not seek the LORD God of Israel should be put to death, whether small or great, whether man or woman.¹⁴ And they sware unto the LORD with a loud voice, and with shouting, and with trumpets, and with cornets.¹⁵ And all Judah rejoiced at the oath: for they had sworn with all their heart, and sought him with *their whole desire; and he was found of them: and the L<small>ORD</small> gave them rest round about."*

When we renew our altar and consecration is when others can see the hand of God in our lives even in a crisis. Entering into a covenant with our God is so very important. The word covenant means to commit oneself or bind oneself. I can think of no-one I'd rather be bound to then the Lord.

When we do this it will require sacrifice. It will mean more time in prayer, reading His Word, and working for Him. We say we want revival but when was the last time you went out of your way to help someone in need that didn't go to your church? When did you last go door knocking to invite people to church?

When did you last spend some real time focused on God allowing Him to change you? I'm not talking about church. I'm talking about where no-one can see you. It is time we make time for the most important relationship we'll ever have. It may mean a few sleepless nights spent on our faces humbling ourselves before God but, oh, when we finish the relationship we will have with Him will surpass anything else in life.

Now it is time to truly renew our personal altar. The sacrifice is more than worth it. Once it's done it becomes something to look forward to every day. I believe this is something we should do every day!

October 27, 2013
What a busy day today. Errands, baby shower, then home for a massage, and my friend, even brought me Berry Berry Yogurt. Delish. Afterwards we went out for a bite to eat. Now I'm home waiting on clothes to dry and then I'll go to bed. So very sleepy... Thank you for the massage and the yogurt!

I'm so hungry for more... more... and more of God!

Now it's time for me to remember all the wonderful things God has done and worship Him. My grief tries to consume me but I will worship God... REGARDLESS HE IS STILL GOD & STILL DESERVES ALL THE PRAISE!

No matter what you're going through WORSHIP HIM! Go to church, draw strength from the body of believers. Let them pray with you and help you. No matter what happens, cancer, job loss, death of a loved one, attacks from others, my God has been faithful to me!!!

As I am sitting here this afternoon trying to write about the past two months the tears stream down my face as I listen to worship music. Service this morning was amazing but it was a service where there was no preaching but weeping. Weeping seems to be all I do these days.
I remember praying with folks who lost loved ones but I had no idea, absolutely no idea what it was like to lose the love of your life. He will never come back... never... Our plans and dreams are now gone, but regardless.... regardless God is still God!!!

The words of the song, "God on the Mountain", are so true fore it's in the valley is where our faith is really put to the test. So today remember, no matter, what you're going through He's still God in the valley!!! God is comforting me. Regardless of how I feel inside I will worship God.

OCTOBER 28, 2013
I am finally on the road to New Orleans. Someone (Debbie Barraza Hahn) called me and said Hurry. I did. They were not ready. At least I have the back seat so I can sleep. Another dentist appointment in the morning then a day of laughter I'm sure...

A comment from Debbie Hahn upon our arrival in New Orleans: Suzie-Bell in the elevator. Doesn't she look great in a hat!!!!!! Just got to our room its 3:22 am and eight o'clock is going to come really early.

They had asked me to "borrow" one of Bro. Craft's hats so they could get him one for his birthday...LOL.

October 28, 2013

Sunday night in Jackson, Mississippi the message Bro. Greg Godwin preached was, "When God Presses Pause".

In my life the past two months I have been on pause. Even though I have felt I have been paused, while paused I've been growing with God in the valley of despair.

God has not allowed me to linger too long in the valley but has sent friends to me to cheer me up and go on short trips. It's been a small break of cheer through the dark clouds.

My God is my sustenance! He is my everything! He is my all in all no matter the darkness of the day or the brightness. God is closer in the valley.

When on the mountaintop it is sometimes hard for us as Americans to let God be God because we tend not to rely on our God as much. While I dislike the valley it is where the closeness, the intimacy with God is and where I learn at His knee when I lean back against Him and can do nothing else but breathe. That is when my God comforts me.

Psalms 47:1-4 , :"O clap your hands, all ye people; shout unto God with the voice of triumph. ² For the LORD most high is terrible; he is a great King over all the earth. ³ He shall subdue the people under us, and the nations under our feet. ⁴ He shall choose our inheritance for us, the excellency of Jacob whom he loved. Selah"

He takes my hand in the dark dreary night. He walks with us most of the time carrying us through the valley. What a wonderful God we serve. I'm still standing. ..I'm still trusting....holding to that unseen hand...

OCTOBER 29, 2013

Psalms 108. I love my morning talks with God. After the day yesterday with Debbie and Denny Hahn which was wonderful and cheered me up so much I spent most of my evening focused on God.

Now that the reality of my loves shortened life has set in I am having new challenges spiritually. But this morning in this passage my God reminded me my heart is fixed. I simply go to prayer when I have new challenges.

Even the apostles were challenged yet they praised God in the midst of their adversities. Sometimes we, when we don't want to, we physically have to take ourselves to God and say mold me, break me once again. It is me in need dear God. As we allow Him to work on us once again we become more and more like Him.

I want to be like Him no matter the sacrifice or the cost. The secret to being molded or at least for me is to worship Him through the process. Rejoicing is easy on the mountain top but can you rejoice in the valley of despair?

It is near impossible but that's when you do what you've been taught to do. You raise your hands glorifying your God. Even with your heart shredded beyond recognition you put yourself to the side and praise Him for everything He's done for you in the past.

Those challenges you're faced with as it says in verse 13, "*Through God we shall do valiantly: for He it is that shall tread down our enemies.*"

He will. So now it is time for me to do what my God has asked me to do regardless of how I feel. He will bring me through again, this time in spite of myself and my faults. He simply loves me and I, well, I love Him!

Psalm 60:1-12, " O God, thou hast cast us off, thou hast scattered us, thou hast been displeased; O turn thyself to us again. ² Thou hast made the earth to tremble; thou hast broken it: heal the breaches thereof; for it shaketh. ³ Thou hast shewed thy people hard things: thou hast made us to drink the wine of astonishment. ⁴ Thou hast given a banner to them that fear thee, that it may be displayed because of the truth. Selah. ⁵ That thy beloved may be delivered; save with thy right hand, and hear me. ⁶ God hath spoken in his holiness; I will rejoice, I will divide Shechem, and mete out the valley of Succoth. ⁷ Gilead is mine, and Manasseh is mine; Ephraim also is the strength of mine head; Judah is my lawgiver; ⁸ Moab is my washpot; over Edom will I cast out my shoe: Philistia, triumph thou because of me. ⁹ Who will bring me into the strong city? who will lead me into Edom? ¹⁰ Wilt not thou, O God, which hadst cast us off? and thou, O God, which didst not go out with our armies? [11] Give us help from trouble: for vain is the help of man. [12] Through God we shall do valiantly: for he it is that shall tread down our enemies."

At the day Ladies prayer meeting I was getting shaky and then I realized I hadn't ate anything since New Orleans. So after prayer I got Captain D's and now I'm sitting outside listening to the water while I research and write...it is so relaxing out here. I'm trying to soak it all in for strength for the days ahead. My God will sustain me as He always does!

He is with me... Jesus has never left me... He's been carrying me and surrounding me with angels as I've worked today on pulling information to write about the past two months I just needed to know I could touch my God... I knew it but sometimes in the valley of despair we forget those things that we have been taught our whole lives. There is nothing like sitting at the feet of Jesus.... He is my comforter...

OCTOBER 30, 2013

Matthew 6:25-34, "[25] Therefore I say unto you, Take no thought for your life, what ye shall eat, or what ye shall drink; nor yet for your body, what ye shall put on. Is not the life more than meat, and the body than raiment? [26] Behold the fowls of the air: for they sow not, neither do they reap, nor gather into barns; yet your heavenly Father feedeth them. Are ye not much better than they? [27] Which of you by taking thought can add one cubit unto his stature? [28] And why take ye thought for raiment? Consider the lilies of the field, how they grow; they toil not, neither do they spin: [29] And yet I say unto you, That even Solomon in all his glory was not arrayed like one of these. [30] Wherefore, if God so clothe the grass of the field, which to day is, and to morrow is cast into the oven, shall he not much more clothe you, O ye of little faith? [31] Therefore take no thought, saying, What shall we eat? or, What shall we drink? or, Wherewithal shall we be clothed? [32] (For after all these things do the Gentiles seek:) for your heavenly Father knoweth that ye have need of all these things. [33] But seek ye first the kingdom of God, and his righteousness; and all these things shall be added unto you. [34] Take therefore no thought for the morrow: for the morrow shall take thought for the things of itself. Sufficient unto the day is the evil thereof."

This morning I awoke with the thought, "Enough". Then God directed me to this passage. Now that I'm alone I sometimes find myself wondering how things will work out. I've never been a worrier before. I've always been optimistic saying God will provide. Even though my circumstances have changed my God will still provide. He never changes!

The promises in the Bible are still true and are for all of us. Mt 6:30 simply says, "Wherefore if God so clothe the grass of the field, which today is, and tomorrow is cast into the oven, shall he not much more clothe you, O ye of little faith?"

Lastly it says in verses 33-34, "But seek ye first the kingdom of God, and His righteousness; and all these things shall be added unto you. Take therefore no thought for the morrow: for the morrow shall take thought for the things of itself. Sufficient unto the day is the evil thereof."

So tomorrow morning when I start my journey back to WV I just have to put myself in God's hands knowing not only will He provide my spiritual needs but my physical needs and protection for the journey. Change is hard on all of us but what we allow it to do to us is where the difference is.

I have decided to follow Jesus. No turning back. I will believe and trust Him. He is my God and I am His child.

Bishop Tommy Craft's birthday is today. I'm so blessed to be spending part of the day celebrating this 82nd birthday with he and Sis. Craft. I love and appreciate them so much.

October 31, 2013

Deuteronomy 31:6-8 *"⁶ Be strong and of a good courage, fear not, nor be afraid of them: for the L*ORD*thy God, he it is that doth go with thee; he will not fail thee, nor forsake thee. ⁷ And Moses called unto Joshua, and said unto him in the sight of all Israel, Be strong and of a good courage: for thou must go with this people unto the land which the L*ORD *hath sworn unto their fathers to give them; and thou shalt cause them to inherit it. ⁸ And the L*ORD*, he it is that doth go before thee; he will be with thee, he will not fail thee, neither forsake thee: fear not, neither be dismayed."*

This morning my God knew exactly what I needed before starting the drive back later today. He knows how hard the next month will be on me so He directed me to a passage of scripture to remind me to, "...fear not, nor beafraid of them: for the Lord thy God, He it is that doth go with thee; He will not fail thee, nor forsake thee."

What a promise straight from the throne room of heaven and then in verse eight it again says, "And the Lord, He it is that doth go before thee: He will be with thee, He will not fail thee, neither forsake thee: fear not neither be dismayed."

Then my Lord reminded me in Malachi 3:6 that, "...I change not.", and in Romans 8:31, "What shall we then say to these things? If God be for us, who can be against us?"

Yet with all these promises straight from God we still sometimes struggle believing He will do what He said He will do. As Bishop Craft ministered to us last night we need to remember the coinage of heaven is faith.

What that should mean to us is that just as we use money to purchase items here on earth when we need anything from God the 'money' that we use is faith.

Lastly Hebrews 11:1-2 defines faith for us, "Now faith is the substance of things hoped for, the evidence of things not seen. For by it the elders obtained a good report."

So today as I journey physically back to West Virginia my God took time to reassure me that He is with me. While I may not have my husband anymore, God is with me. He let me know regardless of what happens He will be with me. All I have to do is trust Him, falling back into His arms letting Him catch me.
He will do it again!

Romans 8:31, "What shall we then say to these things? If God be for us, who can be against us?"

Hebrews 11:1-2 " Now faith is the substance of things hoped for, the evidence of things not seen. [2] For by it the elders obtained a good report."

As I am leaving Jackson I am crying and it is raining. .. I don't want to go through the next week but God is with me and on Him I will depend. Next stop... Birmingham, Alabama for dinner

It is time to enjoy dinner before getting back on the road. Loving living and working for God. I stopped to visit with a friend's parents. His father was diagnosed with Pancreatic Cancer. We talked for a long time. This is what is hard is knowing that without a miracle the man I just met won't be alive long. I pray God gives him a miracle!

It has been great! I'm just now leaving...a long night ahead but God moved. That's what it is all about.

I'm stopped for the night. As veggietales would say, "The old grey mare, she ain't what she used to be." Whenever I stop to get a motel room my friends know to pray. I have to be sick or so run down I just can't go on. I'm one of those people that set impossible or near impossible goals and meet them.

November 1, 2013
This morning my Bible fell open to this passage in Philippians 2:7-14 where my love's picture is in my Bible. God has been talking to me through this passage. While I will always love Mike and cherish the memories of our life together it is time for my focus to be on God.
Verse seven says, *"But what things were gain to me, those I counted as loss for Christ."* Loving and being loved is so wonderful in our lives but when we lose that person who meant so much to us our focus is changed. It's up to us whether we put that focus on the right things.

If I wanted to bury my grief and not deal with my overwhelming emotions I could call a headhunter and go back to corporate America with 12-16 hour days only existing in this life. That is no life when we know God has chosen and called us to work for Him. A job like that would be gain to me but loss for Christ. Anything we allow to come between us and what God wants is loss for God.

Finally verses 13-14 of his passage where it says, *"Brethren, I count not myself to have apprehended: but this one thing I do, forgetting those things which are behind, and reaching forth unto those things which are before. I press toward the mark for the prize of the high calling of God in Christ Jesus."*

I'm not saying I'll forget the wonderful years of life I had with my husband. Very few have probably known such unconditional love and acceptance in a marriage. However, now I need to reach forward to the things God is placing in front of me.

I am pressing toward God for the prize of the high calling. It is a high calling to work for God. It's a privilege yet we run from it. It's time to look, really look at our lives and our priorities. God must be first. Living by faith is not for the faint of heart. When things happen, as they will, we will gain even more closeness with God. There is nothing I want more than to do His will and know Him more and more each day

This month is the month of thankfulness. I live my life in a state of perpetual thankfulness. But this month I focus on it as many others do. I'm thankful for the comfort God has blessed me with the last nine weeks or so. There is nothing like the comfort of the Lord.
Exhausted but stopped for tonight. Thank you to all my friends and family who knew how hard this trip would be emotionally and supported me either in prayer or by calling to encourage me. Love you so much!

November 2, 2013
Matthew 16:9-18. *"⁹ Do ye not yet understand, neither remember the five loaves of the five thousand, and how many baskets ye took up? ¹⁰ Neither the seven loaves of the four thousand, and how many baskets ye took up? ¹¹ How is it that ye do not understand that I spake it not to you concerning bread, that ye should beware of the leaven of the Pharisees and of the Sadducees? ¹² Then understood they how that he bade them not beware of the leaven of bread, but of the doctrine of the Pharisees and of the Sadducees. ¹³ When Jesus came into the coasts of Caesarea Philippi, he asked his disciples, saying, Whom do men say that I the Son of man am? ¹⁴ And they said, Some say that thou art John the Baptist: some, Elias; and others, Jeremias, or one of the prophets. ¹⁵ He saith unto them, But whom say ye that I am? ¹⁶ And Simon Peter answered and said, Thou art the Christ, the Son of the living God. ¹⁷ And Jesus answered and said unto him, Blessed art thou, Simon Barjona: for flesh and blood hath not revealed it unto thee, but my Father which is in heaven. ¹⁸ And I say also unto thee, That thou art Peter, and upon this rock I will build my church; and the gates of hell shall not prevail against it."*

What a passage of scripture! At verses 9-13 it talks of those who saw Jesus after He rose from the dead. Then they went and told those that had been with Him but they did not believe. When He appeared unto the disciples He yelled at them for their unbelief and hardness of hearts. Is that not just like us?

God does great and amazing things for us yet, we, when we have another need, we question the ability of the Almighty to do what He said He would do. Thankfully, that is not the end of the story. In verses 15-18 Jesus gives them promises even though they, who had walked with Him, could not believe He was alive.

These promises are for us, even though we doubt His ability to do what we need or ask. He tells them to go into all the world. Then Jesus says in verses 17-18, *"And these signs shall follow them that believe; In my name shall they cast out devils; they shall speak with new tongues; They shall take up serpents; and if they drink any deadly thing, it shall not hurt them; they shall lay hands in the sick and they shall recover."*

I see no maybe's in this passage but a whole lot of shalls. So why aren't we doing more of this? We have the power. Our churches are known for it. It's time we took the authority Jesus, Himself, gave us.
We've got to step out on faith speaking with authority and watch God do the impossible for many. I'm finally starting to get better at this.

It simply doesn't matter where we are. If someone needs a miracle in a restaurant or a grocery store it's time to step out with dignity, grace, and authority taking dominion over it in Jesus name. That's when we will see impossibilities become possibilities.
So let's go be what God wants and step out on faith! He walks and talks with us. Let's show the world who our God really is!

Miracles, signs and wonders are waiting to happen!

Thankfulness is a state of mind. No matter your situation or problem you alone choose your reaction to it. Today I'm thankful for a God who has blessed me with the teaching of consistency, consecration, commitment and courage to thank Him regardless of feelings. So when I worship my God through the valley I'm walking know that this is just who I am. It is as necessary as breathing is to me. I don't know any other way. What a wonderful heritage I've been blessed with. Thank you Jesus!

Packing to head out shortly. I Love how God is ordering my footsteps.
I can truly say I never lost my praise. ...

November 3, 2013
Since yesterday morning I have not been able to get away from this passage in James 4:7-8.

"⁷Submit yourselves therefore to God. Resist the devil, and he will flee from you.
⁸Draw nigh to God, and he will draw nigh to you. Cleanse your hands, ye sinners; and purify your hearts, ye double minded."

Now that things in my world have sort of calmed down over the past few weeks I've been in a new battle. God knows and has it under control.

In a message I listened to yesterday the minister reminded me in James 4:7, *"Submit yourselves therefore to God. Resist the devil and he will flee from you."* Unfortunately most tend to focus only on the part of the verse about resisting the devil but we need to remember the first part.

This is what God has been talking to me about for me and for others. We need to really submit ourselves to God. Then when we resist the devil he will flee from us. It's a promise to us.

Lastly verse 8 says, *"Draw nigh to God and He will draw nigh to you. Cleanse your hands ye sinners; and purify your hearts, ye double minded."* In order to draw nigh to God we must cleanse ourselves by purifying our hearts and minds.

Holiness is so much more than outward appearance. Oh, I believe it is all necessary. However, our minds and hearts must be clear before Jesus. I remember as a child my pastor, Sister Clark always saying right before church was dismissed, "Are all hearts and minds clear before Jesus?"

So before church this morning ask yourself and spend some time searching it out. Is your heart and mind clear before Jesus?

November 3rd 2013

I am so thankful for the security the Lord gives me. He changes not and I'm engraved in the palm of His hands. There is no security like the security the Lord gives us. I'm so blessed to know the security of the Lord.

What an amazing service tonight! Bro. Harper preached & the power of God moved in. I'm so blessed to be able to be in such amazing services. Then Cheri Sandy called me right after she got out of surgery. I'm so thankful it went well. Please join me in prayer for her to have a quick uneventful recovery in Jesus name!

November 4, 2013
This morning I woke up with the thought speak with authority. It seems we have so many who are sick with major illnesses. Then God started to talk to me about a few things.

First He brought to my attention Jeremiah 18:1-6 where it speaks if the potter's wheel.
"The word which came to Jeremiah from the LORD, saying, ² Arise, and go down to the potter's house, and there I will cause thee to hear my words.³ Then I went down to the potter's house, and, behold, he wrought a work on the wheels.⁴ And the vessel that he made of clay was marred in the hand of the potter: so he made it again another vessel, as seemed good to the potter to make it. ⁵ Then the word of the LORD came to me, saying, ⁶ O house of Israel, cannot I do with you as this potter? saith the LORD. Behold, as the clay is in the potter's hand, so are ye in mine hand, O house of Israel."

For weeks now God has been bringing this passage to me daily. God has been reminding me He wants to use all of us. But who among us is willing to be broken in His loving hands?

Who wants to be torn apart so that you can be remade into a vessel that seems good by Him to be of daily use by the Master? Who among us will allow and ask Him really meaning it? Most of us, including myself, have said the words never thinking about the costs associated with it.

Now that I have been on the potter's wheel for a while and know that I will be there for a while I literally want not to be a beautiful vessel but the ugly one that is used every day. I want to be the one Jesus picks up knowing I will simply be the vessel that will bring Him honor.

Then in Matthew 14:23;"*And when he had sent the multitudes away, he went up into a mountain apart to pray: and when the evening was come, he was there alone."*

In the midst of the miracles Jesus was performing He took Himself into the wilderness and prayed. When wonderful things start happening in our ministries we have to remember to go into the wilderness apart to pray. Every day I need my quiet time with my best friend who just happens to be the Lord of Lords and Kings of Kings!

Last night at church when asked to lay hands on someone and pray for them I heard God tell me to speak with authority. Then He reminded me of Acts 3:6-10 and the Apostle Peter's authority in ministering and the miracles that occurred under His ministry.

"*[6] Then Peter said, Silver and gold have I none; but such as I have give I thee: In the name of Jesus Christ of Nazareth rise up and walk. [7] And he took him by the right hand, and lifted him up: and immediately his feet and ankle bones received strength. [8] And he leaping up stood, and walked, and entered with them into the temple, walking, and leaping, and praising God. [9] And all the people saw him walking and praising God: [10] And they knew that it was he which sat for alms at the Beautiful gate of the temple: and they were filled with wonder and amazement at that which had happened unto him."*

When we learn how to put ourselves on the potter's wheel, take ourselves apart to pray is when we will gain the authority that has already been given us by God through His Word. Then the miracles will just happen. There are some who have already gotten it but now the rest of us need to get it.

I think it's time to pray. ..

This week especially I want to be hid away with God. So many memories and on Saturday we finally lay to rest my love's remains. A chapter will close in my life. A new chapter begins... I just don't know if I'm ready for the next chapter yet...Whether I am ready or not doesn't matter it's here and I must walk on... I just pray I'm hid with God...

So hard to believe that twenty five years ago on November 6th we met, then eloped on February 18, 1989 and had a big wedding Memorial Day weekend 1989. I miss him so much. The memories are flooding me this week.

Tonight I'm thankful for the strength of the Lord. As it says in Psalms, Yea, though I walk through the valley of the shadow of death I will fear no evil for thou art with me..." He is simply with us. It's not complicated. When you need God He is available to you and me.

November 5, 2013
Today I'm so thankful for my God taking time out to sweep into the room I'm sleeping in to sweep in with His majestic presence. He wakes me up gently and we spend time together talking. I remember when this first started happening about a year ago all I wanted was sleep.

Now I crave more of Him. I can sleep anytime. I want to be available to God. Thank you Lord for your presence.

The song, "Thankful" by Byron Cage has ministered to me many times. Tonight I'm sending it to my friend Cheri Sandy who is in the hospital. Love you, praying for you. God is unfolding His perfect will in y'alls lives. I can't wait to see and hear about the next great thing He has y'all doing.

I will lift up mine eyes to the hills from whence cometh my help for my help comes from the Lord! This morning God woke me up amazingly early but what a wonderful way to start my day.

Then in Luke 7:12-17 *"¹² Now when he came nigh to the gate of the city, behold, there was a dead man carried out, the only son of his mother, and she was a widow: and much people of the city was with her. ¹³ And when the Lord saw her, he had compassion on her, and said unto her, Weep not. ¹⁴ And he came and touched the bier: and they that bare him stood still. And he said, Young man, I say unto thee, Arise. ¹⁵ And he that was dead sat up, and began to speak. And he delivered him to his mother. ¹⁶ And there came a fear on all: and they glorified God, saying, That a great prophet is risen up among us; and, That God hath visited his people. ¹⁷ And this rumour of him went forth throughout all Judaea, and throughout all the region round about."*

God started talking to me about rumors on this wise. What rumors are circulating about you? Look at the rumors that circulated about me and then tell me why you care so much about what others think.

In this first passage of scripture it talks of the rumors that Jesus was a great prophet that was visiting the people. Then later in this same chapter in verses 33-35 Jesus, Himself says, *"For John the Baptist came neither eating bread nor drinking wine, and ye say, He hath a devil. The Son of man is come eating and drinking; and ye say, Behold a gluttonous man, and a winebibber, a friend of publicans and sinners! But wisdom is justified of all her children."*

So in my little simple mind it was like God was saying to me it is time to quit caring about what others think of you. They will never get it no matter what you do or how hard you try to please them. He was letting me know beyond a shadow of a doubt that it is time for me and you to hit our knees and find out what He thinks of us.

So do you know what Jesus thinks of you and how you are living your life?

It's so hard to believe tomorrow would have been his 51st birthday and he's not here. Oh, I do miss you, your laugh, your voice, your warmth..... there is a hole in our family.

Today is going to be a full day. Spending part of it with two people I love dearly then headed to my house for tonight. Tomorrow... well.... tomorrow....we'll tell you about tomorrow.... tomorrow... LOL

November 6, 2013

Romans 6:1-12; I John 4:4-5. In these two passages this morning God was reminding me of some landmarks in my life.

Romans 6:1-12 " What shall we say then? Shall we continue in sin, that grace may abound? [2] God forbid. How shall we, that are dead to sin, live any longer therein? [3] Know ye not, that so many of us as were baptized into Jesus Christ were baptized into his death? [4] Therefore we are buried with him by baptism into death: that like as Christ was raised up from the dead by the glory of the Father, even so we also should walk in newness of life. [5] For if we have been planted together in the likeness of his death, we shall be also in the likeness of his resurrection: [6] Knowing this, that our old man is crucified with him, that the body of sin might be destroyed, that henceforth we should not serve sin. [7] For he that is dead is freed from sin. [8] Now if we be dead with Christ, we believe that we shall also live with him: [9] Knowing that Christ being raised from the dead dieth no more; death hath no more dominion over him. [10] For in that he died, he died unto sin once: but in that he liveth, he liveth unto God. [11] Likewise reckon ye also yourselves to be dead indeed unto sin, but alive unto God through Jesus Christ our Lord. [12] Let not sin therefore reign in your mortal body, that ye should obey it in the lusts thereof."

In the passage of Romans I was once again reminded why I live a different lifestyle that is clean and wholesome while seemingly the world we live in today is on the fast track to justifying everything the Word of God teaches against.

Verses 1-2 says it plainly and says it best, "What shall we say then? Shall we continue in sin that grace may abound? God forbid. How shall we that are dead to sin, live any longer therein? "

Here I believe God was telling me Don't you know? Don't you get it? How are you going to continue sinning saying I'm living by grace.

We all live by grace, however, you are dead to sin. I'm not saying we won't make mistakes but they should be mistakes. We shouldn't sin with the idea we will ask for forgiveness after the fact. I'm amazed some actually think that. If you're dead to sin you can keep sinning.

Then verse twelve sums it up by saying, *"Let not sin therefore reign in your mortal body, that ye should obey it in the lusts thereof."* We have to grow up. We have to realize some things we just can't do. If these sins keep coming at us we need to separate ourselves and pray.

Do we really want to go to heaven? Are we so happy here on earth that we don't want to pay the price to make heaven our eternal home? There is a hell to shun but I fear a lot of us have forgotten that fact. Our walk with the KING of KINGS and the LORD of LORDS should be the most important thing in our lives.

Finally I John 4:4, *"Ye are of God, little children, and have overcome them: because greater is He that is in you, than He that is in the world"*.

When we obey Acts 2:38 by repenting, being baptized in Jesus name and being filled with the Holy Ghost as evidenced by the outward speaking in other tongues we have the power of God resident in us so that we can say, Greater is He that is in us.

God has given us everything we need to live a clean wholesome life. Why then do we make it so complicated? I am not super spiritual or super holy.

Daily I have things I battle but I've made a choice to live a certain way. Will I make mistakes? Most likely but the secret is in knowing how to do better with much prayer putting God first and not intentionally doing wrong.

So every day I pray and ask God for His help. You see when others see me I want them to see a reflection of Jesus. So something has to be different about me. The closer we get to Him the more we will want to be like Him.

The question you need to ask yourself today is the same one I have to ask myself daily. Do I really want to be like Jesus? Am I willing to pay the price it will cost me?

On the road again...In Maryland...

On our way... We had to stop. The old lady with me had to use the facilities. For some reason she didn't want to use the port a potties for the construction workers. LOL
A Comment from Ronda Dalton Notice it says venture off the highway...lol we have had an adventure....lol
Susan D Wine Smith Most definitely. .. a lot of laughter and adventures...

Sis. Ronda Dalton in the bushes...wonder why???? — with Ronda Dalton.

A comment from Ronda Dalton You have heard of the Bush country in Africa, I may never experience it but I have found Bush country in Maryland at a rest area...lol

At "A Call To War" conference in Annapolis, Maryland with Bro. Wright preaching! Awesome!!!! Today has been a good day and just what I needed. It would have been my love's 51st birthday and I almost didn't come to this conference but I could hear him telling me, "Susie, Do this! You know this is what God wants so do it!"

So I have come to this conference and going to pursue what he and I both knew God wanted for us. I just so wish he was here with me. If I had done what I wanted I would have stayed home and spent the week in solitude. That's not good and not what God or my love would have wanted.

I am so thankful for a God that provides what we need even when we don't know we need it. I think this month of November I'm going to try and find every way I can to thank God for all the many ways He has blessed my life.

At the hotel after church! Wow, what a service. No singing or music, just straight teaching/preaching and travailing for hours.... loved it. Old time Apostolic church at

its best! Tomorrow morning starts at 9:30 a.m. and will probably go until 3:00 or 3:30 p.m. with one break for snacks.... a long day but oh, what a wonderful anointing in the services with such prayer and worship!
Needless to say at this conference for me it's about soaking it in and letting it change me so I don't think that I will have many, if any pictures. And for now I am signing off to get some sleep before time to pray. Love y'all... have a great blessed and safe night.

November 7, 2013
Mark 14:50-54. "[50] And they all forsook him, and fled. [51] And there followed him a certain young man, having a linen cloth cast about his naked body; and the young men laid hold on him: [52] And he left the linen cloth, and fled from them naked. [53] And they led Jesus away to the high priest: and with him were assembled all the chief priests and the elders and the scribes. [54] And Peter followed him afar off, even into the palace of the high priest: and he sat with the servants, and warmed himself at the fire."

After yesterday's amazing services and the way God is stretching me I had no idea where He would take me this morning in prayer. One of the things I learned last night that there have been many times in my life I have been like the disciples in Mark 15:50 where it says, *"And they all forsook him, and fled."*

They didn't just leave the one was their Lord and King but they had watched do miracles they fled when adversity came. In my mind I see people running from Him. Isn't that just like us? Oh, God forgive me....

Even Peter in Mark 14:54 says' *"And Peter followed Him afar off..."* Peter, an apostle with great power struggled. We beat ourselves up so badly when we are human. All we have to do when we realize we have fled or are afar off is take ourselves to our knees and talk to Jesus.

When I think of the choice I made to follow Jesus it was a choice to follow afar off. But now I have chosen to be as close as I can possibly be to Jesus. There is a price that has to be paid for that type of closeness with God.It's a life of humility, submission and obedience. All of my friends know I have had problems with all of those, however, now the only thing that really matters is following Jesus no matter the cost or sacrifice. I think what God wants me to do is look at every aspect of my life and see if anything in my life is causing me to follow Him from afar.

What about you? What are you letting keep you afar off from God?
Time to head back to church! I can't wait to see what God has for us today. This is not for the faint of heart. It's for people who really want more... and more... and more of Jesus.

I so loved being at "A Call To War" conference. What revelations!
We just left church and now to find something to eat before taking a nap and heading back for more preaching.

November 7, 2013
What do i say about today's services? I really don't know where to start except to say that I'm starting to understand myself. It seems like I've always been a square peg trying to fit into a round hole.

Let me explain. By that I mean and I'm not saying this to make you think more of me or less of me but I want to explain how this conference is helping me and continuing to mold me. Being on the potter's wheel is not pleasant. Let's just say my knees will never be the same. I'm learning how to eat carpet in a whole new way. I wouldn't change it for anything. Getting closer to God is all that matters.

Ever since I was a child it seemed like I was always the last one at the altar that I couldn't get enough prayer. Worship it seemed came easy to me. I couldn't understand why others didn't worship or pray like I did. Believe me I'm human and have many faults but God for some reason wants me to share these thoughts with you.

Now I've been with a group of people who (and I LOVE MUSIC) don't need music to worship or pray. It's like things are finally starting to fall into place and I'm beginning to understand more about this journey God has me on. What's so wild is that there are other's just like me. I know there are more out there than not. I feel like I'm finally becoming what I always thought I was, Apostolic....

Think about the Upper Room and how many people first got the Holy Ghost. From that little group of people 3,000 more souls were added to the church that day. No fancy programs, No fancy musicians, just worship.... When is the last time you got lost in worship or prayer of the King of Kings and the Lord of Lords.

Please don't misunderstand me in this I'm talking about me and finding my roots so that I can be everything God wants me to be and live completely in the fullness of His Spirit. Let's not settle for the same old, same old. Let's stretch ourselves and watch what God will do.

I love all of you, my friends, I just want you to get closer yet to your God, Jesus! So think about it. Think about getting lost in worship of Jesus or the Spirit of travail.... So excited to be headed back to church. .. to war... can't wait to be wrung out by God once again!

Today I haven't yet done my thankful post but I am so very thankful for a God who orders my steps each and every day. Each morning when He wakes me up to talk with Him sometimes I am woke up very early by 3:30 a.m. or earlier then the phone sometimes will ring with someone needing prayer or a request will be sent to me to stop somewhere while I'm traveling.

I'm so blessed to know God loves me enough to allow me to share with others my walk with Him and how it has changed me. Not only that when I go to these cities and pray for others God works miracles. It's amazing. I can never say enough about what God does. I love Him so very much!

NOVEMBER 8, 2013
I've repacked to head home after the first morning session of "A Call to War" Seminar but to me this has been better than church. God moves in and you're on your face in deep prayer. There is nothing like it. Oh, how I have enjoyed this. I so wish we could stay but real life intervenes. At least I will be able to watch the sessions I will be missing online.

Tomorrow afternoon we lay my love's remains to rest at the cemetery in Fayetteville, West Virginia at 3:00 p.m. A door will close when we do that and then it will be time for me to put my focus completely and totally on God and the things He has for me to do. I ask for prayer today for traveling mercies as we (Rhonda and I) journey about 3 1/2 to 4 hours to Morgantown and then I journey another 2 1/2 to 3 to my house. God is with me and on Him I depend.

This morning God took me to Isaiah 45:9-10, 18-19 and asked me the question, Why do you argue with me when I am fashioning you after my will?"

Verse nine and ten says it best, *"Woe unto him that striveth with his maker! Let the potsherd strive with the potsherds of the earth. Shall the clay say to him that fashioneth it, What makest thou? Or thy work, He hath no hands? Woe unto him that saith unto his father, What begettest thou? Or to the woman, What hast thou brought forth?"*

The Word says it very plainly here but to make sure you understand the conversation God and I were having here's what I felt He told me. He basically said why do you keep arguing with me about this. You think you know more than I do. Who died and made you God? Its time we remember who God is.

It is going to require us to step out by faith with no guarantees of financial stability and trust Him on a level we as Americans don't understand. We've got to become pioneers of the gospel holding nothing back, NOTHING! This means we let God be God.

I'm not saying go off the deep end but know that God will order your footsteps. He will provide. He does know what's best for us.

Lastly verses 18-19 remind us who He is. Why do we keep having to be reminded? It is time to obey Him and quit arguing with Him. I know I now need to pray.

A comment from Aurelia Hopkins "...step out by faith with no guarantees of financial stability and trust Him on a level we as Americans don't understand." I LOVE THIS STATEMENT!!!
I believe HE is calling HIS children to this Act. If the USA economy continues to fail then the BEST PLACE TO INVEST what we have is in THE WORK of GOD! Your Interest Gains will be beyond all your EXPECTATIONS! -

At the last session of "A Call to War" conference that I will be privileged to attend

On the road again.... headed back to WV. Ronda Dalton (otherwise known as Louise) is so thankful we made it back to Morgantown...LOL. She thinks I have a lead foot. I'm just trying to be transported where I need to be...

A Comment from **Melony Pennington** So are you Thelma?
Yep, I'm Thelma...lol
A comment from Ronda Dalton May I just say this one thing, if you want to see how to make a turn without brakes with a sharp curve into a parking lot, I now understand why there is a time to just get out kiss the ground and say thank you oh God in control of all things...I truly understand the need of prayer especially traveling....Oh the stories to tell but God is so good....

Today's thankful post. Today I am so thankful for the safety the Lord provides for us, as His children. Tomorrow when I am in the midst of enemies I know my God goes before me.

As it says in Psalms 23:5, *"Thou preparest a table before me in the presence of my enemies: thou anointest my head with oil; my cup runneth over. Surely goodness and mercy shall follow me all the dsys of my life: snd I will dwell in the house of the Lord for ever."*

I know I will have friendly faces tomorrow also. I am so grateful for those supporting me in prayer. Please lift us up in prayer all weekend. I know God has got this all under control.

I am standing and will continue to stand on the promises of God.

NOVEMBER 9. 2013
This morning my thoughts are lingering on the past two months and the past twenty-five years. What drastic changes I've been through.

Anyway God took me to II Corinthians 4:8-18 and finally to II Corinthians 5:6-8. In reading this it was like I was reading my own thoughts this morning. While I am troubled because I'm human I'm not perplexed because I have a confidence in my Lord and Savior. It is hard to explain but I know my God will carry me through this day and the others that will come after it.

Then verse sixteen to eighteen. In Gods eyes my storm is a light affliction. When going through the storms in our life we need to look at the problem from God's point of view. What we see as insurmountable God looks at and sees something very small and insignificant.

Because we have learned to trust Him we won't faint. Oh, we may pause as the blows of life hit us but our God renews us day by day. Because we all face storms/problems in life we have to remember everything in this life is temporary.

We need to be able to see the things that can't be seen. Believe me I know how hard it is to do this when your personal storm is raging but we serve a God who calms the wind and the waves. Why, then, do we have so much trouble believing He will do it in our situation when He has done it for so many others?

Lastly in II Corinthians 5:6-8. This morning it was like God was telling me it's going to be okay. You walk by faith not by sight. It's high time we actually did this. Yes we will still struggle with our flesh but when the storm rages we can be calm knowing God is in control.

So no matter your storm/problem know your God is carrying you and has already given you everything you need. Just reach out to Him.
I'm so impatient. My children are almost here and it seems like time is crawling....

Almost time.... Life can be so hard. Closing the chapter on a life I loved more than anything is so hard. God is good and will be holding me this afternoon.

Tonight I'm thankful for the closeness of my walk with God. Today I had no doubt God would wrap me in His arms and He did. Not only that but God gave me another miracle today.

Jesus is so very, very wonderful!
 I went to sleep listening to Wrap me in your arms. A great comforting song. Keep me wrapped in your arms dear Lord....especially tonight and throughout the holidays.

NOVEMBER 10, 2013 This past week has been amazing in so many ways. It has had high highs and low lows but through it all one thing never changed. God was with me!

I couldn't talk about the graveside service yesterday because I was too emotional but today I will go over the details. Many family issues for some reason has given some of the family the idea that I don't know how to coordinate a graveside service. Thankfully, I have many friends that are ministry and three ministers showed up, one with his wife.

As I got to the funeral home my husband's sister was waiting on me. I had arranged for my children to be with me and asked them to ride with us to the cemetery. I felt I needed to be protected, not from bodily harm, but just protected. I wanted no missteps.

When we got there I was walking over to the car where my former husband's mother was getting out of the car with a man who is not a family member. Introducing him to Bro. Lloyd Hart with Treasa Dickinson standing on one side of me he said, "I thought I was the one in charge here today."

I became so angry from the months of pressure they had put me under that while holding my husband's ashes I almost dumped them over his head. Yes, I can get mad. I saw RED!!!

Thank God Bro. Hart was there. He put his hand on my hand and looked me in the eye willing me to calm down. I think they could see that was the straw that broke the camel's back. My former husband's mother was paying for the graveside service but I was still the widow.

Bro. Hart calmly said, "When would you like to speak." They arranged the service so the ministry that I had invited could speak. My children and I went over and sat down. During the service while that 'wonderful' man was speaking the wind started blowing when he was trying to convince us of things we did not believe in and that my children had not been raised to believe in. Then, I think even God had enough!

Yesterday at the graveside service towards the middle of that man speaking a big buck with at least a 10 point rack seemingly came out of nowhere. He cleared a six foot fence with barbed wire. To me it seemed like he stopped and looked at me to let me know I'm going to be ok. It was almost like God let my Mike come back and look at me telling me, You're going to make it. My Mike was always the rebel. He loved to stir up trouble. This would have been his way of interrupting his own graveside service.

Then a friend called to check on me and reminded me we had seen one Friday in Annapolis, Maryland that jumped out right in front of us in the city. He made it across eight lanes of traffic. I had forgotten about him racking it up as insignificant.

Then she reminded me of one of my favorite passages of scripture, Psalms 42:1-4. Basically to me it is me thirsting for God in my day of trouble just as the psalmist did.

As the hart panteth after the water brooks, so panteth my soul after thee, O God. [2] My soul thirsteth for God, for the living God: when shall I come and appear before God? [3] My tears have been my meat day and night, while they continually say unto me, Where is thy God? [4] When I remember these things, I pour out my soul in me: for I had gone with the multitude, I went with them to the house of God, with the voice of joy and praise, with a multitude that kept holyday.

How many times does God try to tell us something or give us a sign and we rack it up as insignificant? Isn't it time we started believing the Bible literally?

Again, don't take me wrong. This isn't about going off the deep end but putting on your spiritual antenna to hear when God speaks to you. Sometimes in the middle of valleys we couldn't hear God if He stood in front of us. I believe God sends signs. He even uses animals like He used a donkey in the New Testament.

In these few verses of scripture it describes me to a T the past few months. Lastly in the fourth verse it says, *"When I remember these things, I pour out my soul in me: for I had gone with the multitude, I went with them to the house of God, with the voice of joy and praise, with a multitude that kept holyday."*

Today is Sunday so today is holyday. As hard as it will be I will do my best to go with the voice of joy and praise even though I don't feel joyful because my God deserves my praise for I am blessed... so very blessed!

This morning when you're making excuses about why you can't go to church realize that since my love died ten weeks ago I've averaged being in four to six services a week. It's not because I am great or super spiritual but because at a young age I learned that's where my strength is.

So I said all that to say quit making excuses and go to church today with the spirit of joy and praise for the one who gave His all for you.
Wow! What a wonderful spirit of worship and praise this morning so far. God swept in and took over. — at Apostolic Life Cathedral.

This is the part of my life I will be focused on going forward. I will be working for God writing, ministering and hopefully with the help of God seeing lives changed by Him for His glory and His kingdom! I want to see people freed by the power of the Holy Ghost!

Today I'm so thankful for the hunger God has given me for the things of the Spirit. Hunger keeps me on my knees and in the Word of God. Hunger for God has helped me so much. Thank you Lord for giving me such a hunger for you...

NOVEMBER 11, 2013
Psalms 126:1-6. Last night I laughed until I cried. It was happy laughter and happy tears.

This morning God woke me up thinking about laughter. Basically I think God is letting me know even though I will continue to have dark times but joy will also be present.

It is time for me as Psalms 126:5-6, *"They that sow in tears shall reap in joy. He that*

goeth forth and weepeth, bearing precious seed, shall doubtless come again rejoicing, bringing his sheaves with him."
Today I'm thankful for the tears I've shed fore it is in the valleys of life where I learn what true strength in God is. When I'm able to worship with tears of sadness rolling down my face is when I know I truly love my God.

Now I am thinking about how cold I am. We are to get anywhere from one to four inches of snow by morning or so they say and a low of nineteen degrees...brrrrr. I've cranked the heat, put on my warmest jammies and socks curled up under an afghan my friend in Texas, Elizabeth Vaughn, made me doing my best not to turn into an ice block.I'm singing oh, how I miss the warmth of the south.....

I finally got semi warm and promptly took a three hour nap. I may not need a toboggan to sleep in to keep my head warm. My bedroom is so warm. I cranked the heat up as high as I could.

You know there is a message in that. When we say we want to be close to God we should crank the heat up in our relationship with Him. How? We do this by spending more time in His Word and on our knees learning of Him sacrificing things that please our flesh to have greater consecration and more power with God.

I think most are satisfied with a surface relationship with our God. Personally I want to continue getting deeper and deeper with Him until there is so little you see of me but so much you see of Him. What about you? What are you willing to do to become closer to your God?

NOVEMBER 12, 2013
Ecclesiastes 9:10-11. This morning I started looking for verses with the word snow in them of which I found several but God directed me to something else. I guess I needed reminded once again.

[10] *Whatsoever thy hand findeth to do, do it with thy might; for there is no work, nor device, nor knowledge, nor wisdom, in the grave, whither thou goest.*

First of all in verse nine whatever we find to do we should do it with all our might and in verse ten it says "*I returned and saw under the sun, that the race is not to the swift, nor the battle to the strong, neither yet bread to the wise, nor yet riches to men of understanding, nor yet favour to men of skill; but time and chance happeneth to them all."*

So today while we sometimes wonder why God hits pause in our lives He is preparing us to be better for Him. Sometimes we get so busy either working for God or taking care of our families and careers that we cannot hear God for the noise in our lives.

I know I have had to de-clutter my mind daily. We have so much media and things that are of this world keeping us from hearing God. Yes, we have to work and take care of our responsibilities but our biggest responsibility usually gets neglected because we are so wrapped up in the cares of this world. Today take some time and spend it focused on God. See what He wants you to know. That's when you really grow with Him.

Turn off the noise in your life every day for just a few minutes. Before you know it you'll be longing for an hour in His presence. Don't limit God to days of crisis or church services.I am walking the dogs in the snow and twenty degrees weather. Now I'm headed to the doctor for blood work of which I will get the results tomorrow.

Back from the doctor. .. It took three needlesticks and they finally got enough blood for testing. .. My arm and wrist are still stinging but It's worth it to simply be alive. Now I'm thinking a small glass of Orange juice and half a bagel so I can say I did eat breakfast. .

Last night for dinner I had ten or fewer triscuits. I did have hamburger helper for a late lunch. I still have no appetite but I'm thankful today for a friend Joyce McCann, who's coming by to take me out for lunch.

I just finished watching Bro. Ron Macey at Royalwood.cc preach a message titled, "There is Hope". Wow, what a message. It was just what I needed to hear today. It seems like this valley I'm in when I catch a glimmer of light at the end another storm comes but I will not quit because in my heart I know worship is the key to victory regardless of my situation or problems. It's the key to yours also. —

Today's thankful post. I'm writing now about the most traumatic time in my life. I'm thanking God for the direction and inspiration He has given me today.

NOVEMBER 13, 2013
As I sit here trying to write and feel Gods will for what is next in this new journey I'm on God reminded me this morning what I need to do.

Luke 10:1-4. *"After these things the L*ORD *appointed other seventy also, and sent them two and two before his face into every city and place, whither he himself would come.² Therefore said he unto them, The harvest truly is great, but the labourers are few: pray ye therefore the Lord of the harvest, that he would send forth labourers into his harvest. ³ Go your ways: behold, I send you forth as lambs among wolves.⁴ Carry neither purse, nor scrip, nor shoes: and salute no man by the way."*

Regardless of our calling or vocation in life if we are filled with the Holy Ghost evidenced by the outward sign of speaking in tongues and having been baptized in the name of Jesus we should be laborers for His kingdom. You should be a laborer wherever God has chosen to place you. Some of us will travel to distant lands while God has chosen others to be effective right where they are. Those that travel should be effective everywhere they go always looking for an open door to lead someone to more of God.

We are the problem, God isn't. We limit Him. It's time to take the Word of God literally and stand upon its promises. So what if you're labeled a radical. Be radical for Jesus.

We want to see more miracles. Well, then, you have to be brave. This is not for the faint of heart. But after you take that first very scary step you will find God, Himself, will guide you.

I can think of no better guide for my life then Jesus Christ, the King of Kings and the Lord of Lords!I'm off for a while. Time to focus on writing. God is changing me so much.

I'm taking a break at the doctor. That is a seriously sad break...lol
Waiting for the doctor and blood work results

Blood work was perfect!

So today I'm thankful for miracles that my God does and prayer!

That is another miracle. Typically someone who has battled pancreatic cancer in the 6% that lives challenges are common but my God does all things well! What an amazing service tonight at Glen Ferris Apostolic Church. The glory of the Lord swept in and for a very long time God worked and then the service continued. I'm so glad God ordered my steps to be there.

NOVEMBER 14, 2013
This morning when I was reading the Word of God He brought me here to II Corinthians 4:8-18 where it talks of light affliction.

[8] We are troubled on every side, yet not distressed; we are perplexed, but not in despair; [9] Persecuted, but not forsaken; cast down, but not destroyed; [10] Always bearing about in the body the dying of the Lord Jesus, that the life also of Jesus might be made manifest in our body. [11] For we which live are always delivered unto death for Jesus' sake, that the life also of Jesus might be made manifest in our mortal flesh. [12] So then death worketh in us, but life in you. [13] We having the same spirit of faith, according as it is written, I believed, and therefore have I spoken; we also believe, and therefore speak; [14] Knowing that he which raised up the Lord Jesus shall raise up us also by Jesus, and shall present us with you. [15] For all things are for your sakes, that the abundant grace might through the thanksgiving of many redound to the glory of God. [16] For which cause we faint not; but though our outward man perish, yet the inward man is renewed day by day. [17] For our light affliction, which is but for a moment, worketh for us a far more exceeding and eternal weight of glory; [18] While we look not at the things which are seen, but at the things which are not seen: for the things which are seen are temporal; but the things which are not seen are eternal.

If you sit and really read each verse it is like you are reading your own thoughts some days. We get confused, distressed, persecuted, cast down (depressed) but never are we forsaken.

Then in verse sixteen is where we are reminded that we faint not. In verse seventeen what we see as so horrible is but a light affliction. To use the teens words it's no big deal and what seems like forever to us is over in seconds.

Lastly this is for an eternal glory. I can't say I've ever looked at my problems or valleys as bringing eternal glory but what if....what if they are? Wow! All of a sudden I can look at the problems of this life a little differently. Then the last verse summarizes it all up with a bow on top where it says, *"While we look not at the things which are seen, but at the things which are not seen: for the things which are seen are temporal; but the things which are not seen are eternal."*

So when life knocks you down, then around, and down some more don't look at it with your earthly eyes. You have to go to God put on your spiritual eyes with prayer and digging into His Word. Then the problems are only temporary. Once you realize that you can get more strength for the rest of the battle. Remember we don't look on what can be seen but on what can't be seen.

God has got your problems and you in the palm of His hands. Now lift up your head and praise your God. It's not over until He says it's over!
As much as I hate to do this because of what God has for me I must start looking for a loving home for Brownie. She is very spoiled, loves to cuddle, and talk to you. She has been a great companion and friend, however, I will be on the road 80-90% of the time. That is no life for a loved pet.

Love my Brownie. She has been fixed and cannot have puppies
I am also looking for a home for my miniature black Labrador Daisy. She is also very spoiled and loving. She cannot have puppies. I need to find a home for both dogs by the end of November.

Some days we just have to remember that we are in gentle hands....
Daisy had a new forever home that same afternoon. I had no idea how much more pain I could handle but I found pain continues.... I had to do something to distract myself from the pain.

That afternoon I went to help make some food at the church. They let the one who doesn't cook hold the pan..lol

Now I need a home for Brownie. ...

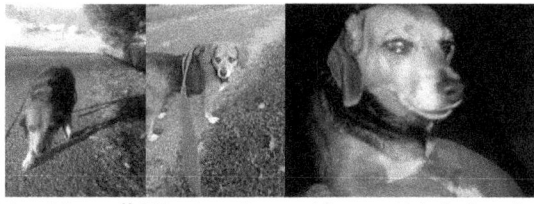

A comment from Sister Vernell Wooten Jones I know this is hard to do. Pray you find her a good home. She is pretty.

Susan D Wine Smith Thank you so much Sister Jones. Yes ma'am it racks right up with being one of the most difficult things I've ever had to do.

NOVEMBER 15, 2013
Grief is like a rollercoaster ride you cannot get off of no matter how hard you try. In my particular situation as one crisis after another has rocked my world. I would be shaken but my roots were firm so that I could say, "I simply trust my God."

This morning God directed me to Isaiah 25:8 where I was reminded,..*He will wipe away tears from off all faces*..." and in the next verse I was reminded what I needed to do. "...*we have waited for Him, we will be glad and rejoice in His salvation.* "

When you don't feel it is the most important time to worship. When the last thing you want to do is pray. That's when you must. Finally in Psalms 27:5-8 God reminded me I'm hid with Him, *"For in the time of trouble he shall hide me in his pavilion, in the secret of His tabernacle shall He hide me;..."* I can think of no safer place to be than hid by God.

So, today, no matter what you are going through remember His promises. Then remember Ps. 27:8, *"When thou saidst, Seek ye my face; my heart said unto thee, Thy face, Lord, will I seek."*

Never give up! Never quit! Keep believing! Victory is around the corner!

Sometimes all you can say is You are God and that's enough for me. Now it is time to paste my smile on my face and do a book signing at Montgomery General Hospital in Montgomery, WV

A comment from Treasa Dickinson-Dickinson Thank you for coming out and supporting our young girls you are always there for them thank you Susan D Wine Smith

NOVEMBER 16, 2013
I'm starting my day as I try to do every day with praise and thanksgiving to God for all His mercy as Psalms 107:1 tell us to. Even with all the trouble King David had he always found praise for God.

Yes, King David got depressed and we read that in the Psalms but what is great is that he would also find praise. Here he talks in verse 5-6 of, *"Hungry and thirsty, their soul fainted in them. Then they cried to the Lord in their trouble, and He delivered them out of their distresses."*

If we would really learn this concept King David tells us about we would always, no matter how bad things may be, know God will deliver us. HE WILL!

Then verses 8-9 says, *"Oh, that men would praise the Lord for His goodness, and for His wonderful works to the children of men! For He satisfieth the longing soul, and filleth the hungry soul with goodness."*

So today if nothing else simply praise God for His goodness and the great things He's done. He will satisfy our soul and fill it with goodness. Believe what the Bible says. Stand on it!

I'm still looking for a home for our loving and loved Brownie. She cannot have puppies. She loves to talk, loves walks and cuddles with occasional belly rubs. She's very calm and mild mannered. She is part beagle part wiener dog. I so wish I could keep her but with traveling 80-90% of the time I am unable to

I'm packing to head to Buckhannon, West Virginia later today. Thanking God for my friends. It's going to be great to celebrate the 35th anniversary of the church in Buckhannon with Bro. William Mooring, Bro. Randy, & Sis. Ann Tenney, Brittany, Kaitlyn, and Larissa.

Love my dear friends. It's a road trip for me and Sis. Joyce McCann.. God only knows what we might get into! LOL.

I am so thankful that God has blessed me with such grace to spend time with Him in a secret place. There is just something so special about knowing that place belongs only to me and Him. That is where I find strength, power and rest with God.

For today I am thankful I am learning what the word sacrifice really means for me. I think most of us have no clue but as God draws us closer yet to Him we are learning and understanding in a deeper way than ever before.

NOVEMBER 17, 2013
So enjoyed being at Bro. Mooring's 35th anniversary service in Buckhannon this weekend! So grateful for good weather! Thanking God for NO SNOW!!!

Here is my view this morning as I study. And it is cold enough to need a fire. It feels so good!

This morning in spending time learning of my best friend, the Lord Jesus Christ, I've been drawn to Philippians 4:10-13; 17-19.

"[10] But I rejoiced in the Lord greatly, that now at the last your care of me hath flourished again; wherein ye were also careful, but ye lacked opportunity. [11] Not that I speak in respect of want: for I have learned, in whatsoever state I am, therewith to be content. [12] I know both how to be abased, and I know how to abound: every where and in all things I am instructed both to be full and to be hungry, both to abound and to suffer need. [13] I can do all things through Christ which strengtheneth me."

When reading this first passage I found that learning to be content no matter our situation or circumstances to be content. The way to do this and not always whine, why me, is to realize we can do all things through Christ which strengtheneth us. ALL THINGS!

Believe me I know what I'm saying. I know how hard it is when your world is reeling. Just a week ago this past Saturday I buried my husband's ashes instead of scattering them as I wished because it was about a family healing not about what I wanted. In giving on this point I was not acting as I wished but how I felt Jesus would want me to act. Because of the strength of God I was able to get through that day. Think about others and what you can do for them.

Believe me, I, of all people get it. They've hurt you. You don't want any more heartache. What if Jesus had thought that way? He was beaten for us. Can we not do the same figuratively? So, what if they attack us verbally and want everything to be about them. Let go and let God be God.

Phillipians 4:17-19 *"[17] Not because I desire a gift: but I desire fruit that may abound to your account. [18] But I have all, and abound: I am full, having received of Epaphroditus the things which were sent from you, an odour of a sweet smell, a sacrifice acceptable, well pleasing to God. [19] But my God shall supply all your need according to his riches in glory by Christ Jesus.*

Lastly, verse 19 you need to remember. It has helped me tremendously. *"But my God shall supply all your need according to his riches in Christ Jesus."*

Trust God to be God!!!

Tonight I'm extremely thankful for having the name of Jesus to call on when things break as they will and did today but when I called on Jesus's name He was there. The Jag and I made it home but barely. God supplied my need. Tomorrow when I get up my nerve I will back it down back and it will be parked for now.... so thankful Jesus took the wheel and got me home.
Time for church!

NOVEMBER 18, 2013
This morning God directed me to a passage of scripture I've had memorized since I was a little girl in Ephesians 6:10-12, *"[10] Finally, my brethren, be strong in the Lord, and in the power of his might. [11] Put on the whole armour of God, that ye may be able*

to stand against the wiles of the devil. ¹² For we wrestle not against flesh and blood, but against principalities, against powers, against the rulers of the darkness of this world, against spiritual wickedness in high places."

I really don't think it needs any explanation but here's how God talked to me this morning. He gently reminded me regardless of all that has happened in my life I need to be strong in the Lord and in the power of His might. It does not say be strong on your own or on your own might.

Then God asked me if I really knew how to be strong in Him and His might. To me that means I step back and give Him everything. I do mean everything I have all the good and all the bad. Plus I go to prayer and reading the Word of God.

In the next verse it tells us to put on the whole armor of God. This is warfare. This is not lay me down to sleep prayers. It's the kind of praying that takes you deep places with God. It means you might spend a few hours or more in His presence battling on your knees. All of us can do this.

If you've never done it before you start out by first of all having a daily prayer time and increasing it. You pray for the lost with a deep burden. Tears will be shed, groanings which cannot be uttered like a woman in travail will come. This is so much more than being a surface Christian.

I was a surface Christian for so many years but I never want to go back to that. I want more of Him. With the way our world is changing so rapidly with sin becoming so much more widely accepted even in the "Christian" ranks the only way we will change our world is on our knees and by showing others Christ through our actions.

BE STRONG IN THE LORD!!!

I am seriously enjoying this gorgeously warm day in West Virginia. I think we will be in the 60's...heat wave. Tomorrow, based on the weather, then it will be back to the deep freeze... but I will enjoy today.

An extra blessing today I was privileged to joy ride in a friends Z today. Love it! So enjoying this rare warm day. Convertible weather!

A comment from **Ronda Dalton** Seriously do they know you are driving or did they let you sit in it for pictures....lol

And my reply: Funny! I did drive it today and no my lead foot did not get me any speeding tickets. I did however spin the tires. I think this is the kind of car I need to travel in. I could pretend I'm twenty instead of forty-eight.

Today has been great! It's amazing how relaxed and normal I feel. No crisis today. It is a beautiful Indian summer kind of day. God answered a prayer today. I still have a few more that need answered by next week but I know a God who specializes in things thought impossible so I will just trust the one who has me engraved in the palm of His hand and knows how many hairs are on my head. Isn't Jesus our Lord wonderful!

NOVEMBER 19, 2013
Last night I forgot to do my thankful post. I woke up this morning so thankful for a loving God who never forgets me and always has me on His mind. He is concerned with everything I do and say. Thank you Jesus for your concern for me and every one that took you to the cross to die for our sins. I love you Jesus!

This morning I woke up thinking about the wounds of words in our lives and how we allow those wounds to shape us into the people we are or are not. Then I went to the Word of God.

In Zechariah 13:6 it says, *"And one shall say unto Him, What are these wounds in thine hands? Then He shall answer, Those with which I was wounded in the house of my friends."* Jesus was not only wounded physically but we read in the gospels of times He was wounded by words yet He never quit because He had a purpose.

We are all here for a purpose for Him. Why then do we allow slights or words to halt us and bitterness to grow? Proverbs 18:14 says, *"The spirit of a man will sustain his infirmity; but a wounded spirit who can bear?"*

I started thinking of all my friends who were hurt by folks in church and how they allowed that pain and hurt to define their future. We all say no, we did not.

Each and every one of us have allowed the pain of hurt to shape us. It's not wrong to allow it to shape us if it shapes us constructively in that it brings us closer to God. But most of allow it to drive us away from Him. He did not hurt us so why do we blame Jesus?

Then in Psalms 112:7-8 the Word of God says, *"He shall not be afraid of evil tidings: his heart is fixed, trusting in the Lord. His heart is established, he shall not be afraid, until he see his desire upon his enemies."*

When our heart is fixed, trusting in the Lord it will not matter what others say. Oh, it will hurt because we are human but we will simply go to our knees and talk to our God trusting Him with our pain.
Lastly, Psalms 112:1, *"Praise ye the Lord, Blessed is the man that feareth the Lord, that delighteth greatly in His commandments."*

King David understood the importance of praise and the security it gives you in your walk with God. When we get that in our hearts we will still hurt when things are said about us that are untrue or we are slighted but our trust will be in God. That trust will keep us going and keep us praising the King of Kings and the Lord of Lords.So today no matter what is going on in your life worship is the key to what makes the difference when someone hurts you so worship your God.

Today I am sorting through precious memories. Boxing up our life together and remembering the good times

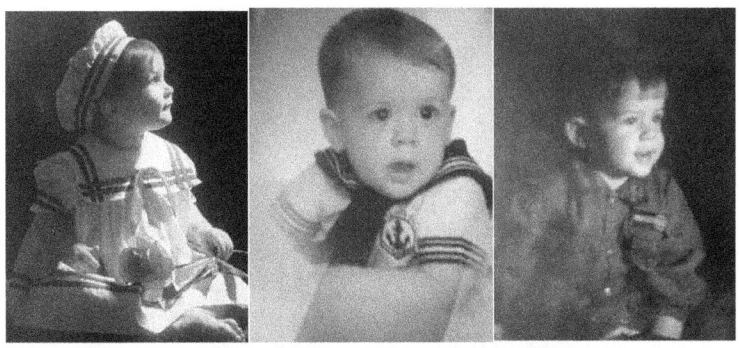

Leah September 1991   J.T. June 1994   J.T. February 1994

Leah March 1995   J.T. & Leah March 1995

Leah Chicago October 2000

Leah and J.T. Fall 2003

J.T. & Leah Easter 1998

I can't quit thinking about the Lord and all the wonderful things He has done for me. And for another fun evening the commode messes up and will not quit running.....trying to turn off the water to it and the knob on the valve is missing... in all things I will give thanks to God even when water is spraying me in the face from the commode.

Comments:
Michelle Marie Leurquin Channon Get a wrench quick! :0)

Susan D Wine Smith My husband's tool belt is missing but a friend is on their way with one. Until then I'm flushing.. What a night!
Robin Fields Harrison Water bill Will go up
Robin Fields Harrison I miss mine to
Susan D Wine Smith No doubt. Finally found the water meter.
Susan D Wine Smith Water is turned off.
Robin Fields Harrison Good
Thanking God for my friend. The commode will soon be fixed and the water will soon be back on — with Lois Procopio Pitsenbarger at Lowes.
<u>**Susan D Wine Smith**</u> And its fixed!
Thank you Lois Pitsenbarger for riding to my rescue tonight! The commode is fixed and the water is back on.
Ronda Dalton Yeah....flush...lol
Susan D Wine Smith Lol
Susan D Wine Smith Paul was unreachable.
David Kevin Price Was a good idea though.
Susan D Wine Smith It was
For today's thankful post. I'm so very thankful for the provisions of God. When things go wrong God provides intelligence, church family, just whatever we have need of. I'm so blessed to serve a God who provides!

NOVEMBER 20, 2013
This morning I started revisiting the thoughts God gave me while I was at the conference in Maryland, "A Call to War". This morning when reading in Nehemiah God directed me to these verses Nehemiah 2:11-13; 17-18; 20.

"11 So I came to Jerusalem, and was there three days. 12 And I arose in the night, I and some few men with me; neither told I any man what my God had put in my heart to do at Jerusalem: neither was there any beast with me, save the beast that I rode upon. 13 And I went out by night by the gate of the valley, even before the dragon well, and to the dung port, and viewed the walls of Jerusalem, which were broken down, and the gates thereof were consumed with fire."

"17 Then said I unto them, Ye see the distress that we are in, how Jerusalem lieth waste, and the gates thereof are burned with fire: come, and let us build up the wall of Jerusalem, that we be no more a reproach. 18 Then I told them of the hand of my God which was good upon me; as also the king's words that he had spoken unto me. And they said, Let us rise up and build. So they strengthened their hands for this good

work.[20] Then answered I them, and said unto them, The God of heaven, he will prosper us; therefore we his servants will arise and build: but ye have no portion, nor right, nor memorial, in Jerusalem."

I really sometimes don't know why God has me post some things. But if the apostles had lived in our day I think they would have used everything that they could to reach their world with the gospel.

So back to Nehemiah in verse 11 he was in Jerusalem three days. In my simple mind that would be symbolic of us holing up in the church but then he goes out in the night.If ever our world is in a night season it's now. Sin is rampant. If we speak against sin we are considered radical and in some places can even be convicted of hate crimes in America.

We have to take the gospel out. It will mean we will have times when we will be the only one. So what? God is with us! Nehemiah obeyed God. He knew what God had told him to do.

How many of us has God given marching orders to? Yet we drag our heels to do His will?

Then in verses 17-18 Nehemiah talks to the others and says basically, look at the problems we have. The devil has attacked us on every side. We've let him win. It's time to get our priorities in order and build the church back up.

How do we build the church back up? How do we put the devil on notice we are not letting him win anymore? This is war!

We start by putting God first (really first) reestablishing family altars in our home, personal devotions, prayer, reading the Bible, cutting out the sin in our lives, travail before God for our families, friends and country. We witness and are open to pray for people with needs no matter where we are. We do God's will not our will.

Lastly in verse 18 he reminds them of the hand of God and His goodness so they respond to him by saying, "Let us rise up and build. So they strengthened their hands for this good work."

So let's rise up and be the church! It's time to see the book of Acts happening today!

Surely soon I will be granted a furlough from the battle... but if not even battered, torn, with blood dripping I will crawl if I cannot stand in Jesus name! Time for CHURCH!!!! — at Solid Rock Worship Center.

Tonight I'm thankful for the battle fore it is in the battle where I've learned to be strong on my knees worshipping my God!

NOVEMBER 21, 2013
Missing Jackson, Mississippi FPC

A favorite portion of scripture this morning that most of us can quote is found in Luke 11:33-36.

"33 No man, when he hath lighted a candle, putteth it in a secret place, neither under a bushel, but on a candlestick, that they which come in may see the light. 34 The light of the body is the eye: therefore when thine eye is single, thy whole body also is full of light; but when thine eye is evil, thy body also is full of darkness. 35 Take heed therefore that the light which is in thee be not darkness. 36 If thy whole body therefore be full of light, having no part dark, the whole shall be full of light, as when the bright shining of a candle doth give thee light."

First of all, this passage talks about how we shouldn't hide our light under a bushel. Of course, every one of us talk about how we should share our Christian testimony with this verse and that is so true but the verse that stood out to me this morning is the next one.

"The light of the body is the eye: therefore when thine eye is single, thy whole body also is full of light; but when thine eye is evil, thy body also is full of darkness."

I looked this up in the NIV version and clarified what I felt God was saying to me. This is talking about singleness of heart in serving God. If your heart is divided then you are full of darkness and so am I. We have to give God our whole heart. We must be clean before Him setting no evil thing before our eyes intentionally. If we come upon something unintentionally we have to be woman/man enough to walk away from it.

We are all guilty of watching and/or reading things we shouldn't. Consecration needs to be so much a part of us that it not only shows up in our outward appearance but in everything we do and say. We can be in darkness and not even realize it.

The next verse says, *"Take heed therefore that the light which is in thee be not darkness."*

Think on that a while. I know I have. We can be walking in the light but covered up in darkness. It's high time we cleaned out our hearts, our minds, our homes (I.e. computers, books, media devices) of anything that we could not listen to or watch if Jesus was beside us.

If you're a Christian He is in you. How can you set that filth before His eyes? You may say this is a bit strong but He died on a cross so that we might have life and more abundantly.

Do you crucify Him afresh every day when you continue in your sin?

Justification for your sin on earth will not get you into heaven. It's time we quit arguing and went to our knees. Each and every one of us know what we are doing that we shouldn't be. Don't you think it's time we truly gave God our whole heart?

The last verse in this passage to me is a promise. If I clean myself up and out then I will be full of light. That is what I want.

That is what we all say we want but do we truly reflect that? Think about it. Then make some changes. Being like Christ requires that we constantly work on us to be more like Him.

Tonight I'm so thankful for the blessings of miracles God gives us from being filled with His presence to healings in our bodies to inspiration to work for Him. We are so very blessed!!!

NOVEMBER 22, 2014
This morning I woke up thinking about deep calling unto deep. So I looked up Psalms 42. One of my favorite verses is the first verse where it says, *"As the hart panteth*

after the waterbrook so panteth my soul after thee, O God."

I'm so thirsty for more of God. I cannot get enough of Him. Then the next few verses talk about how the problems are affecting him. I feel the same way. While I'm trying to be cheerful and normal a lot of the time I'm simply overwhelmed by grief.

I always am thankful for all the blessings I've been given. If I never received another blessing on earth I can still say I've been blessed more than most.

Verse seven, the one I woke up with on my mind and then researched says, *"Deep calleth unto deep at the noise of thy waterspouts: all thy waves and thy billows are gone over me."*

What I found in research was that David was comparing his problems to waves and billows basically swallowing him. That's what grief and problems do to us whether we allow them to or not. It's like you can't catch your breath. You don't know how to go on but you keep putting one foot in front of the other.

What makes us different from people that don't believe in God is the last part of verse 11 where it says, *"...hope thou in God: for I shall yet praise him, who is the health of my countenance, and my God."*

Hope in God and Praise are our secret weapons. Whether we feel hope and praise we keep doing it. Then as it says in Ps. 30:5, *"...weeping may endure for a night but joy cometh in the morning."*

We just need to remember the God we serve and His promises.

JOY IS ON THE WAY!!!!

I am thankful to serve an on time God. I may not understand His timing but His timing is always perfect.

November 23, 2013
Today my God needed to remind me of Isaiah 40:31 and Hebrews 11:1. No matter the challenges facing us these two verses offer us a wealth of promise.

Isaiah 40:31 simply states, *"But they that wait upon the Lord shall renew their strength; they shall mount up with wings as eagles; they shall run and not be weary; and they shall walk and not faint."*

When life overwhelms you as it sometimes will hang on to the promises of God. They are true and will keep you.

Lastly, Hebrews 11:1, *"Now faith is the substance of things hoped for, the evidence of things not seen."*

We have to continue to have faith no matter how bad or long the night gets remembering that no matter what crosses our minds that Jesus will never leave us or forsake us.

He is with me and you. On Him we can depend! Have now faith!
I wasn't sure if I should post this or not but last night on my way to Huntington the speedometer on the expedition quit working. When I would turn the lights off the speedometer would work. Then the windshield wipers would work sporadically.

So I can deduct it's either a fuse or a short. I'm praying it's an inexpensive fix and that it is able to be fixed today. Please pray that it is easily fixable.

So far we found that when my husband replaced the battery in July for some reason he did not clean the corrosion off of the battery cables. It's cleaned off now but based on how it's acting we think it needs a speed sensor... lol... maybe not... we'll see.

I might try changing it myself after watching a youtube video... LOL... or not.

November 24, 2013
I'm thankful for the God I serve who cares so much for me that when vehicles break down He always makes sure I am in a safe place with someone who can help me. What a wonderful God we serve. So plans are changed but God has a reason so I trust in Him while I rejoice in thankfulness that He loves me enough to take care of me.

Oh, the expedition would not start today. So it was another issue entirely. Speedometer is still not working. I ordered the part last night. It will be in today. Almost $127 but there is a garage close by that can probably put it in if someone here can't. It's a small 15-20 minute job if you know what to do or so I'm told. I thought about doing it myself... LOL...can you see that. I did find a youtube video but I have a feeling that would be quite the experience if I did that....

Well, we'll see tomorrow morning how much they'll charge me to install it if someone else doesn't volunteer.... lol.. or I don't decide to try and do it myself.

It is not the speedometer itself but the little thingy that makes it work.

A comment from Lois Procopio Pitsenbarger Susan Smith you know you can get a GPS that shows your speed??
My reply: I know but it also controls the antilock brakes.... I can pick up the part today and get it put in tomorrow hopefully.

This morning I woke up thinking about how much God loves us and cares for us. Psalms 91:5-16 reminded me best. Verse five says, *"Thou shalt not be afraid for the terror by night; nor for the arrow that flieth by day;"* There is so much more in this chapter but that really stood out to me.

Anyone that goes through deep grief knows that it is during the night when it is worse. For some reason everything seems worse at night.

Then the new attacks that come during the day. Things break and other things happen. But our God loves us enough He wanted me and you to know He is with us.

Why is God with us? Because we made a decision as it says in Psalms 91:9, *"Because thou hast made the Lord, which is my refuge, even the most High, thy habitation;"*

To define habitation it says, "the state or process of living in a particular place". Bad things happen to everyone. It is not what happens to us that defines who we are but what we do when those things happen.

When you make that decision to have a close walk with Him you live in Him. Then when things happen or go wrong you're already there in your refuge where He can be God in your situation.

What I mean by this is that you know in your heart He will take care of you. There is already a trust established.

For those that don't yet have that it's so easy to get there. All you have to do is call on His name. Your crisis may not always be fixed immediately but He will be with you and help you through it.
Finally verse 11 is the verse I woke up with on my mind, "*For He shall give His angels charge over thee, to keep thee in all thy ways.*"

For example when my vehicle started messing up it literally could have quit right where I was in the middle of nowhere. I knew to pray. While it wasn't immediately fixed God kept it running.

Then in the middle of a downpour the wipers quit working. God gave me the thoughts about turning them off every few minutes. I had them part of the time. Thank God I was able to make it to my destination. Plans for the next couple of days have had to be changed. Perhaps God has something for me this weekend in a different place. If I was completely absorbed in woe is me I might miss what He has.

Therefore we have to realize some problems and/or detours are to help us. We just have to open our eyes most of the time and realize the huge disaster God kept us from.

So this morning in your devotions and in church don't focus on the problems focus on the promises of God. Think about what He has kept from hurting you.

Then you can do as it says in Psalms 100:4, "*Enter into His gates with thanksgiving, and into His courts with praise: be thankful unto Him, and bless His name.*" That's what I plan to do today.

I decided a long time ago that Jesus would be my habitation. So now I have angels taking care of me. It truly is that simple.

Well if I had to be stranded for the weekend and I couldn't be in Jackson, Mississippi or Houston, Texas well, Huntington at Apostolic Life Cathedral was the next best

thing. God swept in during the worship service and everything just stopped for a while as spontaneous worship erupted. What a wonderful presence of God.
Then Bro. Harper preached a great message titled, "The Secret that the Rich Fool Knew" from Luke 12:16-21. Wow.... what an amazing service! One of those I won't soon forget. I'm still singing, "The Harvest is Ripe...." We've got to go to the fields.... We've got to compel them to come! You can't reap a harvest if you don't go to the fields where the crops or in our case the people are.

NOVEMBER 25, 2013
So... who will go and work for God today. If He calls you...would you go... or would you put limitations on it? Would you dare to try and tell God why you couldn't do what He asked? Would you bargain with Him? When souls are dying and He's asked you to help what would you do? What will I do? God is preaching me a message tonight... and I'm probably not the only one.

I'm going to try and get some sleep. Hopefully later today the Expedition will be fixed and I'll be well on my way to Fayetteville for at least a couple of days before hitting the road again. God knows and He has it all under control. I'm so blessed with wonderful people who are helping me. So I've got several books I need to finish writing but God gave me an idea for another book tonight. Soon I'll get some of these books to my editors because three or four are close to being done but I keep getting drawn away to something else God gives me. When inspiration flows you go with it and it will be okay.

This morning I felt drawn to Philippians 1:6; 21-23. We quote Philippians 1:6 all the time, *"Being confident of this very thing, that He which hath begun a good work in you will perform it until the day of Jesus Christ.:"* I believe that, however, we need to remember Paul was a prisoner when he penned these words. God started talking to me this morning about so many of us that are in prisons of our own making.

How, you ask?

Well we could have unrealistic expectations for our futures or our family's futures. We could be in a prison of debt, work, grief, sickness or anything that keeps us from obeying God.

Yes we have other prisons that are physical with bars but I think we allow the prisons we have created by choices we have made to entangle us so much we think we can never be used of God. That is a trick of the devil to keep you from obeying God.

Then verses 21-23 where the Apostle says (NIV), *"For me to live is Christ, and to die is gain. If I am to go on living in the body, this will mean fruitful labor for me. Yet what shall I choose? I do not know! I am torn between the two: I desire to depart and be with Christ, which is better by far;"*

Yes, I realize this is not a complete thought out of Philippians but I just wanted you to see even a great Apostle struggled with what he wanted and what the church needed. Our struggles with the will of God in our lives are normal. It is not the struggle that is the problem. It is in how long we allow the struggle to derail us from the mission God has given us.

He was torn, like as we are. We love our comforts. Who wants to sacrifice? However, when we do is when we will see great things happen for God.

I know I've weighed the sacrifice as I'm sure each and every one of us does but I think God is telling me and you it's time to quit making excuses and obey what He has told us to do. That is when we will be truly free of the prisons we have created for ourselves.

Remember I Samuel 15:22, *"...Behold to obey is better than sacrifice, ..."*

I am On my way to get the Expedition fixed. It's running again!! Hallelujah! The Expedition is fixed. It cost absolutely nothing to fix. I do believe God just wanted me where I was for a few days. I've walked Brownie. I'm going to miss her so much but I still do need a home for my loving baby girl.

Tonight I'm thankful for the thirst and hunger I have for more of God and to do more for God. I thirst to be a lowly servant of the most high King of Kings and Lord of Lords!

NOVEMBER 26, 2013

What will we do when we hear Jesus is in the house?

This morning I was drawn once again to a passage that most of us know well, Mark 2:1-4. *"And again he entered into Capernaum after some days; and it was noised that he was in the house.² And straightway many were gathered together, insomuch that there was no room to receive them, no, not so much as about the door: and he preached the word unto them.³ And they come unto him, bringing one sick of the palsy, which was borne of four.⁴ And when they could not come nigh unto him for the press, they uncovered the roof where he was: and when they had broken it up, they let down the bed wherein the sick of the palsy lay."*

Verse one tells us that word spread he was there. Then verse two shows us the hunger of the people in the area. The place was so full that no room was left for anyone else to get in. Then someone was desperate to get to Jesus. Are you desperate yet? If you've never been desperate you'll not understand what they were doing or why.

When you have no other options, no other way that's when you'll do anything to get to Jesus just to feel His touch on your life. Because of their desperation they did what they had to in order to get to Jesus, *"And when they could not come nigh unto Him for the press, they uncovered the roof where He was: and when they had broken it up, they let down the bed wherein the sick of the palsy lay."*

What God quickened to my heart this morning was if you and I get truly desperate to be close to Jesus we will do whatever it takes to get to Him. Nothing, and I do mean, NOTHING will stand in our way. As Americans we want the easy way out. If it's going to cost something we back off.

In this passage they made their obstacle become the way to Jesus. Could you do that? Could I? So they couldn't get in, big deal. Most of us would have stopped right then. Not them, they looked around and even though it was difficult they did it.

Then they literally let down the problem to Jesus. Give Jesus your problems, challenges and illnesses. Then let Him be God. We are not God we do not know what is best but He does. Trust Him to know what you need.

Know that in your hour of desperation He is available. Then watch with expectation of the miraculous He will do for you. As we have heard it said many times God is no respecter of persons but He does recognize desperation.

Trust God to be God!

I'm packing to leave for Nashville Tennessee this afternoon to do a book signing at the ALJC Youth Convention at the Grand Ole Opry Hotel. Plans have been changed to leave a day earlier than planned before the weather gets bad. Praying God does great things this week in Nashville and for traveling mercies for all that are traveling this week in Jesus name!

As I was leaving the Expedition began acting up again. I pulled off in Beckley, West Virginia because it appeared to be having problems shifting. I called Bro. Fred Ray and talked to him. I told him what was going on. It appeared that if I turned the lights off the wipers would work. It also seemed that if I would turn the wipers and the lights both off I would have heat and if I turned all of them off it would shift okay. What you need to understand is the Jaguar had just broken down and as at the mechanics making unidentifiable noises but I had somehow limped it to the mechanics. Now the last vehicle I had was acting up.
Bro. Fred Ray prayed for my Expedition and said, "You know God told you to go. God will protect you, so go. We'll be on the phone if you need us.

This was a real leap of faith to start out in a vehicle that did not want to shift gears. I had no gas gauge and was driving several hundred miles from West Virginia to Nashville Tennessee with a heater that could only be used if I turned off the wipers and lights. Unfortunately due to the weather moving in I needed both the wipers and the lights. It was a long drive with only one stop in 8 hours.

When I stopped to get gas I just put what I thought it needed and continued on down the road.

Well.... now that's a deep subject. .. tonight I'm thankful for traveling mercies. ...and praying friends!!!!

I'm in Nashville at my high school friend, Silver Treft's, house. I wish it would have worked out where we could have seen each other but I'm so thankful she opened her home to me. Thanks so much!!!
A comment from Silver Treft So sad I missed you.. Weather! Make yourself at home!!!

When I arrived I wasn't sure I was at the right house. I had never been to her house. Silver and I had not seen each other since our high school reunion that summer and prior to that since high school. This was a real leap of faith. I did not have money for a hotel. I went to Nashville on a shoestring in a car that was having problems. When I arrived at Silver's and parked I turned the Expedition off and it kept running. I thought that was strange so I went to turn off the lights and the engine turned off. Then I went to put the car in reverse and it wouldn't go but the engine kept trying to start itself. I really didn't know what to do. So I finally got it turned around so if it started itself and decided to drive itself it would total itself...LOL

I really thought the devil had a hold of that car. I do think the devil was putting every obstacle in my way to keep me from being at the ALJC Youth Convention. God wanted me there and had provided the means and the way.

Now, let's go back to me staying with my friend Silver. She had left her house unlocked so I could get in. However, I wasn't sure I was at the right house. I'm horrible with directions even with a gps. So after I got the car at least semi-calmed down I got out and walked in the back door yelling as I went in just in case I was at the wrong house. Are you getting this picture?

Imagine, Me, a former banking executive who used to fly in private planes and ride in limousines staying in a strange house in a strange city driving a car that appeared to be possessed.

So, I continued walking through the house and met the dogs. I finally go into the master bedroom and thank God I see a picture on the dresser of her with her fiancée. Thank you Jesus I was in the right house! I almost shouted!

So I go back to the car and get my luggage out hoping and praying the expedition will run the next day.

Part of a facebook conversation I had with my friend Silver once I got settled in at her house.
Me to Silver, Your home is beautiful. I feel guilty enjoying it.
Have a safe trip! Enjoy your family Thanksgiving!
Silver Treft Please enjoy.. It's home! And grand central station!

Susan D Wine Smith Oh, I am. Your son and Mariah just got here and are cooking. I love it! Can't wait to try Peroggia's.... Smells so good!

Below is my next facebook post. I did not post about the car. Too many would have worried. God and I needed to deal with it. In other words I needed to pray and trust God so I just asked for prayer.

Please pray for me. I have an extremely urgent request. God knows and God can work it out.

NOVEMBER 27, 2013

After my night of travel last night and finally arriving in Nashville safely. God impressed upon me Luke 24:13-17; 31-34; 41-43.

Luke 24:13-17

[13] And, behold, two of them went that same day to a village called Emmaus, which was from Jerusalem about threescore furlongs. [14] And they talked together of all these things which had happened. [15] And it came to pass, that, while they communed together and reasoned, Jesus himself drew near, and went with them. [16] But their eyes were holden that they should not know him. [17] And he said unto them, What manner of communications are these that ye have one to another, as ye walk, and are sad?

In the first few verses they are sad because Jesus has been crucified. What they don't see is their miracle walking right beside them. He even asks them, "...*What manner of communications are these that ye have one to another, as ye walk and are sad?*"

They were so sad they didn't recognize the miracle even when He spoke to them. In the next several verses they explain to Jesus why they are sad. Is that not like us? We think He has no clue yet He walked and perhaps even carried us through the storms.

Then in verses 31-34 their eyes were opened and in verse 32 even say, "...*Did not our hearts burn within us, while He talked with us by the way, and while He opened to us the scriptures?*" In our hearts I believe we do recognize Jesus is with us in the storms of life but our minds can't quite get there.

Finally after He has left them they spread the word that He is risen. Even when He appears to those in verse 41 it says, "*And while they yet believed not for joy, and wondered, He said unto them, Have ye any meat?*"

In order to get them to believe it was He, King Jesus, alive and well He had to eat in front of them.

In the margin of this passage of my Bible I had written the words, Courage to go on. When you are buffeted by the storms of life we tend to forget who walks and talks with us.

This has given me renewed courage. I hope it helps you this Thanksgiving season. Jesus is with you and me. On Him we can and should depend!

Today I'm so thankful... so very thankful! My focus today is on being thankful for a God that loves us enough to let our dreams come true. While I've had a lot of tragedy this year I am remembering that God has let my dream come true of being an author. There's no God like our God. He cares about the smallest details of our lives. Know that He cares for you and wants the best for you!

Zach and I at our book table.

NOVEMBER 28, 2013
Happy Thanksgiving to all! I pray you have smiles, hugs and laughter with your family this day. I thank God for the memories of all the Thanksgivings I had with my family. I was indeed blessed for many years with wonderful Thanksgivings.

This year my life has changed radically but I am still blessed far more than I ever should have been. I am so thankful for the memories God is allowing me to revisit tonight. The hugs and kisses of little arms, Thanksgiving with my love, Thanksgivings as the children grew... how blessed I am... hold your family close for no tomorrows are guaranteed. Jesus is with me and on Him I depend.

Today is about Thanksgiving. I have chosen to be alone today. I'm not sure if that was a smart or stupid decision but it was my decision.

Today Psalns 100:1-5 gave me a swift kick where I needed it. I had been having a pity party for myself when Psalms 100:1-5 says, *"Make a joyful noise unto the Lord, all ye lands. Serve the Lord with gladness: come before His presence with singing. Know ye that the Lord He is God: it is He that hath made us, and not we ourselves; we are His people, and the sheep of His pasture. Enter into His gates with Thanksgiving, and into His courts with praise: be thankful unto Him, and bless His name. For the Lord is good; His mercy is everlasting; and His truth endureth to all generations."*

So today I'm thankful for a God that has blessed, yes, blessed me with good health, two healthy children, a son-in-law, living parents and countless other blessings including the fact that I can be thankful with tears streaming down my face. It truly is not about what happens to us but how we allow it to shape and mold our futures.

I will never forget the happy family holidays but I'm in the process of figuring out once again how to put a shattered Humpty Dumpty back together. Forgive me if sometimes the smile doesn't quite reach my eyes or when I worship it is because I know I need to.not because I feel it right now.

I do know... I know that I know....I must keep singing praises and worshipping God with thankfulness. One day the smile will reach my eyes again and the worship will be because I feel it. I know that there are many who have suffered great loss and are in pain today. God will be your comforter as He is for me.

So today in the quiet find a place to worship your God regardless of your circumstances. Know that He has not moved. He's waiting on you. He loves us so very much!

Have a Happy Thanksgiving all! Be blessed of the Lord.
PRAISE GOD!!! PRAISE GOD!!! PRAISE GOD!!!!

God sent my Brownie someone to love her and care for her. Thank you so much for calling me. I am so happy to bring her to you in Jackson, Mississippi.

God cares so much for the details of our lives. I so needed this today! Thank you Lord for taking care of the details of my life!
I am almost ready to head back to the Gaylord Opryland Resort for night two of the ALJC Youth Convention and my book signing. I am so enjoying being here. I so miss my love today. He would have enjoyed Nashville. I've talked to J.T. and I'm hoping to hear from Leah Simpson yet today. Love them both muchly!

A comment from Aurelia N John Hopkins Glad how God works all things out and you are out and busy in The Lord's Kingdom.

It is time to get to the book signing and then church. I'm so blessed my life is literally centered on God — at Gaylord Opryland Hotel & Convention Center.

Where is God?

Job 9:11
[11] Lo, he goeth by me, and I see him not: he passeth on also, but I perceive him not.

When we, like Job, don't think we can find God in our storm because of all the things that are happening to us is precisely when He is carrying us providing our needs. These may be needs we have no clue we need. It may be confirmation for the journey coming. God keeps us in the palm of His hands.

Isaiah 49: (KJV)
"[16] Behold, I have graven thee upon the palms of my hands; thy walls are continually before me."

Wow! What a meeting God orchestrated! When God orders your steps He orders your steps or in this case my steps!

NOVEMBER 29, 2013
After a meeting with two wonderful ladies from New Orleans last night I knew why I had to come to Nashville for this conference. So this morning I woke up thinking about God ordering our steps.

That led me to Psalms 37:3-7; 16-18, 31-33; 39-40. When reading this passage this morning I realized God has brought me to a whole new level of trust with Him.

Psalms 37:3-7
"[3] Trust in the LORD, and do good; so shalt thou dwell in the land, and verily thou shalt be fed. [4] Delight thyself also in the LORD: and he shall give thee the desires of thine heart. [5] Commit thy way unto the LORD; trust also in him; and he shall bring it to pass. [6] And he shall bring forth thy righteousness as the light, and thy judgment as the noonday. [7] Rest in the LORD, and wait patiently for him: fret not thyself because of him who prospereth in his way, because of the man who bringeth wicked devices to pass. [16] A little that a righteous man hath is better than the riches of many wicked. [17] For the arms of the wicked shall be broken: but the LORD upholdeth the righteous. [18] The LORD knoweth the days of the upright: and their inheritance shall be for ever. [31] The law of his God is in his heart; none of his steps shall slide. [32] The wicked watcheth the righteous, and seeketh to slay him. [33] The LORD will not leave him in his hand, nor condemn him when he is judged. [39] But the salvation of the righteous is of the LORD: he is their strength in the time of trouble. [40] And the LORD shall help them, and deliver them: he shall deliver them from the wicked, and save them, because they trust in him."

I listen to that still small voice and walk by faith. Sometimes I have no idea why I go certain places or I think I'm going for one reason and end up going for another reason.

The meeting last night involved tears and an impromptu prayer meeting right in the halls of the Gaylord Opryland Hotel when we met and shared what God had shown us. I cannot wait to see what comes of all of this. The two ladies I met are from New Orleans, Louisiana. When I saw their billboard with the continent of Africa I wanted to know what they were doing. They were raising money for an orphanage in Uganda.

As we talked I found out we were ordained by God to meet at this conference and not only was I driving a car that the devil was trying to possess but they had been driving a vehicle with the same symptoms as mine all the way from New Orleans to Nashville.

Then they asked me what I was doing and I explained about the books and that I had been invited to Kenya to minister to a group explaining how to live for Jesus more fully. When I explained why I was going to Kenya the one lady started crying and praying. I looked at her with questions in my eyes and she said, "Stop, let me explain."

Then she told me that on the way to the conference God had spoken to them and told them they would meet someone there that was going to be influential for God in the continent of Africa. "
She then said she had told God, "We only have two days at this conference so we need to meet this person fast."

I'm not too bright most of the time so I said, "I hope you meet this person before you leave."

She then said, "Let me tell you about a dream I had. I dreamed we were in Africa and had been asked by a priest to explain to a Catholic church in Uganda what it meant to live for Jesus more fully."

When she said that I started to cry and shake because her words were the words Sis. Valentine from Kenya had used when talking to me about coming. As we continued to talk about the way God had ordered our steps it led to a powerful prayer meeting right there in the hallway.

When we put our WHOLE TRUST in the Lord it is amazing how He not only orders our steps but lets us know without a doubt we are in His perfect will for that moment. Oh, how I love Him! He is my breath, my sunshine, my all in all!

Trust Him with your life and watch where He takes you! You must realize though that doing this requires you to get out of the boat like the Apostle Peter and keep your eyes on Him.

It takes trust in God to a whole new level when things don't work out as we sometimes think they should but we just have to remember, He's got this! Tonight I'm thankful for the way God continues to let me know I am walking according to His will for my life. When you step out by faith God will let you know you are in His will for your life.

NOVEMBER 30, 2013
This morning I woke up thinking about the drive back to WV. I'm trusting, praying and believing God for traveling mercies not just for me but for all who are on the roads today.

When I read Luke 12:25-34 a passage many of us can quote God gave me a thought from verse 29, *"And seek not ye what ye shall eat, or what ye shall drink, neither be ye of doubtful mind."* The thought God gave me was, Neither be you of doubtful mind.

It's hard when in the midst of the battle to not doubt but Jesus paid the price and promises us in verse 28, *"If then God so clothe the grass, which is today in the field, and tomorrow is cast in the oven; how much more will He clothe you, O ye of little faith?"*

These are the words of Jesus. Think about these words. Now remind yourself of them and the God you believe in, He will provide for you.

Lastly, when getting rid of our doubtful mind, the only way to do this is through

prayer. You need a daily walk with God. Your walk should be one where you recognize His voice and He recognizes yours.
How long has it been since you really talked with Him?

Pray right where you are. Quit making excuses. He wants to be your very best friend and your God. Remember Luke 12:34, *"For where your treasure is, there will your heart be also."* When taking care of our doubtful mind we need to take inventory of our souls. Where is your treasure? Is it on earthly things or on the things of God?

December 1, 2013
Brownie is so excited I'm home and that we are going for a walk she just doesn't know what to do...love her... missing my family this morning.

I am enjoying our walk in the brisk air with snow still on the ground. Then I'm thinking we will have pizza for breakfast.

Time for CHURCH!!! — at Solid Rock Worship Center.

It's been a great afternoon starting with lunch with my son, walking Brownie, a trip to Walmart, washing clothes and now a nap before Sunday night church. I love Sunday night church. For me it is the best service of the week! I can't wait to see what God will do tonight!
Prayer is the best armor against all trials!

This evening God dropped II Peter 3:9 in my mind. It states, *"The Lord is not slack concerning His promise, as some men count slackness: but is longsuffering to us-ward, not willing that any should perish, but that all should come to repentance."*

So if you've slipped find an altar wherever you are. God is waiting for you to call out. He loves all of us!

December 2, 2013
This morning I woke up thinking about the power source. In the night I realized my tablet was lying beside the plug but not plugged into the power source. If I didn't plug it in it would be useless today.

So I did some research in the Bible and went back to Luke 5:17-26. Verse 17 is the kicker for me. A partial quote says, *"and the power of the Lord was present to heal them."*

The power was present to heal them. It was simply there.

If you read the whole passage it talks of the man they brought to Jesus to be healed that was lowered through the roof. They questioned who Jesus was when He forgave the man's sins. When Jesus healed him they sounded just like us.

Verse 26 says, *"And they were all amazed, and they glorified God and were filled with fear, saying, We have seen strange things today."*

What this passage doesn't say is that all were healed. We don't know. We only know of the one who was healed.

What if? What if on that day many others needed healing and weren't healed? They were in the room with the source of all power but couldn't believe He would do what they needed.

Let's bring it to today. People sit in churches sick, needing saved, needing the power of the Holy Ghost. The power is all around them but if you and I don't plug in to it and believe that God can we will not see our needs met or find that walk with God we've always craved.

We have to do something. They broke the roof up to get the man to Jesus. They were desperate. How desperate are you and I to have a close walk with God or that miracle in our life? I don't think we have a clue what desperation is.

We have to plug in daily to the power source through reading the Bible, prayer and worship. When our consecration to God becomes valuable to us as a treasure of great price we will see changes in us.

Don't simply sit beside the power source you need to plug in and be part of the great things God is doing!

Do not give up! The beginning is always the hardest.

Hold on! God will make you stronger.

I hate waiting... but for some reason that's all I do these days. I'm waiting now to go spend some time with my son tonight. Tonight and tomorrow morning will be hard. I'm so excited for him to be embarking on his dream of military service in the Air Force but oh how I will miss him.

My love should be with me tonight as we say our goodbyes to J.T. Has it really already been three months since he died? It doesn't seem possible but life does go on.

What words do I share that a Father would share with his son on the eve of his dream? I have no clue but I will cover him in love and prayer.

Tomorrow morning will be about the excitement of his dream and seeing him sworn in. Please remember us in prayer tonight and tomorrow morning.
I already miss hearing from him every day. Tomorrow he heads for his exciting future!

Tonight I'm so thankful for a loving God that blessed me with a handsome intelligent son and beautiful intelligent daughter. Now it's time to watch them soar into their futures.

Ronda Dalton They will be okay, momma, you and Mike have taught them to spread their wings and fly.
Beverly Hand Haygood Well said!

DECEMBER 3, 2013
God knows what is best. Isaiah 55:9
Waiting for J. T.'s swearing in — with Joyce Mccann at Beckley MEPS.
Today God directed me to Ecclesiastes 3:1-7. Verse one sums up life in a nutshell, *"To everything there is a season..."*

As young people we can't wait to grow up and have families of our own. Once we grow up and have children what we don't realize is from birth we are giving them skills to be independent and leave. That is the cycle of life.

While today is hard for me as a mother on the flip side of that coin I am so excited for him to soar into his future in the U. S. Air Force. When you pray please add my son, Joseph T Smith to your prayers that God will protect him and grant him favor in the coming weeks and months.

I'm now at a different season in my life trusting God in a new way. In every season we learn not just more about ourselves but more about the God we serve and the benefits we have in Him. Today I'm blessed knowing God is with me and He even sent my friend, Joyce Mccann to be with me today.

And he has sworn in…

So hard to believe he's now an Airman.

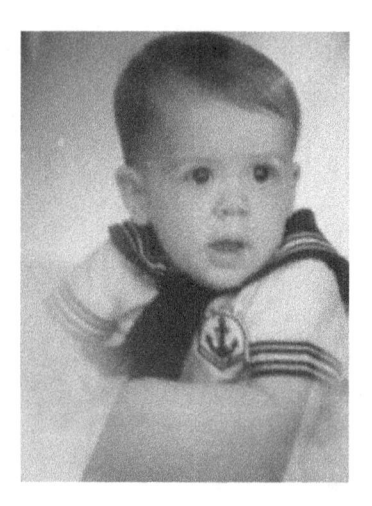

Thank you Joyce Mccann. Everyone should have a Joyce in their life.

And soon he will be on his way. I am missing him already.

He just landed in San Antonio. It was so good to hear his voice. Please pray for him over the coming weeks for good health, favor from God, mental and physical stamina to make it through boot camp in Jesus name. Thank you in advance for your prayers.

December 4, 2013
If you're up in the midnight hours perhaps God wants you to pray. I was just awakened by a phone call from some friends in Alabama. A great man is fighting the battle of his life with Pancreatic Cancer Stage IV.

Without a miracle he will be going home to be with Jesus. He's one of the many God has placed in my path and burdened me with the pain they and their family are going through. Please pray for a miracle and then pray for the family that God will strengthen and be with them in Jesus name. We serve a miracle working God!

Today and for a few days this verse in II Corinthians 5:7 has been on my mind.

"(For we walk by faith, not by sight:)"

This concept is foreign to us as Americans. We want a five year strategic plan with goals clearly enumerated and sub goals identified. Then we need an action plan that will identify possible problems and the resolutions to those before they happen.

Our God, however, really does want us to walk by faith and not by sight. We want to clearly see when sometimes the sky is cloudy or we may run into fog. At those times when driving you can barely see one foot in front of you let alone five years. That's when you follow the lines on the edge of the road. Those lines were put there to keep you from going over a cliff to your death.

That's the same way with living a Christian life. To some rules are restrictive. While in reality rules are like the lines painted on the edges of the road. They're put in place to keep you from harm and safe from the enemy.

So in walking by faith, and not by sight, we have to realize when in the fog and we can't see the way clear Jesus is taking us step by step. When frustration and doubt creep in that's when all we have to do is call on the name of Jesus. He will be there with us. So, in life, as in death, trust God to be God. He won't let us down.

I think I needed this today more than anyone else with all the changes and challenges in my life. I will continue to trust God to be God.
Lastly, I will be taking a break from Facebook for a while. It has been a very hard few months. I feel it is now time for me to hibernate.

I remember the tears would not quit running down my face during this time. Breathing was hard. Just getting dressed was a feat that I could go several days without doing. Depression was becoming my best friend. At one point the pain was so intense I started hitting myself with my fists. This is when I realized I needed to get a grip on me. Sometimes the emotional pain is so great physical pain is welcomed because the physical pain takes your mind off of the emotional pain.

When Bro. & Sis. Craft would call, and they called daily, I would not answer until I ate. They were calling to make sure I was eating and still breathing. I had several friends like that who were so close to me that some would stop by and bring me food while others would try to get me to go places to just be normal. But in my mind I would never be normal again.

Both of them had traveled this road before and knew the depths of depression that I had to go through. As my pastor and wife but also as people that I love like parents they wanted to assure themselves I was okay. Many prayers were prayed for me throughout these months. I will never ever be able to say thank you enough.

December 10, 2013

I'm b-a-c-k! I woke up to a winter wonderland this morning. The weather outside is frightful and since I really have nowhere to go let it snow, let it snow. The countdown has begun ten days until I head home to Jackson, Mississippi and hit the road again evangelizing and doing book signings!

This morning in my devotions John 2:24-25 really spoke to me. Then as I studied it I was led to I Chronicles 28:9.

John 2:24-25, "[24] But Jesus did not commit himself unto them, because he knew all men,[25] And needed not that any should testify of man: for he knew what was in man."

In the first passage I felt like Jesus was telling me in the past I couldn't be as close to you as I wanted to be because I knew the real desires of your heart. We pray and tell God we will do anything go anywhere yet we let obligations stand in our way.

These obligations are not matters of eternity. Yes, we have a responsibility to take care of our families. However, if Jesus has called you to do something for Him do you not think He can take care of you? After all He is the King of Kings and Lord of Lords!

Jesus knows what is in us. He knows if we truly mean what we pray. Sometimes we allow other voices to overshadow the voice if God in our lives. When this happens we need to pull away and go to our knees. He will get us back on track.

Lastly I Chronicles 28:9 says it so well, "And thou Solomon my son, know thou the God of thy father, and serve Him with a perfect heart and with a willing mind: for the Lord searcheth all hearts, and understandeth all the imaginations of the thoughts; if thou seek Him, He will be found of thee; but if thou forsake Him, He will cast thee off for ever."

Sometimes God will turn your life upside down to get you into a place to help someone else get their life turned right side up.

December 11, 2013

I really thought God was just talking to me through this passage the last few days but after the latest crisis God again brought it to my mind this morning.

Luke 13:11-13; *"And behold there was a woman which had a spirit of infirmity eighteen years, and was bowed together, and could in no wise lift up herself. And when Jesus saw her, He called her to Him, and said unto her, Woman, thou art loosed from thine infirmity. And He laid His hands on her: and immediately she was made straight, and glorified God."*

When God was talking to me the past few days it wasn't about physical infirmity (illness) but about my spiritual illness. This morning I felt God impress me that many of us have spiritual illnesses that have gotten us to where we cannot lift ourselves up just like this woman. It doesn't matter what caused it but that it has crippled us spiritually.

Do we even recognize that we are crippled? Have we gotten so used to being bowed low that we think feeling this way is normal?

Verse 12 says, *"And when Jesus saw her, He called her to Him,..."* He's calling us to Him. Evidently she went because the latter part of the verse says, *"and said unto her, Woman thou art loosed from thine infirmity."*

Can you imagine what those words meant to her? After being bowed together for eighteen years to hear those words? Yet, she, was not completely free until in verse 13 where it says, *"And He laid His hands on her: and immediately she was made straight, and glorified God."*

It was like God was telling me even though I promise you in my Word that you are healed of your illnesses whether they are spiritual or physical yet that's not enough for most. When Jesus touched her by laying His hands on her then she was made straight! Not only that but she glorified God.

Yes, I realize sometimes we are so bowed down we probably couldn't hear Jesus telling us we are whole but we know the touch of the Master's hand. When He touches us we are made straight.

So no matter how long you've been in this spiritual condition or illness know that the Master is with you to touch you and release you from it. Then you need to glorify Him! Such freedom and rejoicing is yours for the asking. Believe it!

In your prayers please pray for my children, J. T. Smith, Evan and Leah Simpson that God will be with us holding us.

DECEMBER 12, 2013
This morning I overslept for me but when I woke up God was still talking to me about being in prison, being bound and about angels. After the drama of yesterday it would be so easy to slip back into that place in my spirit but God does not want that for any of us.

I know I have never heard this passage used like this but it makes sense to me and the way God is using it to motivate me. Look particularly at verses 18-20 in Acts 5, *"But the angel of the Lord by night opened the prison doors, and brought them forth, and said, Go, stand and speak in the temple to the people all the words of this life."*

First, we get cast into prison whether that prison is physical, financial or emotional, it is a real prison to us. Sometimes these prisons are of our own making but other times the devil puts us there with discouragement on top of the tragedy we have gone through.

The hope God gave me was that in the night when it is the darkest is when the angel of the Lord showed up and brought them forth. The angel didn't just stop at that but gave them direction as to what to do next.

We do well and rejoice when we are rescued from the prison but I don't think we do so well with the direction God gives us. Do you think you were only rescued to sit on a pew? Really?

We are all called to work for God and to be soul winners. If you never share what God has done for you how can you help someone else?

Can you imagine with me for a moment the devil discovering you're out of the prison he put you in? His despair that you're out but then he realizes you don't want anyone to know what happened because you're embarrassed at how others might look at you! Oh how happy he is because he's still won.

One night while ministering and sharing parts of my testimony I shared an ongoing problem. Afterwards a lady came to me and thanked me because she said you look like you live a blessed life and wouldn't understand continual struggle. If you can continue so can I.

It's not about us it's all about Jesus! If I have to open up about things I'd rather not share but it helps one person find Jesus and/or a closer walk with Him its more than worth it.

Now verse 23 says, *"Saying, The prison truly found we shut with all safety, and the keepers standing without before the doors: but when we had opened, we found no man within."*

That's what the devil needs to find when he goes seeking you and me in our self-inflicted prisons. Bad things happen to everyone. It's not what happens to us but how we deal with it. If we let God be God we are victorious no matter how dark the night. So put your praise on. Tell others of the goodness of God. Then see what God does. He is always there. It's just most of the time we are so wrapped up in self-pity we can't see it. Get your eyes back on Jesus. Watch miracles happen in your life and others!

I am sitting here waiting on a phone call. Patient I'm not! LOL but in this situation I have to simply wait. Well, I got the phone call and it is still a mystery. That's all I can say. Please continue to pray for our family.

DECEMBER 13, 2013
This morning God wants all of us to know as in Isaiah 14:3, *"And it shall come to pass in the day that the Lord shall give thee rest from thy sorrow, and from thy fear, and from the hard bondage wherein thou wast made to serve."*

Rest from sorrow will come. When in the midst of the valley of grief when fear along with chains of struggle are all around you rest will come. Trust in your God to deliver you. He simply will.

Psalms 23 which we all love to quote in the first three verses spoke to me this morning, *"The Lord is my shepherd; I shall not want. He maketh me to lie down in green pastures: He leadeth me beside the still waters. He restoreth my soul: He leadeth me in paths of righteousness for His name's sake. "*

To be able to lie down in green pastures and have my soul restored. What a promise! We can't fathom it when struggling but it's still our promise! No matter what you're going through God is with you. Rest in His promises.

Lastly Zechariah 10:12, "And I will strengthen them in the Lord; and they shall walk up and down in His name, saith the Lord. "
So when the blows of life come at you and you feel as if all strength is gone, God, Himself is strengthening us. Think about that for a while. Then we will walk up and down in His name. Can it get any better?

Valleys will come to us in life. We just have to hang on to the promises of God. So today place your trust in Him. He will provide your needs. That includes peace and rest for a battle worn soldier of the Lord.

I just finished walking Brownie. We are having a heat wave. I think its 30 degrees. I'm almost packed to hit the road tomorrow for Tennessee. A week there and then on home to Mississippi for a few weeks and then Texas!

DECEMBER 14, 2013
This morning in my devotions this passage in John 20:1-2; 11-18 ministered to me.

When we have our miracle sometimes we simply do not recognize that we have it. That was the case here. In verses 1-2' *"The first day of the week cometh Mary Magdalene early, while it was yet dark, unto the sepulchre, and seeth the stone taken away from the sepulchre. Then she runneth and cometh to Simon Peter, and to the other disciple, whom Jesus loved, and saith unto them, They have taken away the Lord out of the sepulchre, and we know not where they have laid him."*

What God was sharing with me was she came in the dark, during dark despair of the valley of losing her Lord and Master. She didn't look in the sepulchre. Instead of walking in to see what kind of problem she had she ran to tell others of the problem. In this situation we need to hit our knees telling Jesus about it.

Even after telling others she still remains outside the miracle as in verses 11 when she finally looks in the tomb. When she does she sees angels! ANGELS!

The angels ask her why she is weeping. She, seeing angels, tells them, *"Because they have taken away my Lord and I know not where they have laid him."*

Then she turns back from the angels. In my mind this is like us seeing our miracle and turning back away from it. Then she sees Jesus and doesn't recognize Him. Whoa! That is us. Jesus steps into our world to let us know the miracle is done yet we don't recognize Him.

Finally in verse 15 Jesus speaks to her but she doesn't recognize Him until verse 16, *"Jesus saith unto her, Mary. She turned herself, and saith unto him, Rabboni; which is to say , Master."*

When He spoke her name is when she recognized Jesus but she still had to turn away from the obvious problem to her and look at Jesus. In our life the problems that come our way we have to turn our eyes off of the problem to Jesus. He's standing, waiting for us to look at Him. He is the solution!

Jesus has all the answers we will ever need!

Well, suffice it to say it looks like I'm not going anywhere today or for a few days. God has got this! It's just ripe for a miracle! I'm trusting God. On Him I can depend!

DECEMBER 15, 2013
God brought two very familiar passages of scripture to me this morning to minister to me. The first one being in I Samuel 17:26-59 and the second one being Daniel 3:13-28.

In both of these Bible stories we see young people who God has called out for a purpose. These young people are obedient to God yet they face what seems like insurmountable obstacles. In David's case his own brother comes against him with words.

In Shadrach, Meshach, and Abednego's case well-meaning folks who have given in to the enemy or who have chosen to not obey God go and tell what they are doing.

The attacks continue with David when he confronts the enemy (Goliath) comes against him basically laughing at him. In the book of Daniel (Ch. 3) the enemy becomes furious at them for being disobedient.

Take that and apply it to our lives today. As long as we walk along never rocking the boat to do anything for God our lives continue with seemingly few major problems. When you or I decide to listen to God at first the devil laughs. Then as we continue and people's lives start being changed the devil gets furious and attacks full force. Sometimes God may lower the hedge to see if we really meant what we said when we said, "No matter the cost I'll do anything God. I'll go anywhere."

Words are easy to say but so much harder to do when adversity comes our way. What will you do?

We are all not called to do the same thing. Some will accomplish great exploits on their knees in prayer while others may travel to distant lands. Whatever God has called you to do you must do it with all your might regardless of the sacrifice or problems that come your way.

Lastly, in the story of David and Goliath David cut Goliath's head off with his own sword. Then in Daniel 3 King Nebuchadnezzar knew he only put three men in the fiery furnace yet four were walking. When they got out not one hair on their heads were harmed. They didn't even have the smell of smoke on them.

We will have difficulties and problems. It's not the problems or difficulties that define us but how much we allow those issues to bring us to a closer walk with God. When faced with the obstacles I've discussed most would have quit.

We have to be so determined in our minds to do the will of God that nothing will stop us!

We may have to catch our breath and keep putting one foot in front of the other but you and I can do this in the name of Jesus! Let's go be soldier's in the army of the Lord!

DECEMBER 16, 2013
At church last night Bishop Hurley came to me with a word from God. He told me, "God has set before you many open doors."
It took me first of all to Hebrews 11:1-3; 8-13, 16 and lastly to Romans 4:13-20. Let me explain something first.

When life throws us curve balls one after the other after a while we still believe God can but sometimes you just want to stay down so when the next blow comes at you perhaps it will miss or at least it won't be as painful. That's just being human but that is when we must pull ourselves back up and remember Hebrews 11:1, *"Now faith is the substance of things hoped for the evidence of things not seen."*

Verse 16 is a promise for all of us, *"But now they desire a better country, that is, an heavenly: wherefore God is not ashamed to be called their God: for He hath prepared for them a city."* I truly want to be one of those that God is not ashamed to be called my God.

Lastly God took me to Romans 4:13-20. This whole passage is so encouraging. What God threw a spotlight on for me was verses 18-21.
"Who against hope believed in hope, that he might become the father of many nations, according to that which was spoken, So shall thy seed be. And being not weak in faith, he considered not his own body now dead, when he was about an hundred years old, neither yet the deadness of Sarah's womb: He staggered not at the promise of God through unbelief; but was strong in faith, giving glory to God; And being fully persuaded that, what He had promised, He was able also to perform."

Abraham had every reason not to believe that God would do what He said yet he staggered not. We need to do the same. No matter what circumstances say our GOD IS ABLE!!!

DECEMBER 17, 2013
I woke up singing Thank you Lord for your blessings on me this morning. When life throws you more curve balls we need to remember to be thankful.

This morning when God woke me it was that I needed to be thankful regardless of situations or circumstances. I was taken to the following passages where God ministered to my soul.

Ephesians 5:19-20, *"Speaking to yourselves in psalms and hymns and spiritual songs, singing and making melody in your heart to the Lord.; Giving thanks always for all things unto God and the Father in the name of our Lord Jesus Christ;"*

What I felt God was telling me was out simply doesn't matter what we are going through we have to speak to ourselves and sing no matter how bad things may seem. We must continue to thank God for His goodness and blessings.

Then I went to I Thessalonians 5:16-18, *"Rejoice evermore. Pray without ceasing. In everything give thanks: for this is the will of God in Christ Jesus concerning you."*

It really doesn't get much plainer than that.
Lastly God took me to Habakkuk 3:17-19; *"Although the fig tree shall not blossom, neither shall fruit be in the vines; the labour of the olive shall fail, and the fields shall yield no meat; the flock shall be cut off from the fold, and there shall be no herd in the stalls: YET I WILL REJOICE IN THE LORD, I WILL JOY IN THE GOD OF MY SALVATION. THE LORD GOD IS MY STRENGTH, AND HE WILL MAKE MY FEET LIKE HINDS FEET,AND HE WILL MAKE ME TO WALK UPON MINE HIGH PLACES. To the chief singer on my stringed instruments. "*

Again that's pretty plain straight from the Word of God. Again, it simply doesn't matter what you are going through God is still God. So have joy in the Lord and believe me I know how hard it is to do that when the world caves in on you. But that is where our strength comes from.

While I am missing my family and some basic needs I have plenty. I am blessed above all because while I may not have some material things, my husband has died and my children are grown I have the most important. You see, that's because I have God. He literally has become my everything. God is so wonderful to me!

While I have wanted to SCREAM some days in the past week because of things that are happening God knows about when I'm there. Out of the sky I have received calls from folks that have been sent to me by professional networks. They have recently been diagnosed with pancreatic cancer for me to give them hope. When you give hope whether you feel hope for yourself or not before that phone call you do afterwards.

You see God is reminding me of all He's done for me. So these new issues are no big deal to God. I have to be reminded that He's got this. So no matter what you are going through remember He's got this too!

DECEMBER 18, 2013
This morning I woke up thinking about the answer is already on the way. God took me to Nahum 1:7, *"The Lord is good, a strong hold in the day of trouble; and He knoweth them that trust in Him."*

He knows us. He knows when we're in trouble. He provides for our needs. After this God took me to Isaiah 26:3-4, *" Thou wilt keep him in perfect peace, whose mind is stayed on thee: because he trusteth in thee. Trust ye in the Lord forever: for in the Lord Jehovah is everlasting strength:"*

So, we need strength to get through the hard days. He is our strength as long as we keep our minds stayed on him. Then I was directed to *Isaiah 49:16, "Behold I have graven thee upon the palms of my hands: thy walls are continually before me."*

Do we really think God doesn't know what's going on with us? Can we forget our children? Can God really forget us? Our problems are continually before him, continually!

This morning God wanted me to be reminded of his promises. Then I was directed to Isaiah 65:24, *"And it shall come to pass, that before they call, I will answer; and while they are yet speaking I will hear."*

Isaiah 59:1, *"Behold the Lord's hand is not shortened, that it cannot save: neither his ear heavy that it cannot hear:"*

Jeremiah 32:27, *"Behold, I am the Lord, the God of all flesh is there anything too hard for me?"*

These are promises, promises to us. Our God hasn't changed. He hasn't moved. Our problems seem bigger to us but to God they are nothing.

Keep your mind stayed on Him and then we will have the testimony as Hebrews 11: 32-34, *"And what shall I more say? for the time would fail me to tell of Gedeon and of Barak, and of Samson, and of Jephthae; of David also, and Samuel, and of the prophets: who through faith subdued kingdoms, wrought righteousness, obtained promises, stopped the mouths of lions, quenched the violence of fire, escaped the edge of the sword, out of weakness were made strong, waxed valiant in fight, turned to flight the armies of the aliens."*

What a testimony!

Wow! Rest in the promises of God! Know that God has not changed! Know He is still God!

Know that your answer is already on the way!

Today's miracle for me is the trees I've wanted to see leave for years are being cut down for free by the power company. Another miracle but yet I need another miracle so continue to pray for me and my children.

And the trees are gone. HALLELUJAH!!!

DECEMBER 19, 2013
This morning from Philippians 2:6-8, and verse 19 God spoke to me.

I'm sitting here waiting on the mechanic to come work on the expedition. It could be something simple like a short or it could need a whole new wiring harness. Whatever it is I just have to have faith that God has got this.

Verses 6-8 tell me to, *"Be careful for nothing; but in every thing by prayer and supplication with thanksgiving let your requests be made known unto God. And the peace of God, which passeth all understanding, shall keep your hearts and minds through Christ Jesus. Finally brethren, whatsoever things are true, whatsoever things are honest, whatsoever things are just, whatsoever things are pure, whatsoever things are lovely, whatsoever things are good report; if there be any virtue and if there be any praise think on these things."*

So this morning, not knowing for sure what's wrong with my expedition I'm going to think about good things. It's a choice we all make. Life throws curve balls at us. As I always say it's not the curve ball life throws at us, it's how we curve to catch that ball.

We can choose to be happy or we can choose to wallow in self-pity. I choose to be happy. I choose to rejoice. I choose with the help of God to do all these and to think on good things because regardless He's simply still God.

Lastly verse 19 gives me a promise, it says, *"But my God shall supply all your need according to his riches in glory by Christ Jesus."* I don't see a maybe. I don't see any hesitation. We need to remember that He will supply all of our need. ALL.

Maybe what we need isn't what we expect him to supply. It's time to be positive regardless.

Give him praise. Give Him glory. Giving Him honor!
So it looks like I will be here a while longer. I have no idea how long. I don't have to know I just have to trust that God knows what He is doing. It's all in His hands.

The parts are ordered for my car. I've decided against fixing the SUV. I'm driving the SUV while waiting on the car to be fixed.

Life is a journey and for now when I drive the SUV I have to hook up the battery each time and plug the starter in. Once it starts I unplug the starter otherwise the lovely SUV keeps trying to start itself and when I get to where I'm going I unhook the battery otherwise it will drain the battery.

Oh, what fun I get to have. I so miss my Mr. Fix It. He could fix anything for anyone and he routinely did. Now I'm learning and gaining scars to prove it.

But I'm so thankful for a God that holds my hand through the good and the bad. He's an amazing God and I love Him so!

DECEMBER 20, 2014

I will give you all. What does giving all mean to you? Are you really willing to give all? If God asked could you walk away from everyone and everything to go somewhere new and start a new work in a new way and depend on God to provide all your needs?

Have we become so comfortable we've forgotten the reason He was born and died not just for us but ALL SINNERS? If we don't step out and let others know by door knocking, by hours spent on our knees, by sacrificing to give to others how will they know? If we keep it to ourselves and only share when they come to us we are in deep trouble with our own salvation. Each and every one of us are called to be soul winners. People need God and are hungry all around us. Find them, help them by giving Jesus your all.

This morning I slept in but I woke up hearing the words to the song, I need a new commitment, I need a fresh touch. Then God reminded me a few things from His Word.

First he took me to Jonah 1:1- 3, and then to Jonah 2:7-10. If you don't want God to change you don't dig into His Word. If you're willing to be changed open your Bible and begin to know your God and He will change you.

"Now the word of the Lord came unto Jonah the son of a Amittai, saying, Arise go to Nineveh, that great city, and cry against it; for their wickedness is come up before me. But Jonah rose up to flee unto Tarshish from the presence of the Lord, and went down to Joppa; and he found a ship going to Tarshisha: so he paid the fair thereof, and went down into it, to go with them to Tarshish from the presence of the Lord."

Are you getting what God was telling me? God told Jonah what to do. Jonah fled from the presence of God. Isn't that just like us? We say we want to know the will of God for our lives. When God tells us and leaves no doubt are we not just like Jonah? Do we flee if it's not exactly the way we want it?

Then Jonah 2:7, *"When my soul fainted within me I remembered the Lord: and my prayer came in unto thee, into thine holy temple."* When we remember, when we faint, then, then we pray. I see a problem with that but that's our humanity. We don't have time to waste anymore.

We've got to get it. That's the only way we can help others find a relationship with God that changes their lives.

God wants to change us but we have to be willing to be changed. Oh we say the right words but we don't mean them. As long as our boat isn't rocked, as long as everything stays the same we will do what he asked but the minute our world is rocked we back off just like Jonah.

Lastly God took me to Luke 9:57-62. I'm only going to quote verses 61 and 62. *"And another also said, Lord I will follow thee; but let me first go bid them farewell, which are at home at my house. And Jesus said unto him, no man, having put his hand to the plough, and looking back, is fit for the kingdom of God."*

The words of Jesus are very strong and require no interpretation. We need to realize the privilege we've been given to work for God, to give Him all! What a privilege! What a blessing!

DECEMBER 22, 2013

Christmas is a hard time of year for those that have lost family members through the year or are alone. I've been told that with time the grief gets easier to bear. Christmas day will be four months since my love died. I still miss him but my grief now comes in waves.

In reading this morning God directed me to Proverbs 18:10, *"The name of the Lord is a strong tower: the righteous runneth into it, and is safe."*

It's like God wants us to know to run to Him in our need. We will be safe because He is always our strong tower.

Then I looked down and saw Proverbs 18:14, *"The spirit of a man will sustain his infirmity; but a wounded spirit who can bear?"*

In other words our bodies/spirit can handle it when we are physically sick but when our spirits are crushed/depressed who can help. Only God can help us.

In thinking back it's been five years this week that I took my first chemo treatment. Because of the type of pancreatic cancer I had I was given end stage chemotherapy. I had never been sicker but through everything I endured my spirit remained encouraged overall.

Now with the death of the man I spent over half my life with. We had our problems but still felt like soul mates, my spirit has been crushed. However, I continually try to encourage myself in the Lord. I was going to go off Facebook until after New Year but God let me know I'm not the only one experiencing this pain.

We need to remember that so many are hurting. They need us to be Jesus to them. When I'm getting down in my spirit God sends me someone to help. When you can't encourage yourself encourage someone else. You'll find by the time you've finished not only did you encourage them but God has encouraged you.

So today in church look around at those who are missing because they can't handle happiness right now. They still celebrate the reason for Christmas but their spirits have to take a break because of their loss. Be it right or wrong it is what it is. Pray for them, love them and let them know you care.

Have a blessed and Merry Christmas!

Make sure to hug them a little closer and always whisper those cherished words, I love you. Have no regrets when it comes to loving your family.

DECEMBER 23, 2013
Last night God started talking to me about broken hearted, specifically my broken heart. Then I was directed to passages of Scripture beginning with Psalms 34:17-19, Psalms 51:17, Psalms 73:26, Hebrews 13:8 and Romans 8:28.

First of all, Psalms 34:17-19 but verse 18 is what really spoke to me. *"The Lord is nigh unto them that are of a broken heart; and saveth such that be of a contrite spirit."*

Then Psalms 51:17, *"The sacrifices of God are a broken spirit: a broken and a contrite heart, Oh God, thou will not despise."*

Then I really wanted to understand what broken hearted meant. It is defined as overwhelmed by grief or disappointment. Those who've lost family understand the overwhelming grief that you feel from that great loss. Psalm 34:18 lets us know the

Lord is close to those that have a broken heart. During the past 4 months I have found that to be especially true for me.

Psalm 73:26, *"My flesh and my heart faileth: but God is the strength of my heart, and my portion forever."*

When in deep grief it feels like our heart can't take anymore. That's when we need to remember God is still our strength. He is our portion. He is our comforter.

It's so hard to remember Hebrews 13:8, *"Jesus Christ the same yesterday, and to day, and for ever."*, when in deep grief. But Jesus doesn't change just because our situation changes. He is still the same. He still loves us. He knows where we are.

Finally, Romans 8:28, *"And we know that all things work together for good to them that love God, to them who are the called according to His purpose."*

God reminded me with Romans 8:28 that although I don't understand why, He does. All I have to realize is that all things work together for the good. That does mean all things!

We just have to trust him. I know how hard that is but I know a God who has never failed me and will never fail you. Let him be your comforter, your best friend, the one that sticks closer than a brother. In the midnight hours of grief He is with you.

So true!

You won't do exploits if you don't attempt exploits. Take a step of faith in God!

DECEMBER 24, 2013

This morning I woke up thinking about blessings. It is Christmas Eve, a day for families and remembering the birth of Jesus.

For those that suffer loss it's hard to think about blessings. When I looked up the definition I found that it's defined as God's favor and protection.

Then I was led to Ezekiel 34:26, *"And I will make them and the place is round about my hill a blessing; and I will cause the shower to come down in his season; there shall be showers of blessing."*

God's favor and protection doesn't change. Showers of blessing mean showers of blessing. It's hard to see that right now but soon there will be showers of blessing.

Matthew 5:3-4, *"Blessed are the poor in spirit: for theirs is the kingdom of heaven. Blessed are they that mourn: for they shall be comforted."*

When mourning our spirits are poor and we need comforted. Jesus will comfort us. During this time we have to be so careful with our souls. We can't allow bitterness to creep in because of our circumstances.

Bitterness defined is shortness of taste, lack of sweetness. It also means anger and disappointment at being treated unfairly; resentment.

When losing a loved one we all eventually feel anger and disappointment. We feel that this was unfair. There's nothing wrong with those feelings as long as we don't allow them to take root in our lives and grow.

Ephesians 4:31-32, *"Let all bitterness and wrath, and anger, and clamour, and evil speaking, be put away from you, with all malice: And be ye kind one to another, tender hearted, forgiving one another, even as God for christ sake hath forgiven you."*

We have to grow up. We have to be adults even in our grief. We have to remember who gave His all for us and put away our childish feelings of unfairness. If anyone should ever think that life wasn't fair it should be God for the way we treated him and continue to treat Him.

In Hebrews 12:15, *"Looking diligently lest any man fail of the grace of God; lest that which is lame be turned away; but rather let it be healed."*

It is ultimately our decision how much we allow Jesus to comfort us during grief. Hebrews 12:15 lets us know God wants to heal us. He wants to heal our broken heart. We have to let him heal us.

Remember, the God we serve is a gentleman. He won't force himself on us or His healing on us. It's easy to believe God for a physical miracle but we won't allow him to heal our spirits.

Then God started talking to me about sacrifice. To define sacrifice it is the act of giving up something you want to keep. Am I saying we want to keep grieving?

I do think we get so wrapped up in our grief that it becomes comfortable to us. It becomes a place that while it hurts is also a way for us to check out of life when we need to check in.

We need to remember why we're here. We're here to be a blessing and to lead others to Christ. How can we do that if we can't be with others?

Then God started talking to me about sacrifice. To define sacrifice is to give up something you want to keep. Do we want to keep grieving? I don't think we really do but we get wrapped up in it. We have to unwrap ourselves. To do that we look at Hebrews 13:15.

"By him therefore let us offer the sacrifice of praise to God continually, that is, the fruit of our lips giving thanks to his name."

Is it easy to worship God and give thanks when your world has crumbled? No. But it is what we must do in order to go on. Our loved ones would want us to remember the blessings we had with them, not dwell on the bitterness of what we've lost.

God wants us to root out the bitterness before it takes root and strangles us. This will not be easy. This will be a sacrifice, but, oh what joy we will find in our worship and praise to God.

DECEMBER 25, 2013

Thank you for your prayers during this time. I'm making Brownie (the dog) and I breakfast. Eggs, hash browns, sausage and toast this morning. Then I will remember the Christmas's my love and I shared. Hug your loved ones close today.

I remember being along in my house on Christmas day. Early Christmas morning my phone started beeping. First I had texts from Bro. & Sis. Craft then they called. I am so blessed.

I waited all day for a call from my children. My son did call late in the day. God was with me. He is teaching me how to rely on Him for all things, ALL THINGS!

I just curled up on the couch with a couple of good books and prayed for the day to pass.

DECEMBER 26, 2013
This morning I woke up with a thought yes Jesus loves me. You know the children's song. Yes, Jesus loves me, yes Jesus loves me; the Bible tells me so, little ones to him belong, they are weak but he is strong yes Jesus loves me.

Love defined in our generation is defined as intense feeling of deep affection. I didn't like that definition so I decided to go to the Bible.

What I found in the Bible was a definition of love that makes more sense. Love is a purposeful commitment to sacrificial action for another with God Himself being our example.

I John 4:7-10 says it best, *"Beloved, let us love one another: for love is of God; and every one that loveth is born of God, and knoweth God. He that loveth not knoweth not God; for God is love. In this was manifested the love of God toward us, because that God sent His only begotten Son into the world, that we might live through him. Herein is love, not that we love God, but that he loved us, and sent His Son to be the propitiation for our sins."*

I know there are some that will want to know what propitiation means so I looked it up online. I wasn't disappointed. What I found was that it is to make up for something I did. So Jesus loves me. He loved you and me enough to leave glory and come to earth to die on the cross because of our sins.

Oh, how Jesus loves us!

I'm so thankful today that my first Christmas without the love of my life and my children is over. I'm also so very thankful for the friends who obeyed God yesterday and in the midst of their family Christmas stepped away to call and encourage me. I will not forget the many text messages. God is so very good to me.

I am out on the town with friends that wouldn't take no for an answer..lol. Then Sister Pat was hunting us in Olive Garden. She thought she was in Cheddars until she called me and asked to find out where she was...lol. I needed to laugh.
We are just now leaving Wal-Mart after two hours. Joyce Mccann and I patiently(not) waited. I think Sis. Patricia Sizemore bought out the store. What an adventurous day we have had! LOL!

I was so exhausted that I got home and promptly fell asleep on the couch about 7 pm. I slept until Brownie woke me up at 10 pm to let her out. Now I'm back in bed...lol.

DECEMBER 27, 2013
This morning I went to Psalms. Sometimes in the Psalms is the only place we can find comfort and encouragement. This morning Psalms 15:5-11 is where God counseled me.

"The Lord is the portion of mine inheritance and of my cup: Thou maintainest my lot. The lines are falling unto me in pleasant places; yea, I have a goodly heritage. I will bless the Lord, who hath given me council: my reins also instruct me in the night seasons. I have set the Lord always before me: because He is at my right hand, I shall not be moved. Therefore my heart is glad, and my glory rejoiceth: my flesh also shall rest in hope. For that how wilt not leave my soul in hell; neither wilt thou suffer thine Holy One to see corruption. Thou wilt shew me the path of life: In thy presence is fullness of joy; at thy right hand there are pleasures for ever more."

Through this God encouraged me. He reminded me that He alone is my portion. It is He who counsels me in the midnight hours. It is He who holds me when there's no one there. In the night my heart instructs me. My heart reminds me the God I serve. I will bless Him.

While I am on this roller coaster ride called grief God has become more real to me. I think the secret to getting through this is like it says in verse 8 I'm paraphrasing, I keep my eyes always on the Lord. It simply doesn't matter how bad things get if we keep our eyes on God. He's there!

When we do this, that's when we'll find we will not be moved spiritually. Then in verse 11 it tells us that in his presence is fullness of joy. Right now there are so many suffering with recent grief and that think you'll never feel joy again.

It's been a little over 4 months and joy comes. There are days I never want to repeat but there are moments when God gives me joy.

Those moments are starting to get longer and the grief while still fresh is not as harsh. Trust in your God to do what He does best... to comfort you and give you joy.

DECEMBER 28, 2013
Trusting in God

I love hearing the Word of God sung...so powerful.
Remember all God has already done. He's taking care of it now.
I'm hanging out with friends! A better outlook means I have to get up and get out of the house! Sometimes the first step out the door is the hardest but oh, so worth it.

DECEMBER 29, 2013
Praise is not only what I do but it's who I am. Through the years I've learned to praise through every storm. Now that it seems like I'm in the midst of the biggest storm I've ever encountered praise is still what I do.

Just because life blows up in your face in unimaginable heartache and pain that's when we should praise God more. We should continue to say like Job, *"Though God slay me, yet will I trust Him."*

In reality it is probably not God slaying us but the hedge around you and me has been lowered to show the devil what we are made of. I plan to show him that even in days I don't know how to stand, that even on the flat of my back I KNOW, I KNOW, HOW TO PRAISE MY GOD FOR ALL HIS BLESSINGS!

Even when in the midst of the storm I'm still blessed and highly favored by God! So praise Him and tell the devil this battle belongs to God!

DECEMBER 30, 2013
Victory is mine in Jesus name!
For the last few days God has been asking me, Why are you in the cave?

So then I went to I Kings 19:4-9 where Elijah, the great prophet of the Old Testament had run in fear and was under the juniper tree for forty days. During those forty days angels brought him food yet he stayed there until he went to a cave.

That's when God Himself came and asked him what are you doing here? We talk faith and say we walk by faith yet sometimes God, Himself, has to ask us why are you hiding.

So, today, why are you hiding?

I'm getting ready now to go. It may still be a few weeks but soon in Jesus name I will be back on the road again giving my all to Jesus.

DECEMBER 31, 2013
Off and on all day I've been thinking about new year's resolutions. What I read in the Bible this morning about new year's resolutions make me think a little harder and still yet I haven't committed any to paper.

James 4:13-15 says it best, *"Go to now, ye that say, Today or tomorrow we will go into such a city, and continue there a year, and buy and sell, and get gain. Whereas ye know not what shall be on the morrow. For what is your life? It is even a vapour that appeareth for a little time, and then vanisheth away. For that ye ought to say, If the Lord will, we shall live, and do this, or that."*

So, in making our new year's resolution, our first resolution, should be that God has a place in every resolution. We shouldn't attempt to do anything unless we first preface it by saying if God wills. If God's will is not in your new year's resolutions why are you making them? God needs to be in every detail of our lives, every detail.

The reason this is so important is it our life is here today and gone tomorrow. I found that out very harshly this year. Now, my life has to be different because I realize just how quickly it can be taken.

Philippians 3:12-14 says it this way, *"Not as though I had already attained, either were already perfect: but I follow after, if that I may apprehend that for which also I am apprehended of Christ Jesus. Brethren, I count not myself to have apprehended: but this one thing I do, forgetting those things which are behind, and reaching forth unto those things which are before, I press toward the mark for the prize of the high calling of God in Christ Jesus."*

In making new year's resolutions I have to forget about the successes and failures of the past. I have to press toward God. I have to set new goals that reflect God's will in my life. We all should do that.

Ps. 51:10-12 is my first resolution, that it will be my prayer each and every day.

"Create in me a clean heart, O God; and renew a right spirit within me. Cast me not away from thy presence; and take not thy holy spirit from me. Restore unto me the joy of thy salvation; and uphold me with thy free spirit."

2013 was a great and a bad year for me. While I don't understand everything that happened I know a God who does. So in 2014 my spirit must be right, my joy needs to be restored, and I need to realize that God will uphold me.

What is so great about all this is that God will not only do it for me. He will do it for each and every one of us. All we have to do is ask. So much has happened in 2013 from extremely high highs of miracles for myself to miracles on the evangelistic field and three more books published to one of the lowest days of my life on August 25th when my husband of 24 1/2 years passed away.

I came back to the house early. Now I'm curled up under a comforter waiting on the new year but I'll probably be asleep before long...lol. It's so cold....brrrr.

January 1, 2014
This morning I wanted to post something about prosperity, love and wonderful things but once again God has focused me on the book of Job, specifically Job 1:8, *"And the Lord said unto Satan, Hast thou considered my servant Job, that there is none like him in the earth, a perfect and an upright man, one that feareth God and escheweth evil."*

Could Job 1:8 be said about us?

Did we ever stop to think that a conversation could be had about you or me in heaven discussing our faith?

What does escheweth really mean? I looked it up online and found it means deliberately avoid; abstain from, have nothing to do with.

Does the definition of escheweth get any plainer? We continue to play with sin. Why? Why do we keep making excuses for our sin? If the Bible says it is sin then guess what? It is still sin!

It's time to take a stand up and be counted for righteousness and God regardless of the price we personally must pay. No matter how much you try the Bible does not change. Either we are living for God or we're not.

So, back to my original question, do you or I have a walk with God that God could say the same things about us without hesitation?
In this new year it's so important to clear the junk out of our lives. Do we truly want to be one, like Job, that God can use as an example? Can you imagine God using you as an example to the devil as one He knows will stay the course regardless of what happens?

So in starting this year off on the right foot with God. I plan to try, no matter how busy I get, to spend more time with him furthering His kingdom for His glory because it's all about Him!

The temperature is to drop and more snow is to come. Therefore, I must go to the grocery store today for a few things. Now that it's just me I'm amazed by how little food I need and by how long it lasts. Yes, I am eating but much less. It now takes three to four days to eat what I used to in one day. So, today I plan to be busy grocery store, laundry, and writing. It's past time for me to publish more books while I'm in this holding pattern.

I feel in my soul its going to be an amazing year with God!

JANUARY 2, 2014

Today Ephesians 4:14-18 is where God led me.

Ephesians 4:14 is as follows, *"Wherefore he saith, Awake thou that sleepest and arise from the dead, and Christ shall give thee light."*

Isn't it time for you and I to wake up? Have you ever thought that while sitting on a church pew and even working for God you could have been lulled to spiritual sleep not even realizing it? Oh, to be spiritually dead and not know it.

That's why our daily devotions are so important. We've got to have that time with God that is the time when He walks and talks with us. I'm not saying be so spiritually minded you're no earthly good but I am saying don't be so earthly minded you're no good for God. It's time to quit making excuses and be about God's business.

Ephesians 4:15-17 says it like this, *"See then ye walk circumspectly, not as fools but as wise, Redeeming the time because the days are evil. Wherefore be ye not unwise, but understanding what the will of the Lord is."*

I think that puts it plainly. It's time for us to redeem the time. Evil is everywhere being shoved down our throats yet we don't spend the time with God that we should or the time telling others of all He has done for us and how blessed we are.

We have the secret to eternal life yet we don't share that like we should. It is time to redeem the days standing up and being counted on the side of the Lord.

Lastly Ephesians 4:18-20 says, *"And be not drunk with wine, wherein is excess; but be filled with the Spirit; Speaking to yourselves in psalms and hymns and spiritual songs, singing and making melody in your heart to the Lord; Giving thanks for ALL THINGS unto God and the Father in the name of our Lord Jesus Christ; "*

When was the last time you were so truly filled with the presence of God you bubbled over onto someone else?

That's what it's supposed to be like. When the Holy Ghost is evidenced in our lives bubbles over revival happens amongst our church body and the people we love and the people that are watching us from afar.

Then the Bible tells us to speak to ourselves. We have deep problems but when we do this is when we find a victory in Jesus that is like no other. So when you're down and feel like you're out start singing one of those old songs. "There's something about the name Jesus", "Victory, victory shall be mine," "In the presence of Jehovah". You'll find victory in Jesus when you do this.

Lastly but most importantly we have to GIVE THANKS IN ALL THINGS! It doesn't matter what is coming at you or me we simply have to give thanks. God is with us all the time, through the good and the bad.

Today, give thanks then talk to yourself and sing whether you feel like it or not. Victory is yours!

I've had a busy afternoon hanging out with Joyce Mccann at her house. We've laughed and had fun while I posted furniture and other items for sale on our local facebook yard sale pages along with calling the local trading papers to have it put in there. Praying everything sells quickly so I can get back to working full-time for God.

JANUARY 3, 2013

My winter wonderland. For some reason I'm pretty sure there is no school today with the condition of one of the main roads in Fayetteville in front of my house looking like a path.

Looking at the snow this morning God started talking to me about sin in a new way for me.

I went to Mark 6:51-52, *"And He went up unto them in the ship; and the wind ceased: and they were sore amazed in themselves beyond measure, and wondered. For they considered not the miracle of the loaves: for their heart was hardened."*

Think about who was on that ship. It was probably the disciples. They walked and talked with Jesus every day. They saw the miracles. Yet their hearts were hardened. In the midst of great revival and great miracles our hearts can be hardened.

How do we fix sin in our lives?

We fix that by finding a place on our knees to repent and remembering Isaiah 1:18, *"Come now and let us reason together, saith the Lord: though your sins be as scarlet, they shall be as white as snow; though they be red like crimson, they shall be as wool."*

The greatest miracle of all is that somehow God takes our nasty sins and washes them until they are as white as snow. Even though, we, even after seeing or having great miracles have a hard time believing He can, He still does. It shouldn't amaze us and make us wonder but it does.

The best promise of all is found in Acts 2:37-39, *"Now when they heard this they were pricked in their hearts, and said to Peter and to the rest of the apostles, Men and brethren, what shall we do? Then Peter said unto them, Repent, and be baptized every one of you in the name of Jesus Christ for the remission of sins, and ye shall receive the gift of the Holy Ghost. For the promise is unto you, and to your children, and to all that are a far off, even as many as the Lord our God shall call."*

What is amazing about this is that those asking the question about what they needed to do had not walked with Jesus. Their belief in God was simple.

We need to go back to when we simply believed Jesus would do what He said. Why do we make everything so complicated? The gospel is simple.

We should be using everything in our arsenal to convince people that what He did for us He will do for them.

If you haven't yet received the marvelous gift of the Holy Ghost or have walked away Jesus is standing with open arms to bless you with this miraculous gift. All you have to do is repent. Ask God to forgive you of your sins then raise your hands in worship. Tell Him you love Him and want His gift. Your tongue will start to say words you don't understand. That's ok it is God.

You will feel joy and happiness like never before. Then you need to be baptized in the name of Jesus and you'll feel so clean afterwards. It is almost unexplainable how wonderful you will feel.

What are you waiting on? Find a place to pray.

JANUARY 4, 2014

We are having a heat wave it is 16 degrees! I'm going to celebrate and have Spaghetti for breakfast..lol

JANUARY 5, 2014

I tried to post this several times yesterday but Facebook was not cooperating. So this morning I'm going to try again because I think it's really important.

Revelation 8:3-4, *"And another angel came and stood at the altar, having a golden censer; and there was given unto him much incense, that he should offer it with the prayers of all saints upon the golden altar which was before the throne. And the smoke of the incense, which came with the prayers of the saints, ascended up before God out of the angels hand."*

Just think about it. We have to pray. Those prayers are a sacrifice. When we pray we are doing battle for the lost, for our families, and for a multitude of other things.

From battle we have smoke. Smoke comes up before the throne of God. We shouldn't struggle to pray. We should always have a prayer on our lips and in our minds. Pray without ceasing.

II Chronicles 7:14 tells us how important our prayers are to God.
"If my people, which are called by my name, shall humble themselves, and pray, and

seek my face, and turn from their wicked ways; then I will hear from heaven, and will forgive their sin, and will heal their land."

We say we want God to change our world yet we don't pray. Here it tells us what will happen when the people of the name will just humble ourselves, turn away from our sin, seek His face, and pray. The promise He gives us is that He will heal our land and hear from heaven.

So, tell me again, what was your excuse for not praying today? I don't think any of us have an excuse.

So before church, before teaching Sunday school or anything else we should all find a place to bow our knees before the King of Kings and Lord of Lords.

Learning that being sick by myself is no fun after twenty five years. ##missing my family

JANUARY 6, 2014

Thanking everyone for the prayers so glad I'm feeling better this morning. Our temperature is dropping like a lead balloon and, of course, it is snowing.

This morning God brought this passage to mind Ephesians 4:26-32. This passage has so much.

"Be ye angry, and sin not: let not the sun go down upon your wrath; Neither give place to the devil. Let him that stole still no more: but rather let him labour, working with his hands, the thing which is good, that he may have to give to him that needeth it. Let no corrupt communication proceed out of your mouth, but that which is good to use of edifying, that it may minister grace to the hearers. And grieve not the Holy Spirit of God, whereby ye are sealed unto the day of redemption. Let all bitterness, wrath and anger, clamour, and evil speaking, be put away from you, with all malice: and be ye kind one to another, even as God for Christ's sake hath forgiven you."

First we can be angry as long as we don't sin because of the anger. The part God really highlighted for me was about not giving place to the devil. In other words don't let him get a foot hold in your life.

Most of us don't want to think about some places the devil may have established a foothold in our lives. As we continue to become more like the world we are allowing the devil to gain that foot hold he has been trying to get for so long.

I hear the arguments. I'm not stupid. We say these things were not really wrong, we were too strict.

However, when you allow your consecration to slip do you realize you will find power with God slips also? I have found when my consecration deepens power with God deepens. How badly do we want to be close to God? Are the things that you think you need to do that important?

A lot will probably get mad at me for what I'm about to say but it's my opinion. In my eyes it's not about the right or wrong it's about my relationship with God and what I don't want standing in the way of that relationship. The closer we get to God the more like Him we will be. So if you find yourself making justifying sin it is time to work on your relationship with God through Bible reading, prayer and fasting.

If every time I try to talk with Jesus I have to clean my mind out of all the junk I have chosen to read, listen to, watch, the way I have talked or thoughts I have allowed to take up residence in my mind then I have a much deeper spiritual problem that needs taken care of. Nobody wants to hear this. We all just want to go on our merry way but it's so much more.

We have got to stop being surface Christians and be true blue from the tops of our heads to the soles of our feet and everywhere in between. We are too close to the end to let anything stand between us and God!

I know I'm crazy but I needed to get out before I'm stuck for a few days. Driving to Wal-Mart in the Expedition the wipers quit working. Have you ever driven in a blizzard with no wipers. Well, it made the drive very interesting. However, I did make it home. One thing I don't think has been mentioned yet is that when I take the Expedition out I have to lift the hood and hook the battery up to start it. Since it still seems possessed it wants to start itself. So, after I hook the battery up I get in and it has started itself.

Never a dull moment in my world!

They said 2-4 inches of snow... well, we've already got that. Someone forgot to quit shaking up the snow globe. My idea of being prepared for a winter storm. Yes I did get bread but I still had milk and eggs. The junk just looked so good, chips, candy, pop tarts, donuts, pizza, and so forth....lol. Now if I will eat it.

JANUARY 7, 2014
Before crawling out of bed I decided to check the temperature its -6 degrees....brrrrr....

I woke up thinking about choices and friends. Not quite the way you might think. God was putting it to me like choosing the will of God for our lives and choosing to be his friend.

Before I post the thoughts God gave to me I have to pray and think about it awhile. I doubt I will share all but I will share some but just think about friendship with God = choosing to do His will.

Well... Christmas break for the kids ended Monday but so far they've not gone back yet in our county (Fayette County WV) because of snow days. Tomorrow is another snow day. So hard to believe my kids are grown now. Wow how time flies.

JANUARY 8, 2014
Choices = friendship with God

The more God has talked to me about this the more time I have spent delving into the Word to let it speak to me as I hope it will speak to you today.

Genesis 12:1-4 when God tells Abram to leave and to go to a land He will show him. Hebrews 11:8 says it best, *"By faith Abraham, when he was called to go out into a place which he should after receive for an inheritance, obeyed; and he went out, not knowing whither he went."*

He obeyed. Then in Isaiah 41:8 because he simply obeyed it says, *"But thou, Israel, art my servant, Jacob whom I have chosen, the seed of Abraham my friend."* In James 2:23 it also talks of Abraham being a friend of God.

So we say we want to be called a friend of God. Do the choices we make in everyday life reflect that?

God had a confidence and trust in Abraham because of the relationship they had established. It was the type of relationship where God knew what choice Abraham would make. Does God have that same level of confidence and trust in you to know regardless you will choose Him.

In Joshua 24:15 where it says (partial quote), *"...but as for me and my house, we will serve the Lord."* Here is another descendant of Abraham making the same choice. Choices you make today will be reflected in generations to come so when you make that decision to compromise on something you've always believed because the Bible spelled it out to you think of how it will not only affect you but those you love.

King Agrippa in Acts 26:28 said, *"Almost..."* Are you going to be an almost Christian... an almost friend of God. Almost isn't good enough. If God has asked you to do something almost doing it won't cut it. You simply must obey.

Lastly John 15:13-14 where Jesus is talking says it best, *"Greater love hath no man than this, that a man lay down his life for his friends. Ye are my friends, if ye do whatsoever I command you."*

Abraham, the Apostles, and many others throughout the Bible laid down their lives understanding this principle. Some won't be asked to do that but whatever God asks you should just simply do it.

God will not ask you to do anything immoral just as the devil will not ask you to do anything to further the kingdom of God. I don't want to be an almost friend of God. I want to be His friend. I want God to know I choose Him.

What about you?

JANUARY 9, 2014

Isolation vs insulation are the words I woke up with early this morning. Immediately I thought I knew what they meant but still decided to look them up. One thing I found was that both words come from the same root word.

Isolation means to isolate. To isolate means cause (a person or place) to be or remain alone or apart from others.

Insulation means the act of insulating something or someone. To insulate means to protect (something) by interposing material that prevents the loss of heat or the intrusion of sound.

Some isolation is good while other is bad. When people are grief stricken they should not be isolated from others. I chose to isolate myself. Thank God for good friends who stepped in and called, dropped by, and/or forced me to get out. But today I'm talking about the good part of being isolated.

Then I went to Mark 1:35, *"And in the morning, rising up a great while before day, He went out, and departed into a solitary place to pray."*

Then to Luke 5:16, *"And He withdrew Himself into the wilderness to pray. "*

Some isolation is good for our souls to be closer to Jesus. That is when we go off by ourselves to pray but we still need to be with the saints and ministry to inspire us and help provide the insulation from the storms of life that will come.

Lastly, I went to Mark 6:45-49, *"And straightway he constrained His disciples to get into the ship, and to go to the other side before unto Bethsaida, while He sent away the people. And when He had sent them away, He departed into a mountain to pray. And when even was come, the ship was in the midst of the sea, and He alone on the land. And He saw them toiling and rowing; for the wind was contrary unto them: and about the fourth watch of the night He cometh unto them, walking upon the sea, and would have passed by them. But when they saw Him walking upon the sea, they supposed it had been a spirit, and cried out:"*

I think what God is trying to tell me is prayer is my insulation from the storms life brings. However, if I'm not careful I can allow myself to use that as an excuse to isolate myself from the people of God where I can draw strength.

The disciples, while together, were isolated in the midst of the storm from Jesus.

They were so isolated the Bible tells us He would have passed by them. They did see him. Because of their focus on the storm they didn't recognize Him but thought He was a spirit when they cried out, probably afraid.

Isn't that just like us? We have every excuse in the book for not going to church. Did you ever think that by isolating yourself from church it would keep you from recognizing your miracle if it stood right beside you?

JANUARY 10, 2014

Today's Miracles (Actually yesterday)

When God opened the windows of heaven today for me He really opened the windows of heaven!

My day started out by singing that old altar call song, Jesus on the mainline tell Him what you want. I changed the words to Jesus on the mainline tell him what you need! I then told Him what I needed. I left my needs at His feet and went on about my day. Problems still happened but, oh, the focus was on the miracles!

A couple of hours later the miracles started happening.

1. The mechanic where my car has been in the shop for 2 months told me the car is fixed and its solid. It just needs a windshield for the inspection sticker. He then said I know you and what you've been going through so pay me when you can. I didn't ask he volunteered.

2. I called the windshield folks where I have been told the windshield would be $900 plus. My insurance would pay anything over $500. They needed to check things out and call me back. I went to lunch with my friend someone else paid for our lunch. While waiting on lunch I told her we needed to pray that the windshield would be less than $300 and I know that's impossible so we prayed. Getting our dessert I got a call from the windshield people and they told me that it would be around $330. I was happy with that but that wasn't really what I asked God for. Going in to use the restroom my phone rang again. It was the windshield people one more time telling me that they applied some discounts and now the windshield would be $279 and

some change. I was overwhelmed, humbled, awed by a God that loves me so much but the day wasn't over yet.

3. I hadn't seen my son in 6 weeks and while I was at my friend Joyce Mccann's he called. I was uploading a picture of a bed I was trying to sell. He was at my house. I hurried there and was blessed to spend a few hours with him.

4. While I was with him my phone rang. Someone that knew me was calling about the bed. They offered full price.

5. While I was still with him my phone rang again another friend was calling to check on me since my SUV wouldn't start earlier. They were coming by to look at it and give me a jump.

6. When the folks came to get the bed. They not only got the bed but everything that went with it, and a keyboard, a chest and a triple dresser. I had more than enough for the windshield when they left.

7. While on the phone I got another message that someone wanted an entertainment center I have. They're to come tomorrow.

Yes, I still have needs BUT I KNOW A GOD WHO SPECIALIZES IN THINGS THOUGHT IMPOSSIBLE!!!!

God has truly blessed me more than anyone else. Oh, how I love Him! How I adore Him, my breath, my sunshine, TRULY MY ALL IN ALL!!!

JANUARY 11, 2014

God started talking to me about miracles yesterday. Then my miracles started happening. They are still happening!

What is a miracle?

As defined by Webster's dictionary a miracle is an unusual or wonderful event that is believed to be caused by the power of God.

We pray for miracles. We ask for them. Sometimes we beg God for miracles.

What did Jesus say about miracles?

Matthew 10:1, "And when He had called unto Him His twelve disciples, He gave them power against unclean spirits, to cast them out, and to heal all manner of sickness and all manner of disease."

Luke 9:1-2, "Then he called His twelve disciples together, and gave them power and authority over all devils, and to cure diseases. And He sent them to preach the kingdom of God, and to heal the sick."

I think the words of Jesus explain it enough. Then what about the price a miracle? We long for miracles but are we willing to pay the price as Jesus explained it in Matthew 17:19-21.

"Then came the disciples to Jesus apart and said, why could not we cast him out? And Jesus said unto them, because of your unbelief: for verily I say unto you, If ye have faith as of a grain of mustard seed, ye shall say unto this mountain, remove hence to yonder place; and it shall remove; and nothing shall be impossible to you. How be it this kind, goeth not out but by prayer and fasting."

Who are the disciples of Jesus? A simple question you think. It can be answered with the names of twelve men but can it?

John 8:31, "Then said Jesus to those Jews which believed on Him, If ye continue in my word, then ye are my disciples indeed."

Have you continued in His word or did you stop when you got what you needed?

Who is a Jew?

I know some of your arguments. Well I'm not a Jew so it isn't talking about me. Well, let's see what the Bible says in Romans 2:29,"*But He is a Jew who is one inwardly; and circumcision is that of the heart, in the spirit, and not in the letter, whose praise is not of men but of God.*"

So we are spiritual Jews if we have done the above. In John 14:12-14 Jesus tells us that we will do greater works than He did but until we get it for ourselves and pay the price we can dream on.

Everything costs something. Tell me, why then, do we expect everything from God for nothing?

In Acts 19:11-12 is a great example of greater things in my mind. Hankerchiefs or Aprons were laid on the Apostle Paul. People were healed when they touched these. That's how much power with God Apostle Paul had. If we want that we will pay a price. Are you willing to sacrifice?

It requires us to grow up first of all and quit being spoiled Americans who consistently say give me, give me, give me! It's about other's, not about us. I Corinthians 13:11-13 sums it up.

"When I was a child, I spake as a child, I understood as a child, I thought as a child; but when I became a man, I put away childish things. For now we see through a glass darkly; but then face to face: now I know in part; but then shall I know even as also I am known. And now abideth faith, hope and charity, these three; but the greatest of these is charity."

When we are truly willing to sacrifice and pay the price so others will receive the miracles they need is when we will see greater things in their lives and our own.

Are you willing to pay the price?

I have lost so much weight a size eight skirt a friend gave to me is almost sliding off and a medium t-shirt is roomy. Thanking God for all his blessings. I guess I'm going to have to do sit ups to get my belly to be flatter....lol.

JANUARY 12, 2014
I so enjoyed my visit tonight with JasonWilden Evans. What great folks!

Today is Sunday. The day we should all be in church worshipping God. This morning I did not want to get up. I felt God whisper in my ear sleep on. That woke me up immediately.

Then I decided to find out what spiritual sleep means. In my mind spiritual sleep symbolizes death just as being awake symbolizes life.

So after that I wanted to know what spiritual death meant and it was exactly as I thought. It is simply man separated from God.

What happens when we fall spiritually asleep?

Matthew 13:25 says, *"But while men slept, his enemy came and sowed tares among the wheat, and went his way."*

In other words while you keep letting other things come between you and your walk with God the devil slips in and starts tearing down until you awake one day to find yourself separated from God.

What will happen while we sleep?

The parable of the virgins in Matthew 25:1-13 tells it best. We will be woefully unprepared when the trumpet sounds because without that daily relationship with God we will not have enough or any oil. Then he will simply say, "...I know you not."

Also the disciples were to watch and pray. It doesn't matter who you think you are anyone can fall spiritually asleep if they don't spend that time with God.

Matthew 26:45 says, *"Then He cometh to His disciples, and saith unto them, Sleep on now and take your rest: behold the hour is at hand, and the son of man is betrayed into the hands of sinners."*

What should we do?

I Thessalonians 5:7 tells us simply, *"Therefore let us not sleep, as do others; but let us watch and be sober. For they that sleep sleep in the night; and they that be drunken are drunken in the night."*

Many times in the Bible we are told to watch and pray. It's so important to have our private time with God just as it is important to be in church worshipping to gain strength and understanding.

Have a great services worshipping and growing in your relationship with God!

My Expedition wouldn't go into gear. My other car is still at the mechanic but I should have it back Tuesday evening or Wednesday morning. If it could go wrong it has gone wrong when it comes to my life but I am still trusting in Jesus.

Lord willing I will be headed home to Mississippi late this week. Automobile challenges have delayed my departure a few times. Everything appears to be coming together in Jesus name. My first stop will be East Tennessee for a couple of days and then I will push on to Jackson, Mississippi by Saturday evening. I'M SO EXCITED!

JANUARY 13, 2014
In getting ready to start packing again or in other words going through everything to make sure that I pack what I will need God gently nudged me to be sure that spiritually I am packed.

By doing that God led me to Joshua 9:11-14.

"Wherefore our elders and all the inhabitants of our counsel spake to us, saying, Take victuals with you for the journey, and go to meet them, and say unto them, we are your servants: therefore now make ye a league with us. This our bread we took hot for our provision out of our houses on the day we came forth to go unto you; but now, behold it is dry, and it is moldy. And these bottles of wine, which we filled, were new; and these our garments and our shoes are become old by reason of the very long journey. And the men took of their victuals, and asked not counsel of the Lord. And Joshua made peace with them, and made a league with them, to let them live: and the princes of the congregation sware unto them."

Then verse 22 says, *"And Joshua called for them, and he spake unto them, saying, Wherefore have ye beguiled us, saying, We are very far from you; when ye dwell among us?"*

There is so much in this passage but I will start with a question. Are we like the Gibeonites?

Do we seek to act as if we are on fire for God when indeed our walk has grown cold and moldy? Yes, they were trying to trick the people of God and were successful because even Joshua didn't seek the counsel of the Lord.

Are we like the children of Israel here not seeking God's counsel because we think we know more than God? Or could it be we know God does not want us being with people who look right and act right but in reality aren't right

The Gibeonites could be like so many who stand in churches near us acting the part but do not have a walk with God of their own.

It's so important that we get it for ourselves and we learn before making decisions we always seek the counsel of the Lord.

Finally in verse 22 it says, *"And Joshua called for them, and he spake unto them, saying, Wherefore have ye beguiled us, saying, We are very far from you; when ye dwell among us?"*

The Gibeonites knew the children of Israel would destroy them if they knew who they were. That's just like the devil. He continues to try and trick the people of God. Sometimes he succeeds but if you stay on fire for God, consistently seeking His counsel you won't be so easily tricked. It's when we neglect to seek His counsel that we get into trouble.

Today seek God's counsel in all decisions. He will not steer you wrong.

JANUARY 14, 2014
Another miracle... windshield being put in right now! Thank you Jesus!

Yesterday God started talking to me about how a person can be so rich yet so very poor. He also brought to mind how some can seemingly have nothing yet have riches unseen.

Then He directed me to Psalms 50:12, *"For every beast of the forest is mine, and the cattle upon a thousand hills. I know all the fowels of the mountains: and the wild beasts are mine. If I were hungry, I would not tell thee: for the world is mine and the fullness thereof."*

That's the God we serve! When we really get whose child we are our problems may not go away but living by faith should become easier. Then God directed me to a passage of promises in Isaiah 40:28-31.

"Hast thou not known? hast thou not heard, that the everlasting God, the Lord, the Creator of the ends of the earth, fainteth not neither is weary? There is no searching of His understanding. He giveth power to the faint; and to them that have no might He increaseth strength. Even the youths shall faint and be weary, and the young men shall utterly fall: But they that wait on the Lord shall renew their strength; they shall mount up with wings as eagles; they shall run and not be weary: and they shall walk and not faint. "

All of us have issues at one point or another with defeat, depression" and discouragement. It is at those times we should hide ourselves in the Word of God and prayer. It is in His Word and prayer where we will find happiness, joy, and encouragement.

Lastly Zechariah 13:9 which has been a scripture God has comforted me with and today I revisited.

"And I will bring the third part through the fire, and will refine them as silver is refined and will try them as gold is tried: they shall call on my name, and I will hear them: I will say, It is my people; and they shall say the Lord is my God."

God never said the road would be easy. Actually in many places we are told it will be hard. However, to appreciate our blessings some valleys and trials must be gone through. But then He will call us His people. How wonderful is that!

Those that are truly rich get this while some with monetary riches may never understand how you can be poor but rich. Poor in this worlds goods should not be a hardship. Happiness and fullness of life in God is when a person is truly wealthier than the richest person on earth.

Count your many blessings name them one by one. See what God has done!

URGENT Prayer Request! Please pray. I'm continuing to trust God! I know that I know that I know that God is in control. In Jesus name He's got this!

Driving home the car started having a funny smell. Well, I managed to get home but the car was making an interesting noise. At least it had quit smoking on the driver's side. So, tomorrow I will call the mechanic.

JANUARY 15, 2014
In a lady's meeting I went to last night as an ice breaker you had to say two things about yourself that were not true and one that was. Then the group had to guess which one was true. A friend of mine's true statement was, "I like to peel skin."

God started talking to me about peeling. In order to eat a juicy orange or delicious banana first you must peel the skin. You could probably eat the skin if you wanted but the taste would not be what you wished for.

After everything that happened last night and praying I would get home safely I remember realizing that this problem is just another bump in the road. I also realized I am ripe for a miracle just as a piece of fruit should be ripe when we eat it.

However, when you peel that piece of fruit that looks wonderful and you take a bite. If the fruit is sour or a rotten spot is in the center it has to be cut out so that the taste will be delicious like you expected.

That is just like us before God. Just because we look right and act right does not mean we are right. King David a man after God's own heart made mistakes yet he learned the secret of repentance and worship.

This morning God directed me to II Samuel 22:1-9 where David worshipped God with thanksgiving, for His deliverance and His blessings. Then verse 6 says, *"In my distress I called upon the Lord, and cried to my God, and He did hear my voice out of His temple, and my cry did enter into His ears."*

So when God starts peeling us back to see if we indeed are as good as we look, what will He find? Will He find problems make us complainers or praisers?

So today I want to praise my God for many blessings and say like in II Samuel 22:2-3, "And he said, The Lord is my rock, and my fortress, and my deliverer; The God of my rock; in Him will I trust: He is my shield, and the horn of my salvation, my high tower, and my refuge, my saviour; thou savest me from violence. "

So, what will you do? Complain or praise? When God peels back your skin what will He find?

I have decided to praise my God!

Walking Brownie in the snow. When the going gets tough, pray and then keep living and worshipping God. I will be taking the car back to the garage tomorrow but in the meantime I will praise God!

JANUARY 16, 2015
To be consistent = being faithful

Definition of consistent is to always act or behave in the same way: by harmony, regularity, or study continuity: free from variation or contradiction.

Definition of faithful is loyal, constant, and steadfast. Strict or thorough in the performance of duty: true to one's word, promises, etc. steady in a allegiance or affection; loyal; constant:

In studying this this morning I found that our God is a faithful God Deuteronomy 7:9. I also found promises to those who are faithful beginning in Psalms 31:23-24

"O love the Lord, all ye His saints: for the Lord preserveth the faithful..."

Psalms 101:6 another promise for the faithful, *"Mine eyes shall be upon the faithful of the land, that they may dwell with me:..."*

Matthew 25:23, *"His lord said unto him, well done good and faithful servant; thou hadst been faithful over a few things, I will make the ruler over many things: enter thou into the joy of thy Lord."*

And I'm stopping with Luke 16:10, *"He that is faithful in that which is least is faithful also in much:..."*

Think about what the Word says. You say you want to be great but you have yet to learn how to be faithful in the little things. I'm talking about those things only you and God see.

Our consecration to Him begins with private prayer and Bible reading. It is so important we get this if we truly want power with God. Everything costs something.

The question this morning is are you willing to pay the price?

This morning the car is back in the garage and I'm waiting to hear what is wrong. While I'm waiting I will remember that God works all things to the good. I will continue to stand upon His promises because I know that He is more than able! I will encourage myself in the Lord. I will remember the many miracles He has done for me. This is yet another miracle that this happened near home. I will worship, praise and thank Him for His many blessings!

So happy my J.T. came to see me for a while today!

And the saga of the car continues. ... parts need to be ordered.. $1,182.82 in parts before labor. The miracle in all of this is that it happened here and not in the middle of nowhere so in every crisis you can find a miracle. When having your pity party thank God for what hasn't happened that could have. Our God protects us so tonight I'm thankful for His protection and praising Him for His goodness. My God has got this! It is just another bump in the road.

As to what's broke. Well it is a 1997Jaguar and the passenger right rear wheel needs the hub, studs, bearings, seals, lugs and speed sensor. Price on the parts are with me ordering them direct. That does not include labor.

I so enjoyed small groups tonight, Bro Randall Pitsenbarger did an awesome job teaching , enjoyed the food n fellowship... Gonna enjoy this group too... Laughter doeth good like a medicine !

JANUARY 17, 2014
Ugly feet, crusty toes, and hairy arms

Last night in small groups when we were fellowshipping we were having fun. Some folks got to talking about things that bug them. On that list were ugly feet, crusty toes and hairy arms. I couldn't get away from it. So I thought about it and God brought some things to my mind. Here are my simple thoughts.

1. Ugly feet

Exodus 3:3-5, *"And Moses said, I will now turn aside, and see this great site, why the bush is not burnt. And when the Lord saw that he turned aside to see, God called unto him out of the midst of the bush, and said, Moses, Moses. And he said, Here am I. And he said, Draw not nigh hither: put off thy shoes from off thy feet, for the place whereon thou standest is holy ground."*

If Moses had been absorbed in his own looks whether he had ugly, pretty, or cute feet he would have stopped to consider all of that before taking off his shoes. Well I took this from a bunch of people having fun but within ugly feet we have a message. When we get so overwhelmed by the presence of God it will not matter where we are or what God asks we will simply obey.

It is time to put aside the issues we may have with certain areas of our body. If you feel God impressing you to take off your shoes did you ever think that because of your obedience to God you could be the catalyst to break that service wide open and see God do great things. All it takes is one person to obey God. One person.

Are you that one person?

Ephesians 6:14-15, *"Stand therefore, having your loins girt about with truth, and having on the breastplate of righteousness And your feet shod with the preparation of the gospel of peace;above all taking the shield of faith, wherewith ye shall be able to quench all the fiery darts of the wicked."*

Sandwiched in a scripture we love to quote it talks about feet. All the greats of the Bible knew the Word of God. If we truly want to be used of God we will be going to the Bible. It will become our friend.

Then we will be able to quote this scripture and know it to be true about us. The day is coming when, if our feet, are not shod with the preparation of the gospel of peace we will not have what it takes to stand.

The Kings in the Old Testament had to know the scripture. Grant it, back then, they only had four to six books of the Bible to memorize. They had to handwrite the Scriptures and know them in and out.

We have so much more, yet do so much less. It's time we dig into the Word along with sacrificing other things to focus time to pray.

How badly do we want to do greater things than the apostles did? Are we willing to sacrifice to make it happen?

So, in thinking about ugly feet, what are your feet shod with?

Do you have what it takes?

Are you willing to get what it takes?

Tomorrow I will talk about crusty toes and crusty souls and finally on Sunday hairy arms.

Watching the snow globe be shaken by God. I wonder how much snow we will have by morning. While I'm not fond of cold weather and snow I do think snow is beautiful. I just wish I only had to see it from a distance.

JANUARY 18, 2014
2. Crusty toes and Crusty Souls

Did you ever stop to think that sin can become like the crust on crusty toes but it will be the crust on your soul?

I've been studying the life of King David, a man after God's own heart. After having finally made it, when he is no longer running from King Saul, that is when his soul takes ease.

When we relax and quit moving forward is when the crust begins to build on our soul/spirit. He didn't even realize it happened. He sent his men to battle. As king, he should have led them to battle. No, but he stayed home and walked on the rooftop.

He was probably looking at all God blessed him with when he noticed a woman. Bathsheba, bathing (II Samuel 11:1-15). If he had just walked away, quit looking, but by dwelling on what he should not have or even looked at; the price for his sin would be great.

The Prophet, Nathan came to King David in II Samuel 12:7-12 and told him, a man after God's own heart, that the sword would never depart from his house, his wives would be taken away, and what he did in secret God would bring it before Israel and the sun.

Before the Prophet came to King David he had been given several months to repent on his own. He ignored his need for repentance.
Are we not just the same? In our minds we can justify anything we want even when we know in our hearts doing it was wrong. By the way, hanging onto bitterness is wrong. So they hurt you. Pray, forgive and move on with God.

No matter how much God blesses us or how great a walk with God we might have if we are not consistent our souls become crusty without us ever realizing what's happened to us. When we ignore the still small voice that says don't do that over and over again is when the crust begins to build.

It gets into the crevices of your soul, those corners where you hold onto that sin or bitterness. If you don't clean it out, it starts to build up, until you can no longer hear God speak to you. That is just like the crust on or between our toes. If we don't clean the dirt out between them it turns to a hard crust that will require some time and work to get out.

I can hear you now. You're saying it will never happen to me. Well, if it could happen to King David, who is a man after God's own heart, what makes you think that you are immune?

I think that's when we really get into trouble. When you think you can't get into trouble because you start to see yourself as righteous. My Bible tells me in Romans 3:10, *"As it is written, There is none righteous, no not one."*

I never want the words to be penned about me that were penned about King David where it says in II Samuel 11:27, *"...But the thing that David had done displeased the Lord."*

I believe that is why God is drilling in my head and I hope yours how important it is to be consecrated to God. We have to have that daily time with Him in repentance, prayer and Bible reading but we also have to be working in the field. It was when King David stayed home during the battle that he sinned. Sin cost him everything that was dear to him.

Before our souls get crusty like the crust on and between some toes we have to start cleaning it out. Crust builds up in our soul and its crevices. We will all make mistakes but make sure it is a mistake and not a choice to go against the Word of God. No matter who we are and what we accomplish we need to find a place of repentance daily.

When we wash our souls with repentance is when we get the crust out of the corners and the dark places. It is just like soaking your feet in water. When they become crusty soaking in the water removes that crust. So now it is time for us to soak in repentance, His Word and in prayer.

Let's clean out the crusty crevices of our toes and our souls

JANUARY 19, 2014
Today is the final segment of ugly feet, crusty toes, and hairy arms. This morning I looked deeply at hairy arms Biblically.

In Genesis 27 hairy arms equals deceit. It is a story we all know well about how Jacob deceived Isaac into believing he was Esau the first born to get the blessing.

What we don't find in this passage speaks louder to me than what we do find. What we don't find is Jacob asking his mother for help in his deceit. However, what we do find is Rebecca making the plan and coordinating it.

She gave Jacob the means and the instructions on how to be successful in deceiving his father. She knew her husband better than anyone. Why would a wife and mother do this? Perhaps she didn't like the way Esau looked or his voice. Who knows? Family dynamics can cause all kinds of problems.

In this passage of scripture God is showing us how important it is to treat our children fairly. Also, what God has brought to my mind today is who or what are you allowing to steal what is rightfully yours?

Do you have peace, joy, and happiness?

Why not? What has taken that from you? So, bad things happened. They happen to everyone. You think it's too much for you. Really?

The devil is still the ultimate deceiver but he can only take what we allow him to have. Let me explain. I'm talking about how you allow losses and pain to affect you. All of us will suffer hurt. Jesus was not immune so why would we think we should be immune?

In looking at the triangle of Rebecca, Jacob, and Esau we find three people in desperate need of repentance. You're thinking, not Jacob. He was the one done wrong. Yes, he was. But he allowed the deceit of his mother and brother to cause him to sin.

Genesis 27:41 (partial quote), *"And Esau hated Jacob..."*. There is more in that verse but hate is as much a sin as murder. When you allow something to cause you to hate someone that is when you need an altar of repentance as much as the person that hurt you.

Matthew 5:23-24 tell us what to do when we go to pray when there's a problem with our brother. Have you ever had to apologize to someone who wronged or hurt you? I have. I argued with God because it was the last thing I wanted to do but the hurt in me was standing between me and God, it had to go. I did not want to do it.

I know there are horrible abuses that occur every day against people along with words that can hurt you. Let the pain and hurt draw you closer to God. You can't hang on to the hate at the cost of your own soul.

Lastly, when you get to thinking you can't continue try hitting your knees and explaining to Jesus why you won't serve Him. He was the one who was not only betrayed by one of his closest, but was beaten and crucified by those he came to save.

Now, what were you saying about why you couldn't live for God or go to church?

I'm so excited to be in Canvas, West Virginia tonight. Barring a miracle it looks like I will be unable to be in Alexandria, Louisiana for BOTT. While I'm slightly disappointed I'm more excited about what God is doing in my life and ministry. Lord willing by the middle of next week I will be on my way home to Mississippi.

Praying in Jesus name that these last parts ordered have fixed the car when they arrive Tuesday or Wednesday and the mechanic puts them in.

JANUARY 20, 2014

Part Two of Hairy Arms
Another hairy man in the Bible that did things differently and seemingly came out of nowhere is one of the greatest prophets in the Word of God.

II Kings 1:8, *"And they answered him, He was an hairy man, and girt with a girdle of leather about his loins. And he said, It is Elijah the Tishbite."*

When and why did Elijah come on the scene?

Seemingly he came out of nowhere to be one of the greatest prophets. God has a way choosing people from the most unlikely places and unlikely situations to use. We wonder, why? We don't see ourselves as anything special.

How long did it take Elijah to obey God? Do you have questions as to why God chose him to be a great prophet? Why not someone with the right last name or someone that oozes talent? On the other hand, why?

Look at people who have had to work for their walk with God. They hold it as a priceless treasure.

Those who have grown up in and around it no longer see the value in sacrifice to have that closeness with God. I do realize there are those who have grown up in and around it that understand sacrifice. However, typically that's where we get into trouble.

Believe me, I know of which I speak. Up until a few years ago I had no idea what it felt like to be a new convert. Oh, yes, I grew up in church and received the gift of the Holy Ghost at the age of seven but that passion to work for God regardless. That, I did not have.

I Kings 17 is the first place we see Elijah. The Bible says he was a Tishbite from the land of Gilead. In researching this I found his village was a remote village in the mountains on the other side of the Jordan River. So based on that, I feel like we can say he came out of nowhere.

Lastly Mark 9:5, *"And there appeared unto them Elias and Moses, and they were talking with Jesus."*

Out of nowhere came Elijah to be one of the great prophets of the Bible. Centuries after he lived he was seen talking to Jesus and Moses. Elijah never died, he was caught up in a whirlwind (II Kings 2:11).

For a hairy man he is a great example to study and be like. He fought depression and battles of life as we do. But he also showed us even with being human we can still have great power with God. So if you feel like nothing but you know God has chosen you to do something great for Him start changing.

How?

Well, it goes back to consistency and consecration. Spend more time in the Word of God learning of Him. Then a lot of time, a lot of time, alone with God, on your knees sacrificing the time you'd rather spend having fun.

Remember with great power with God comes great sacrifice and great consecration. Be available to your leaders to serve in whatever role in your church they may need you for. That may mean cleaning the commodes, sweeping, teaching Sunday school, driving the church van, passing out tracts, door knocking and so forth. There is so much more than just being on the platform.

We should all strive to be a servant of God. That is the highest calling.

The Apostle Paul wrote in I Corinthians 9:19, *"For though I be free from all men, yet have I made myself servant unto all, that I might gain the more."*

JANUARY 21, 2014
I Need My Monthly Bath (Part I)

At the in group Bible study during fellowship this was part of the conversation last Thursday evening. God started talking to me about the spiritual implications of repentance.

To repent is turning away from sin; being sorry for your sin.

For days I have thought on this and finally am able to share a few things God has talked to me about.

Acts 2:38, the foundation of our church. The first thing Peter tells us to do is REPENT.

What we don't always realize is this needs to be a daily thing and for some of us a moment by moment thing.

How long has it been since we, who consider ourselves Christians, have bathed our souls with repentance and tears?

We consider ourselves righteous. Really? Are your thoughts righteous? Do you have self-control? I could go on and on but I will stop there. You know what God wants you to stop doing or change. What is stopping you?

What does the Bible say?

Isaiah 1:16, *"Wash you, make you clean; put away the evil of your doings from before mine eyes; cease to do evil;"*

Jeremiah 4:14, *"O Jerusalem, wash thine heart from wickedness, that thou mayest be saved. How long shall thy vain thoughts lodge within thee?"*

Hebrews 10:22, *"Let us draw near with a true heart in full assurance of faith, having our hearts sprinkled from an evil conscience, and our bodies washed with pure water."*

Psalms 51:7, *"Purge me with hyssop, and I shall be clean: wash me, and I shall be whiter than snow."*

Now let's consider hyssop. When researching it I found it was a herb used for cleaning. In Bible times it was also used to sprinkle lepers to signify they were clean.

In some of my research I found Psalms 51:7 where some say King David was wanting to be cleansed like they did clothing. He wanted the desire for sin to be beaten out of his soul by God. What a desire to be clean before God?

Do we have that same desire?

Lastly, Proverbs 30:12, *" There is a generation that are pure in their own eyes, and yet is not washed from there filthiness."*

I believe we are living in that generation. I do not want to not see my sin. I want to repent continually always striving to do better. This is in no way justification for sin. It's time we really clean ourselves up and we do it every day. We should be like King David and want even the desire for sin to be beat out of our souls by God.

So, I said all of that to say, it's time for my monthly bath in repentance to become a daily bath and a consistent change in thought patterns and a way of life.

It is snowing today in Fayetteville, West Virginia. Brownie and I enjoyed our walk before the snowplow came through the neighborhood.

Then I played basketball even with the snow and I have some shots of Brownie complaining. She so wanted my attention but I'm trying to work off my belly.

Hopefully we will do it again this afternoon. Two 1/2 mile walks then 20-30 minutes of shooting hoops and doing layups while we worship God.

Still snowing!

I received a delivery of all but one of the parts needed for my car. The last one should be here tomorrow. Hopefully by the weekend I will be in Jackson, Mississippi. I'm so ready to have a view that does not include snow.

JANUARY 22, 2014
I Need My Monthly Bath (Part 2)

This morning I'm going back to the foundation Acts 2:38, *"Then Peter said unto them, Repent, and be baptized every one of you in the name of Jesus Christ for the remission of sins, and ye shall receive the gift of the Holy Ghost."*

First, let's define remission. Remission is the cancellation of a debt, charge, or penalty.

For those that have been or are currently sick let's look at remission from cancer. What I found online is that it means when there is no trace or sign of it on scans or when the doctor examines you.

Now let's define baptism. It is an immersion or sprinkling of water that is symbolic for spiritual purification.

However, baptisms in the Bible were immersions including Jesus. Matthew 3:16 says, *"And Jesus when he was baptized, went up straight way out of the water..."*

Also Acts 8:38, *"And he commanded the chariot to stand still: and they went down both into the water, both Philip and the eunuch and he baptized him."*

Colossians 2:12 says it best, *"Buried with Him in baptism, where in also ye are risen with him through the faith of the operation of God, who has raised him from the dead."*

When you are fully immersed in the water in the name of Jesus all your sins are washed away. That is why Jesus died.

Why is baptism so important?

Our sins are washed away.

Acts 22:16 says, *"And now why tarriest thou? arise, and be baptized, and wash away my sins, calling on the name of the Lord."*

Romans 6:3-4 says, *"Know ye not, that so many of us as were baptized unto Jesus Christ were baptized into his death? Therefore we are buried with him by baptism unto death: that like of Christ was raised up from the dead by the glory of the Father, even so we also should walk in newness of life."*

Gal 3:27 says, *"For as many of you as have been baptized into Christ have put on Christ."*

Colossians 3:17 , *" And whatsoever ye do in word or deed, do all in the name of the Lord Jesus, giving thanks to God and the Father by him."*

So, by being baptized in the name of Jesus, we are putting on Christ. When we put on Christ we live differently, we walk differently, and we talk differently.

What I mean is that from that point on Jesus is living inside of us. So everything we do and I do mean everything we do we should always think can I do this with Jesus?

If you can't watch it or do it with Jesus then why are you doing it?

You only need to be baptized once in the name of Jesus for your sins to be gone. Once they are gone then He can fill you with the gift of the Holy Ghost. The outward symbol is of speaking in other tongues as God gives the utterance.

Once you feel God's presence in this supernatural way you will never be the same again.

You'll be changed!

While I have been talking about a monthly bath in jest the spiritual implications are huge. We have to keep ourselves clean before God with daily and sometimes moment by moment repentance. I'm not making excuses for sin.

Actually Romans 6:1-2 says it best, *"What shall we say then? Shall we continue in sin that grace may abound? God forbid. How shall we, that are dead to sin, live any longer therein?"*

I'm waiting on the last part to be delivered so I can take them to the garage and hopefully have my car within a day or two. It's so cold Brownie and I are staying in for today much to her dismay.

The last part did not come in today. If it doesn't show up by tomorrow afternoon I will call the specialty auto parts place I ordered it from. I'm trying to be calm and roll with the punches but I'm starting to get tired. Please pray it is delivered tomorrow afternoon. Thanks for the prayers.

I'm tired of crying... I think in the past five months I've shed enough tears to fill an ocean. I know it is okay to do it and God knows I will shed more tears but I'd really like to be joyful...truly happy. . You know where when you smile it reaches your eyes and your soul. One day in Jesus name!

JANUARY 23, 2014
Waiting for take off!

Have you ever been on a plane sitting just waiting for the go ahead to take off?

Time passes by ever so slowly. One time in Chicago years ago when I was there on business God prompted me to take a minute and grab a burger and some fries. We spent 3 hours sitting on the tarmac. Because I listened to that prompting from God I was one of a very few that had something to eat.

You know when the plane is cleared for takeoff it will not take you long to reach your destination. However, what you do and how you act while waiting, could affect you for a very long time...

We have so many typical examples of waiting. I'm only going to focus on Elijah. I really like him because he was nobody until God raised him up. He was from a remote village so basically he was from nowhere. Let's look at I King's 17:1-7.

"And Elijah the Tishbite, who was of the inhabitants of Gilead said unto Ahab, As the Lord God of Israel liveth, before whom I stand, there shall not be dew nor rain these years, but according to my word. And the word of the Lord came unto him, saying, Get thee hence, and turn thee eastward, and hide thyself by the brook Cherith, that is before Jordan. And it shall be that thou shalt drink of the brook; and I have commanded the ravens to feed thee there. So he went and did according to the word of the Lord: for he went and dwelt by the brook Cherith, that is before Jordan. And the ravens brought him bread and flesh in the morning, and bread and flesh in the evening; and he drank of the brook. And it came to pass after a while, that the brook dried up because there had been no rain in the land."

Provisions of God

When the brook dried up what happened?

What I don't see in this passage preaches louder to me than what I do see. Elijah did not complain because the brook dried up. He was just there waiting on the Lord. When God places us by a brook what do we do when it dries up?

Elijah came out of the remote village. In that remote village is where he cultivated a deep relationship with God. He probably never thought he would do the things for God that he did. He was a lot like each of us. The difference between Elijah and most Christians is the friendship he had with God. I believe that is why when the brook dried up we don't read of him complaining. He is just there.

Then because of this friendship and trust that was built by Elijah with God, God speaks.

I Kings 17:8-10 says, *"And the word of the Lord came unto him, saying, Arise, get thee to Zarephath, which belongeth to Zidon, and dwell there: behold, I have commanded a widow woman there too sustain thee. So he arose and went..."*

Relationships are built with consistently spending time with the other person. You want to know them so you talk to them, do things with them, and involve them in every part of your life. God wants to have that type of relationship with us.

That is how we will be able to do as it says in I Thessalonians 5:17, *"Pray without ceasing"*. Your relationship with God becomes who you are. That is when you don't even realize it but you automatically consult him on all matters in your life and then you simply do what God tells you to do.

So while sitting in the plane waiting for God to give the all clear for takeoff build that relationship with Him.

Let your consecration become so deep that when God says Go, you Go!

Then, as Elijah, when you need God to do the supernatural for you or for others he does it. It is really that simple.
****
I'm so excited. I just got home from a late lunch/early dinner with Sis. Lois Pitsenbarger. When I got home the last part was here! HALLELUJAH!!!

I still think it will be sometime next week before I head south. Too many snowstorms coming our way to safely leave this weekend. If it was a four wheel drive I'd go ahead and go but not in a rear wheel drive. I've had enough things happen to me that I am trying to be smart. Don't laugh...I can be smart occasionally....

JANUARY 24, 2014

So today regardless I am blessed above all and without measure.

I just received a call from my mechanic....more parts are needed. Please pray for God to make a way once more....
We can return some parts to make up some of the $900 cost. There is a lot more money to this and I still need the miracle for labor and the amount left on the part but I know a God! Enough said!

Thank you Lord for your blessings on me!

BROKEN

Job 2:8
"And he took him a potsherd to scrape himself withal; and he sat down among the ashes."

JANUARY 25, 2014
HUMILIATION versus HUMBLENESS

Yesterday God started talking to me about these two words. They come from the same root word. In one way their meanings are completely different yet in another way very similar. I know I'm speaking in circles so read what I've written and think about it.

Define Humiliation

Some one feels ashamed and foolish because their dignity or self-respect has been injured.

Now let's look at the Bible and see what it has to say. We'll start in Acts 8:32-33 where it talks of Jesus being humiliated.

"The place of the Scripture which he read was this, He was led as a sheep to the slaughter; and like a lamb dumb before his shearer, so opened he not his mouth: In his humiliation his judgment was taken away: and who shall declare his generation? For his life is taken from the earth."

Jesus suffered humiliation for us. When we start to suffer persecution for what we believe and we feel humiliated we are identifying with Him in another way. It's not in what happens to us, it's in how we handle what happens to us.

We may think we have been humiliated. Consider what Jesus went through. We struggle with persecution but we must get stronger because as wickedness prevails the persecution will also become more prominent.

Nobody wants to talk about this but its coming. It is as much a part of the last days as the great revival. In times past when great revival was poured out great persecution and troubled times were also in abundance.

As Americans, we are all so blessed with our abundance. We are soft. James 1:10 speaks of humility in a different way. How will we react when we have nothing but God?

James 1:10 says, "But the rich, in that he is made low: because as the flower of the grass he shall pass away."

HUMILITY BEFORE THE LORD

Lastly, on humility I want to go back to Ezra 9:5. The word humiliate is not in this passage but its meaning is clear.

When we really humiliate (truly ashamed for our sin, sins of our country) ourselves before the Lord is when we grow the most spiritually. Humiliation of this type is healthy spiritually. Ezra shows us how.

Ezra 9:5-6

"And at the evening sacrifice I arose up from my heaviness; and having rent my garments and my mantle, I fell upon my knees, and spread out my hands unto the Lord my God, And said, O my God, I am ashamed and blush to lift up my face to thee, my God: for our iniquities are increased over our head and our trespass is grown up into the heavens."

What God is talking to me about here is the sin of our generation, our country. You can legalize drugs. You can say its okay for people to live together before marriage. We can ignore gossip and backbiting as normal today. People can even say homosexuality is not a sin. But we will still put people in prison for murder and the Bible is very plain that all of these are sin.

Why did I go there?

Because it's time, it's time we get serious about our walk with God. We have to fall on our faces in embarrassment for the sins that have become acceptable in our country and our generation.

When we want revival, really want revival, we won't argue with people. That is when we will go to our knees, we will go door knocking, we will travail before God because of our sin and theirs. The way we have acted towards them is also sin but no one wants to mention that.

We can hate the sin but we must love the sinner.

How do you treat people who are different from you?

Would Jesus be ashamed of you?

Tomorrow I will share what God has been talking to me about humbleness and then on Monday how the two are similar yet dissimilar.
So thankful I heard from my son today. He is with my daughter and our nephew today. I wish I was with them.

Each milestone since my love's death brings a wave of fresh pain but I'm finding I rest easier as each month passes in the comforting arms of Jesus. Five months ago today my world rocked precariously but my God reached His hand out to me and calmed me in the midst of the rocking.

That's the God we serve. He's with us on the mountaintop and even more so in the turbulence of the valley.

For some reason it seems I have an undetermined stay in the valley of life. In this valley I only hope and pray I find what God is wanting me to find and I learn what he is wanting me to learn. I also pray that no matter what the devil sends my way I continue to worship God. You have to know when you are weak and need help in order to ask for help from a God that loves each one of us more than life.

God is shaking up that snow globe again.... then it's back to the deep freeze...I wonder if the kids will get to be in school at all next week.

And it continues to snow...

I'm praying our power does not go out. It has flickered a couple of times. It's to be blue cold so I'd prefer electricity. I like being warm.

I do believe it looks like a good old fashioned blizzard outside. I can't even see the neighbor's driveway across the road. With the way the wind is whistling I am praying the power stays on. It's snowing so hard it looks like a sheet of white coming down. It will be interesting to see how much more snow we have by morning.

JANUARY 26, 2014

HUMILIATION versus HUMBLENESS (Part II)

We say we want to be humble before God but do we really understand its full meaning? This morning I'm focused on humbleness, yesterday it was humiliation. Let's see where this takes us.

Define humble

Having or showing a modest or low estimate of one's own importance.

Now let's see what the Bible has to say about being humble.

Proverbs 29:23 says, "*A man's pride shall bring him low: but honour shall uphold the humble in spirit.*"

Matthew 23:12 "*And whosoever shall exalt himself shall be abased; and he that shall humble himself shall be exalted.*"

John 3:30. "*He must increase, but I must decrease.*"

Micah 6:8, "*He have shewed thee, O man, what is good; and what doth the Lord require of thee, but to do justly, and to love mercy, and to walk humbly with God.*"

There are so many passages in the Bible on being humble. Being humble does not mean you allow others to walk all over you. All it means is that you're not proud.

We have to work at this. It is a daily thing. As humans we are naturally proud of our families, proud of what we've accomplished, proud of who we are but we cannot allow pride to come between us and God. We must be humble.

We must realize that everything God has blessed us with and allowed us to accomplish has come from God. When we realize that and we give God the glory for all He has done that's when our relationship with Him changes. When somebody applauds you for what you've done you need to turn that applause to God.

When people have honored me for accomplishments that's when I have to take myself off to pray. I have to get down on all fours. I have to be as low as I can get in the presence of God. I have to make sure that I become as humble as possible and then try to be more humble.

Colossians 2:18 says it best, *"Let no man beguile you of your reward in a voluntary humility and worshiping of angels, intruding into those things which he hath not seen, vainly puffed up by his fleshly mind."*

If we are not careful we can become so important in our own minds that we try to put ourselves in God's place. This passage lets us know that we should not be puffed up in our own minds so it's very important that we learn how to humble ourselves or God will humble us.

WHAT IS TRUE HUMBLENESS?

Psalms 51:17 says, *"The sacrifices of God are a broken spirit a broken and a contrite heart, O God, that wilt not despise."*

We should all humble ourselves in the presence of God.

Tomorrow I will show the comparison between humility and humbleness. Please understand this is how God talks to me and effects change in me. I pray it helps someone to come closer to God.

On a snowy wintry day what does one lone adult fix for herself and her spoiled pooch for dinner... Why, fried chicken, deviled eggs, and her favorite macaroni and cheese. Then much later tonight perhaps a slice of The Cheese cake Factory plain cheesecake.

Why, yes, I do believe that will be my meal for the day with the spoiled pooch probably eating 75% of it since I'm still not eating that much. At least the pooch will be full.

URGENT Prayer Request - Please pray for Bishop James Kilgore. (JANUARY 26, 2013)

To this day when I am putting this book together I remember getting the call that he had fallen and was unconscious. Then they texted me and told me he was in surgery for his brain. I couldn't believe another tragedy was striking so close to home. I immediately began to pray for him and his family posting that simple message above.

JANUARY 27, 2014

Praying for this wonderful man of God tonight. He has impacted so many lives with encouragement and an anointed ministry. I have been privileged to call him my pastor, mentor and friend. Please lift him, his family and his church family up in prayer.

So far I've heard nothing new. He is critical. Today and tomorrow are crucial as they are watching for swelling of the brain. Please continue to pray.

He fell outside of a restaurant and hit his head on concrete. Brain surgery yesterday. A small portion of the skull was removed for swelling.

HUMILIATION versus HUMBLENESS (Part III)

HOW ARE THEY ALIKE?

Humbleness is when we show or feel a modest or low estimate of our own importance.

While humility and humbleness are alike they're also very different. Humility in my eyes = shame while humbleness = not prideful.

We want God to do great things among us but we have to understand the importance of humility and humbleness before him. I think to get a real grip on this we need to understand sanctification (consecration) before God.

SANCTIFICATION (CONSECRATION)

Joshua 3:5 says, "*And Joshua said unto the people, Sanctify yourselves: for to morrow the Lord will do wonders among you.*"

- How do we sanctify ourselves?

We don't. God does. However, this is a process that we have to allow God to work on us. Humility and humbleness before God are integral to this process.

We have to remember that no matter what we think of ourselves or how righteous we may appear it only matters what God thinks. Isaiah put it in the best perspective. We say our perception is our reality.
- What about God's perception of us?

Isaiah 64:6 says, "*But we are all as an unclean thing, and all our righteousnesses are as filthy rags;...*"

--Brokenness

If we truly want to be as Jesus, it will cost us. There will not be too many who are willing to be placed on the potter's wheel. God truly wants to make and mold us after Him but we are so unwilling to be molded. No one likes pain. To be molded you must be broken. To be broken causes excruciating pain.

Jeremiah 18:4 says, "*And the vessel that he made of clay was marred in the hand of the potter: so he made it again another vessel, as seemed good to the potter to make it.*"

We want it to seem good to us. It doesn't matter what we want. It only matters what

God, our potter, wants. What may seem good to us may be the exact opposite to God.

SANCTIFICATION THROUGH THE WORD OF GOD

John 17:16-17 says, *"They are not of the world, even as I am NOT of the world. Sanctify then through thy truth: thy word is truth."*

--Our reasonable service

True humility and humbleness before God will take us to our knees for we will do as Romans 12 verse 1 says, *"I beseech you therefore, brethren, by the mercies of God, that ye present your bodies a living sacrifice, holy, acceptable unto God, which is your reasonable service."*

We must remember if we walk away from everything to do the work of God we are just doing our reasonable service. It is the same as being broken on the potter's wheel. We have to realize it's all about Jesus.

Whatever talent you possess or don't possess belongs to God. If people put you on a pedestal you are responsible for giving the glory back to God. More importantly, you are responsible for humbling yourself in humility before God.

-- Deeper consecration

When we really understand this is when we will see our consecration to God deepen to a new level. Our ministries will grow. We will be led by the Spirit of God into new dimensions and greater heights. But first, we must remember how Ezra went before God.

Ezra 9:5-6 says, *"And at the evening sacrifice I arose up from my heaviness; and having rent my garment and my mantle, I fell upon my knees, and spread out my hands unto the Lord my God. And said, O my God, I am ashamed and blush to lift up my face thee, my God:..."*

How long has it been since you or I went before God like this?

Please continue to remember Bishop James Kilgore in prayer. So far today there is no new news of his condition and it will probably be a couple of days. The Kilgore family needs to also be lifted up in prayer. God knows the situation and we must pray for God's will.

I'll never forget him praying for me. The day I was told I was dying I called him and he said you've prayed for us now it's time for us to pray for you. So today it's time for us to pray for one of the greatest, humblest, most compassionate men of God whose ministry has touched and changed untold thousands of people

JANUARY 28, 2014
Is your spiritual thermostat in a downward spiral like America's?

With everything that is going on in our country or not going on when it comes to standing for morality I have to question whether, we as Christians, are hot or cold? Or, God forbid, have we become lukewarm?

Do we even know our own spiritual temperature and its implications?

Revelation 3:15-16 says, *"I know thy works, that thou art neither cold nor hot: I would thou wert cold or hot. So then because thou art lukewarm, and neither cold nor hot, I will spue thee out of my mouth."*

Do you know who you are spiritually? Do you know what you stand for?

When God started talking to me about the spiritual temperature in a free fall downward I wondered where He would take me. Well, He took me also to II Peter 2:4-8 where it says,.

"For if God spared not the angels that sinned but cast them down to hell, and delivered them into chains of darkness, to be reserved unto judgement; and spared not the old world, but saved Noah the eighth person, a preacher of righteousness, bringing in the flood up on the world of the ungodly, and turning the cities of Sodom and Gomorrah into ashes condemned them with an overthrow, making them an ensample unto those that after should live ungodly; and delivered just Lot, vexed with the building conversation of the wicked: (For that righteous man dwelling among them, in seeing and hearing, vexed his righteous so from day to day with their

unlawful deeds;)"

Lot chose to live next to sin. He raised his children where it touched them day in and day out. We allow things in our lives and homes that touch us and our families never realizing the price we will have to pay.

I wonder how many watched the Grammy's and were not offended with the display of gay marriage and witchcraft? I agree we should love the sinner but we also must take a stand against sin.

Have we become so weak in our walk with God that we do not know how to let people know that while we love them we will stand against their sin? Are we afraid of the price we may have to pay?

It's time to say, ENOUGH!

You won't be able to do that if you don't know where you stand with God. How do you know? Well, through prayer and reading His Word. It's called daily consecration. Every day start your day and end your day with God.

The question today is are you hot, cold or in that awful place of lukewarmness?

I love working for God and sharing about the miracles He has blessed me with.

I just got off the phone from another call the pancreatic cancer action network sent to me. That's three families across the U.S. I've talked to about pancreatic cancer, encouraged and shared God's love with.

That is what it's all about giving our all so people will be drawn to Jesus

For those that have watched as my world has spun out of control I have had my highs and a lot of lows. However, every morning I do my best to open my mouth and simply say, Jesus, I love you.

Well, today the emptiness of the house got to me. Yes, my husband passed away but our children.. that's all I will say about them... God knows.

I began to wonder what's the use, I'm tired, take me. I'm all alone and useless. Yes, God has blessed me and given me great miracles but I'm human and tired. Then I started studying and found I'm in good company. Many great people of God have felt this way.

So instead of letting it get the best of me I'm studying and will probably write a three part study on Depression, Despondency, and how to overcome it.

But today I will encourage myself in the Lord by listening to songs and reading the Bible

JANUARY 29, 2014
There are some things that are classic Bro. Kilgore. One of those things is how he sings when he preaches. When sharing dinners or celebrating with what he called 'his kids' he would also sing and pray. He taught us we were diplomats for Jesus and how to have a relationship with God that consistently took us closer to the cross.

JANUARY 30, 2014
It's a great day at the O.K. Corral. 8 whole degrees today. I'm praying it warms up. Even with heat tape on my pipes and plugged in it appears the water is frozen. Please pray no busted pipes.

****

Depression, Despondency and How to Overcome It (Part I of III)

Define Depression

Severe despondency and dejection, typically felt over a period of time and accompanied by feelings of hopelessness and inadequacy.

Depression is scattered throughout the Bible. Do not think you are alone when you feel this way. It is not what you feel but in how you handle those feelings. Take them to your God.

Elijah, David, Abraham, Peter, Jacob, Job, Jonah, Paul, Isaiah, and many others battled with depression in the Bible.

Biblical Examples

--David

Psalms 40:1-3 (I didn't and usually I don't but David did)

"I waited patiently for the Lord and He inclined unto me, and heard my cry. He brought me up also out of an horrible pit, out of the miry clay, and set my feet upon a rock, and established my goings. And He hath put a new song in my mouth even praise unto our God: many shall see it, and fear, and shall trust in the Lord."

--Moses

Numbers 11:14 (Burden of the people too heavy for him.)
" I am not able to bare all this people alone, because it is too heavy for me."

--Jonah

Seemingly depression is always worse after a great victory when other problems seemingly happen. Jonah is one great example. This is after he came out of the whale of the fish and after Nineveh repented.

Jonah 4:3
"Therefore now, O Lord, take I beseech thee, my life from me for it is better for me to die then to live."

Yes, after having experienced all of that he became so depressed all he wanted to do was die. When depressed things don't make sense. Reasons to live evaporate. That's when you speak his name, Jesus.

--Paul

II Corinthians 7:5-6
"For when we were come in to Macedonia, our flesh had no rest, but we were troubled on every side; without were fightings, within were fears. Nevertheless God, that comforteth those that are cast down, comforted us by the coming of Titus."

GOD HEARS

I don't want to just leave you with depression today so here's one little jewel to help you if you're battling depression. Remember all you have to do is call that name. That name is Jesus. He will deliver you just like it says below:

Psalms 34:17
"The righteous cry and the Lord heareth, and delivereth them out of all their troubles."

He will deliver us!

WATER!!! I have water... the pressure is not what it needs to be but I have water!!! HALLELUJAH!

Now I'm having toilet issues... the water won't quit running in the toilet. Oh, well, never a dull moment...

Comments below:
Amanda Riley turn the water off to the toilet under it should be a shutoff valve
Susan D Wine Smith Yes there is a shutoff valve but it is stripped. Tried that the last time.
Melissa Harris Sorry Sis Susan D Wine Smith- I was shouting for joy for ya - now back to prayer & thawing out the bottom of my hot water tank - lol !!
Susan D Wine Smith Well I will be praying for you that yours thaws out and at least mine shouldn't freeze tonight with water running constantly.
Melissa Harris Lol - I love that you're positive Sis Susan D Wine Smith!!
David Kevin Price take the top off the tank see if it's running over the overflow tube. bend float arm to sink float into water a little more
- **Susan D Wine Smith** David Price I did all that after watching a youtube video. I will be calling my homeowners insurance to see if any of this is covered especially the frozen busted pipes... @Amanda my last part is due in for my car so I'm hoping and praying Lord willing to be somewhere south.
Robin Fields Harrison It will run your water bill up high
Susan D Wine Smith Turning off the water at the meter. Hopefully one of my friends is coming soon to help me do that but she's in a class right now. I'm praying my homeowners insurance will cover this but I will find out tomorrow.

God works all things to the good even frozen and busted pipes.... ALLL THINGS.....

So I've filled every pan with water I can find and I'm working on filling up the tub now.
I keep saying God works ALL THINGS TO THE GOOD whether I can see it or not

Thanking God for Bro. Randall Pitsenbarger and Sis. Lois Pitsenbarger who were my knights in shining armor and got the water turned off. God always provides for His children.

JANUARY 31, 2014
Depression, Despondency, and How to Overcome It (Part II of III)

- Define Despondency

A state of low spirits caused by loss of hope or courage.

After studying depression, despondency seems to me the next step down. This is where we have to get a grip. We have to get a handle on us and a handle on our God. Let's look at some Biblical examples of despondency.

--Abraham

Genesis 17:15-17 says, "*And God said unto Abraham, as for Sarai thy wife, thou shalt not call her name Sarai, but Sarah shall her name be. And I will bless her, and give thee a son also of her: yea, I will bless her, and she shall be a mother of nations; kings of people shall be of her. Then Abraham fell upon his face, and laughed, and said in his heart, shall a child be born unto him that is an hundred years old? And shall Sarah that is ninety years old, bear?*"

Talk about despondency. God, himself, was talking to Abraham yet he laughed and in his heart mocked the promise God gave him. You think you're the only one hopeless. Abraham was sure he had the market cornered. God gave him a promise he never expected God to fulfill.

What about you? Has God given you some promises you don't think He can fulfil? He is still God!

What made Abraham think he knew more than God? What makes you or I think that?

--Hezekiah

Isaiah 38:9-12 , "*The writing of Hezekiah king of Judah, when he been sick, and was recovered of his sickness: I said in the cutting off of my days, I shall go to the gates of my grave: I am deprived of the residue off my years. I said, I shall not see the Lord, even the Lord, and the land of the living: I shall behold man no more with the inhabitants of the world. Mine age is departed, and is removed from me as a shepherd's tent: I have cut off like a weaver my life: he will cut me off with pining sickness from day even tonight wilt thou make an end of me.*"

People get sick all the time. For some reason when Christians get sick if we don't get well immediately we think God has deserted us. What if? What if we have to go through the valley to be what God wants us to be and to go where He wants us to go?

--Elijah

I Kings 19:4, 9 , 4. "*But he himself went a day's journey into the wilderness, and came and sat down under a juniper tree: and he requested for himself that he might die; and said, It is enough; now, O Lord, take away my life; for I am not better than my fathers.*"

9. "*And he came thither unto a cave, and lodged there; and behold, the word of the Lord came to him, and he said unto him, What doest thou here, Elijah?*"

I love Elijah. He is so human. After great things have happened he goes out into the wilderness to die. This is a man that called fire down from heaven and killed soldiers, over 50 at one time and he did it more than once! All of a sudden he's become a chicken.

Then if it doesn't beat all God comes to him after he continues to run and hide. Now, he's in a cave and God wants to know why?

Are you running from something that you shouldn't be afraid of? Is God hunting for you to ask you why? Is God hunting for me to ask me why?

That's really got to be hopeless. Angels touched him and fed him. Do angels not touch us and feed us when it is necessary? God had done amazing things already in his ministry yet he was scared. Put yourself in his shoes.

Why are we afraid?

--Paul

Acts 27:20, *"And when neither sun nor stars in many days appeared, and no small tempest lay on us, all hope that we should be saved was taken away."*

Everyone, at some point, has feelings of hopelessness or despondency. That's when the scriptures we have written on our hearts should help us.

Psalms 27:1, *"The Lord is my light and my salvation; whom, shall I fear? the Lord is the strength of my life; of whom shall I be afraid?"*

It's going to be one of those days that will try my patience. I called my homeowners insurance now I'm waiting on a claims adjuster to call me back. Hopefully, in Jesus name, the last part will be in this afternoon for my car. Please Jesus let the car be fixed completely today! And, Jesus while you're helping me let the insurance folks call me back quickly. Thank you Jesus!

February 1, 2014
Depression, Despondency and How to Overcome It (III of III)

OVERCOMING DEPRESSION AND DESPONDENCY

Define overcoming
succeed in dealing with a problem or difficulty

Before we start I need to put a disclaimer for those that think only substandard people battle this. I've got news for you! Some of the most successful highly motivated people battle this routinely. No one is exempt.

You know I actually feel sorry for folks who have never battled this. Today this is the last thing I want to write about but it is important because they're so many people battling it. I am one of those. You really get to know Jesus by going through trials and tribulations that bring you to the point of depression and despondency.

Don't think for one minute I'm giving you an excuse to stay hopeless. I'm not! God gave this to me to give me a swift kick in the backside. So, I battled one of the, if not the most deadly form of cancer, my children backslid, my husband died of a prescription drug overdose, car problems, in law problems, insurance issues, frozen pipes and the list goes on.

BIG HOOEY!

It is nothing in God's eyes. It's time we were truly overcomers and not just for looks. You know what I mean, most of us don't have a clue what being an overcomer really is. Let's take a journey through the scriptures and see what they tell us.

-First, how do you learn to be an overcomer?

-- search the Scriptures DAILY

Acts 17:11 says, *"Those were more noble than those in Thessalonica, in that they received the word with all readiness of mind, and search the Scriptures daily, whether those things were so."*

It is not good enough to just search the Scriptures but you have to have a readiness of mind. In other words you have to be open to what God is telling you. Then you have to do something about it

There is so much more to this so tomorrow I will go into what the Bible teaches us about how to be an overcomer. Sorry this was just a teaser but these posts are getting so long and I don't want to bore you too much.

In the meantime study the scriptures with a mind open to the things of God.

I am walking Brownie this cool wintry morning. Then it will be time to start carrying stuff out and ripping up carpet. Lord willing I will have a car tonight and water. My goal is to at least stop mold from starting to grow where the pipes froze and burst.

You know when you get good and mad it is amazing what you can lift and do by yourself. I've got a bed out, chairs, big boxes of movies and dishes. I still have a couch to go, computer desks, more boxes then to rip out the sheetrock in the bathroom where the leak was.

Unfortunately I have asthma and even in anger I have enough sense to stop for a break until my chest quits hurting. In an hour I will get back at it.

I am headed to Lowes for pipe. Thank God for Sis. Lois Pitsenbarger. The calvary is on the way in the form of David Price. When I get back ripping up carpet, getting the couch and tv out, and fixing the pipes. Well. Sister Lois will be fixing the pipes. We all know the only mechanical ability I have is to break things not fix them.

So many frozen and busted pipes in the area Lowes is sold out of what I need.... story of my life these days. But on a good note Kevin is there ripping out carpet. Thank God.

55 degrees roasting in WV after below zero temps for weeks. I'm sure some are in their flip flops today

One leak fixed and we found another one. They're working on it now. My asthma is acting up so I came out to give my lungs a break.

Fixed that leak and alas we have another one. Thanks, Sis. Edna Myers Kincaid for telling us The Store might have pipe. They did. Now working on multiple leaks. Thank you David Price and Lois Pitsenbarger. Everyone needs friends like them. They told me to leave I know it's because of my lungs. I hate being needy.

Leaks are finally fixed. Water is back on. Before bed a hot shower. I'm making a frozen pizza right now for dinner for Brownie and I.

I ache all over. I don't know what I would have done without David Price and Sis. Lois Pitsenbarger helping me today. The car is still not fixed but they're working on it. Lord willing I'll get out of here early next week. ..like Monday or Tuesday.

FEBRUARY 2, 2014

Depression, Despondency, and How to Overcome It (Part IIIA of III)

Yesterday I started sharing what God had given me about how to overcome when you're swallowed up by depression and despondency. First thing of course is to search the Scriptures daily.(Acts 17:11) Now to continue the journey God took me on.

What does the Bible teach us?

-To be an overcomer STAND and BE QUIET

Sometimes standing still is all you've got. The Israelites love to compare how wonderful they had an Egypt when they were slaves. Do we do that to God?

It might look as if the enemy will soon have you down for the count but sometimes what our enemy and we haven't counted on is the God we serve. Right before the children of Israel crossed the Red Sea they were ready to go back to the bondage God had liberated them from.

Aren't we just like that?

Exodus 14:13-14 says, *"And Moses said unto the people, Fear ye not, stand still, and see the salvation of the Lord, which he will shew to you to day: For the Egyptians who ye have seen today, ye shall see them again no more forever. The Lord shall fight for you, and ye shall hold your peace."*

Think about this? Can you imagine never seeing your enemy again?

NEVER!!!!

The other part of this, well actually both parts get me into trouble. I hate standing still but the next part is near impossible for me. Being quiet always gets me into trouble.

Why do we not want to be quiet and listen to his still small voice. When I listen to that voice I learn so much. He's always right on time. Even when I think he's late he's on time.

Today I'll leave you with this last thought from Jeremiah.

Jeremiah 29:11 says, *"For I know the thoughts that I think toward you, saith the LORD, thoughts of peace, and not of evil, to give you an expected end."*

Tomorrow and probably for the next few days I'll continue to take you on this journey with me. God really talked to me a lot about this. I hope it helps you as much as it has helped me.

Time to head to the house of God. No matter what kind of aches, physical pains, spiritual pains and heart pains from family hurts the house of God is where you will find refuge and encouragement for your spiritual soul! So get up, get dressed and even if you'll be late GO!

JESUS IS WAITING!

Church this morning was beyond amazing. I walked into the Holy of Holies. It was just me and my God!

I'm headed back for Round Two of a Super Bowl with God! Nothing remotely touches what I feel in the presence of God.

Turn off the SuperBowl and find a Sunday Night Apostolic Church Service. Now, that is truly a SUPER BOWL!!!

FEBRUARY 3, 2014
Depression, Despondency, and How to Overcome It (Part III B of III)

To be an overcomer you must be determined!

Determined means having made a firm decision and being resolved not to change it.

The Bible tells us to be determined. I Corinthians 9:24 says, *"Know ye not that they which run in a race run all, but one receive it the prize? So run, that ye may obtain."*

This passage is talking about our Christian walk. It is encouraging us to run the race so that we may obtain the prize of being with Jesus.

Take a look at a couple of Bible greats who had this kind of determination. First, let's take a look at Daniel in Daniel 1:8, *"But Daniel purposed in his heart that he would not defile himself with the portion of the Kings meat, nor with the wine which he drank:..."*

Can you imagine how hard that was? For most of us we wouldn't even try. It doesn't matter how hard it is for us to be determined it is something we must do if we truly want to know what it feels like to be an overcomer.

Now to Isaiah in Isaiah 50:7 where it says, ."*For the Lord God will help me; therefore shall I not be confounded: therefore have I set my face like a flint, and I know that I shall not be ashamed."*

When we get truly determined it won't matter what trial or what valley comes our way we will not waver. The storm will buffet us but determination keeps us on course with God. That is when our minds are already made up.

That's when you simply say I know that I know that I know that my God has this. I know He's in control. It doesn't matter what it looks like. You just have to know that you know!

When you get there you're different, you've changed. You've gone deeper in God than you ever dreamed. So, today, get determined that no matter what comes your way you will not change unless it's to grow deeper in God.

My car is ready. I'm hopefully going to go get it soon. Making plans to Lord willing head out of WV this weekend. I might get to be home in Jackson Mississippi this Sunday night!!!

FEBRUARY 4, 2014

"Who loves Jesus More?"

So many memories tonight of a wonderfully anointed man of God, Bro. James Kilgore that I was privileged to call pastor and friend. He is not a perfect man but he is a man that loves Jesus more.

He has shown us how to love like Jesus and how to be a diplomat. He always made us feel like we were the most important person in the world when he talked to us. He showed us how to love people by loving Jesus more.

He taught us to be humble and to always give any glory or honor received right back to God. He gave anyone close to him a mind for foreign missions to love Jesus more.

To this day I look at things and wonder how much money could be raised to spread the gospel on foreign soil if they were sold. I've seen him sell cars and give the money to foreign missions showing us how to love Jesus more.

He taught us by example. The greatest honor we can give to our beloved Bro. Kilgore is to teach the next generation those principles by how we give, live, walk, and talk. They must be shown how to love Jesus more.

We need pioneers of the gospel from our generation that know how to sing the songs of old in all night prayer meetings like he has. Those prayer meetings are where lives are changed and calls of God are placed on lives to go, to love Jesus more.

He taught us to love the Word of God by singing, I have a wonderful treasure, It's given to me without measure, So we'll travel together, My Bible and I. We need a revival of loving the Word like he taught us so then we can stand with firm conviction raising our Bible in pulpits across America asking the question he routinely asked us,

"Who loves Jesus More?"

To all the family thank you for sharing your sweet Dad, Grand Dad, Great Dad, family member with all of us that he adopted into his family. I love and appreciate all of you and along with countless others will be lifting you all up in prayer tonight and in the days ahead.

Depression, Despondency, and How to Overcome It. (Part IIIC of III)

To be an overcomer you must have PASSION!

Passion means intense, driving, or overmastering feeling or conviction; or strong and barely controllable emotion.

God keeps expanding my thoughts on how to be an overcomer. This journey could take days as I discover more God wants me to know.

Numbers 13:30 says, *"And Caleb stilled the people before Moses, and said, Let us go up at once, and possess it; for we are well able to overcome it."*

Caleb had a passion that we need to get ahold of in our spiritual journey. No matter what others thought, he stood against the crowd. He not only said they were able to come overcome it but he said they were well able to overcome it. Would you have that much conviction against your peers if there was no doubt God had told you to do something.

Ruth is another great example of someone with passion. Ruth 1:16 says, *"And Ruth said, Intreat me not to leave thee, or return from following after thee: for whither thou goest, I will go; and whither thou lodgest I will lodge: thy people shall be my people, and thy God my God."*

The last example I'm going to share this morning is straight from the mouth of Jesus in Luke 9:62, *"And Jesus said unto him, No man having put his hand to the plough, and looking back is fit for the kingdom of God."*

So, tell me again, Christians shouldn't be passionate. All things have to be done decently and in order. However, we have taken that to the extreme and lost passion somewhere along the road.

If we want our walk with God to be passionate our worship must be passionate. It will show in every facet of our lives. People will be drawn to us because of the Spirit of God they feel when near us.

You probably think I'm being a bit extreme. Why not? The world is extreme in shoving they're liberalism down our throats.

It's time we become extreme for Jesus. We have to stand for something or we will fall for anything. Rediscover your passion for Jesus. Then show others through love how to have a passion that not only changes you but changes those you come in contact with.

Let's not just be overcomers but passionate overcomers!

Please add my dad, Joseph Wine to your prayers. He has been admitted to United Hospital in Bridgeport, West Virginia with chest pains.

FEBRUARY 5, 2014
Depression, Despondency and How to Overcome It. (Part IIID od III)

--TO BE AN OVERCOMER TRUST GOD TO BE GOD

Trust means a firm belief in the reliability, truth, or strength of someone or something.

Before I even go into the passages God brought to my attention on trust I want us to stop and really think about the definition. When you think about your relationship with God how does trust affect it?

Ask yourself the following questions in relationship not only to your walk with God but in your effectiveness to being an overcomer.

1. Do you really believe that what happened in biblical times could happen today?

(For example: Elijah calling fire down to consume troops. The sea parting for Moses and the children of Israel to walk on dry ground. God being the fourth man in the fiery furnace and not a hair being singed. I could go on and on but you get the picture. Do you believe it could happen today?)

2. Do you really believe God equals truth?

3. Do you believe God is reliable or do you question it because he didn't answer a prayer the way you thought he should?

4. Have you ever wondered how trusting God affected your ability to be an effective overcomer?

Now I'll take you on that journey God took me on this morning.

Proverbs 30:5, *"Every word of God is pure: he is a shield unto them that put their trust in him."*

Psalms 56:3-4, *"What time I am afraid I will trust in thee. In God I will praise His Word, in God I have put my trust; I will not fear what flesh can do unto me."*

In order to be able to say things like these two passages I've quoted we have to really trust God. It can't just be words we say. It's got to be so much more.

While studying on over coming and everything I've gone through with depression and despondency since my husband passed away I am changed. My trust in God is at a new level.

Yes, we will all still have days when we wonder. That is called being human. But on those days you have to get a hold of yourself . Shake yourself. Take you to an altar and re-establish your trust in God.

All of us should strive to trust God with every part of our lives every day of our lives. It doesn't have to make sense. Gods economy will never make sense in our economy.

So why do we limit God and what he can do for us?

Please continue to pray for my dad, Joseph Wine. He remains hospitalized at United Hospital in Bridgeport, WV in stable condition.

He did not have a heart attack. Tomorrow they will be doing a stress test and changing some medications. He will remain in the hospital for at least the next couple of days.

More snow.... will it ever stop?!

James and Imogene Kilgore were reunited today, February 5, 2014, at 2:25 a.m.

I lost not only my pastor but a great friend, a mentor, a counselor and someone who prayed for me daily. When I was evangelizing the last couple of years he would call me to check on me, pray with me and just to talk. I'll never forget those times God gave me with him. Before he died in the spring of 2013 he prayed a blessing over me. We spent three hours together that I will treasure forever. If I had known it was one of the last times I would see him alive would I have treasured it more? Think about that with your walk with God.

.

FEBRUARY 6, 2014
Snowing again! Those snow clouds look like they might stay all day.thick and heavy.

Depression, Despondency, and How to Overcome It. (Part IIIE of III)

To Overcome Please God

First, I think we need to have a clear understanding of the word please.

Pleasing means to cause to feel happy or satisfied.

Now, let's say that again.

To overcome you need to cause God to feel happy or satisfied.

Did you ever think about it that way? I hadn't.

In studying being an overcomer and the many different sides of it God is showing me where I have missed it. So when we are going through a valley or trial and we get stuck in depression and despondency we need to try to please God; to make him feel happy or satisfied.

Then the next question is how do you please God?

Hebrews 11:6, *"But without faith it is impossible to please him:...."*

Hebrews 13:16, *"But to do good and to communicate forget not: for with such sacrifices God is well pleased."*

Proverbs 10:5, *"He that gathereth in summer is a wise son: but he that sleepeth in harvest is a son that causeth shame."*

Mark 12:33, *"And to love him with all the heart and all the understanding, and with all the soul, and with all the strength, and to love his neighbor as himself, is more than all whole burnt offerings and sacrifices."*

Romans 12:1-2, *"I beseech you therefore, brethren, by the mercies of God, that ye present your bodies a living sacrifice, holy, acceptable unto God which is your reasonable service. And be not conformed to this world but be ye transformed by the renewing of your mind, that ye may prove what is that good, and acceptable, and perfect, will of God."*

II Corinthians 5:9, *"For whether we labour, that, whether present or absent, we may be accepted of him."*

Why is it so important to please God?

Galatians 1:10 answers that question clearly.

"For do I now persuade men or God? or do I seek to please men? For if I yet please men, I should not be the servant of Christ."

The highest calling is to be a servant of Christ. If we seek to please men over God we can't be the servant of Christ.

So in this journey you're going on with me about learning how to be an overcomer it digs in the corners of our hearts. For those of us who have never wanted to rock the boat it's hard to realize but sometimes pleasing God is the exact opposite of pleasing people. Its like this, either stand for something or fall for anything.

Anything valuable will cost you something. Going through the valley is one thing but learning how to sacrifice to come out of the valley is a whole new realm of closeness with God.

Think about it. Apply it to your life. Look at what the scriptures say. Then find yourself a place to pray.

Please continue praying for my Dad. They are doing a heart catheterization today. He seems to be feeling some better but the doctors are trying to get to the bottom of his pain.

FEBRUARY 7, 2014
Tomorrow is the service honoring Bro. James Kilgore who chose to live his life living, working, and giving to God. Because of his choice countless lives were changed and will continue to be impacted as those of us who were blessed to sit under his ministry continue to work for God.

Depression, Despondency and How to Overcome It. (Part IIIE of III)

TO OVERCOME BE JOYFUL AND REJOICE

Joyful means Feeling, expressing, or causing great pleasure and happiness.

Rejoice means to feel or show great joy or delight

Here we go again. We're to cause God great pleasure and happiness, great joy and delight!

In the trial or valley you are going through how do you show not just joy but great joy or delight? All trials and valleys are hard. They are not measurable from person to person or circumstance to circumstance. It does not matter whether you are a teenager or nearing the end if your journey whatever trial or valley you are going through is big to you.

I Peter 4:12-13, *"Beloved, think it not strange concerning the fiery trial which is to try you, as though some strange thing happened unto you. But rejoice, inasmuch as you are partakers of Christ's sufferings; that, when his glory shall be revealed you may be glad also with exceeding joy.*

In other words why do we think we are the only one? Why do we think no one has ever been through this before? Friends may even tell us we must be doing something wrong. This must be the judgment of God. That's what they told Job.

What if?

What if in order to know exceeding joy in Jesus we have to go through certain trials? Is it worth it? You bet it is!

So, in our valley of despair what we must do is shake ourselves!

We must lift up holy hands and worship the one who gave all that we might have hope!

Tomorrow I will talk about joy with patience. To me those two words shouldn't even be in the same sentence. Today, even in your despair, find joy in Jesus!
****
My Dad's heart catheterization is over. He has no blockages and needs no stents. I am praying that the chest pains are just a needed medication change. Please keep him in your prayers.

URGENT PRAYER REQUEST!!!

Please pray for my dad.

Earlier today my Dad had a heart catheterization which showed no blockages and no stents needed. He was up walking and preparing for discharge home tomorrow or Sunday when late this afternoon he had an episode where Rapid Response was called on him. He is now in CCU in critical but stable condition. He is on a ventilator at this time. All labs are normal and tests are being run. We hope to have some answers tomorrow and him off the ventilator. In the meantime we ask that you pray for him and my mother.

FEBRUARY 8, 2014
I am walking Brownie on the fresh snow while praying for my Dad, the Kilgore family and all my church family that is grieving today. I will continue to trust and rely on God for direction with the latest crisis I am facing. I know that my God has got all these situations in his hands.

God is so good to me. I just talked to my mom. Dad is doing much better and is no longer on the ventilator or oxygen. The doctors say he had a bad side effect to medication. He should be home in a couple of days. TO GOD BE THE GLORY!

FEBRUARY 9, 2014
If my plans had worked out this morning I would be somewhere between Knoxville and Chattanooga on my way home to Mississippi. However, my dad is still critical so I'm headed north to the hospital in Bridgeport WV. Please remember all of us in your prayers.

Thanking and praising God I made it to the hospital and am staying with my dad tonight. He has been moved to a regular room. It was so good to see my friend Cheri Sandy, Zach Sandy, his cousin, Pastor Doug Joseph and his son. I'm blessed with so many who are praying around the world for my Daddy. He's sitting on the edge of the bed talking to us right now. Thank you Jesus!

I love this picture of my dad and me relaxing on an outing when I was battling pancreatic cancer and in the middle of chemotherapy.

It is time to try and get a little sleep here in my dad's hospital room tonight. Listening to him breathe I know how blessed I am to still have him in my life. Please continue to pray for him, especially for a restful night. He is doing better but we still have some challenges.

FEBRUARY 10, 2014
So since Daddy is still awake I think I'll write the thoughts down I'm having in my tablet. Believe it or not with everything that's happened I never saw this coming. I don't think my Dad has been in a hospital for over thirty years. So tonight while I'm laying here praying in Jesus name he drifts into a deep sleep because even with medicine the human body needs rest to heal.

I'm getting the feeling it's going to be a power nap kind of night for my Daddy and me.

Keep the prayers coming. Its every fifteen or twenty minutes.

I remember having newborns and being this tired but I had someone to share the tiredness and the work with. It's hard to believe that there are still a few hours left in this night.

Wide awake once again....

In our family when I was growing up there were things that were hidden from outsiders. A family that is dysfunctional or has some form of abuse whether it be verbal, physical or both is detrimental to the psychological growth of the child.

If you are raising your children in that environment you need to seek spiritual and professional guidance. The reason I am discussing this is that in the home I grew up in while it wasn't daily the abuse did occur. When judging someone for not going home often or for not being available to parents realize that things are not always as they seem. The only people that know what goes on in a home are those that live in the home.

This night in the hospital in trying to get my father to go back to bed he reverted to his old personality. He started throwing punches at me. Because the nurses were in the room they stepped in between us and put me in another room while they put my father in a strait jacket. When I say, I'm broken before God. I mean I'm broken. In that other room I prayed as this episode brought back memories I did not wish to deal with. However, they needed to be dealt with in order for me to continue to grow in God.

Depression, Despondency, and How to be an Overcomer.

TO BE AN OVERCOMER NEVER EVER GIVE UP

Luke 18:1, *"And he spake a parable unto them to this end, that men ought always to pray, and not faint."*

Galatians 6:9, *"And let us not be weary in well doing: for in due season we shall reap, if we faint not."*

I learned how to stand and be a true overcomer when I understood that on my knees in prayer is when I truly stood. We want things to come the easy way. As I've set in the hospital this night and dealt with many situations and memories I know God is cleaning another corner of my heart out.

It is in those times we not only need to pray but to take ourselves to the Word of God for the answers we seek about our situation(s). Then seek the Godly counsel of your pastor.

Most of the time well-meaning friends look at the situation from the outside not understanding or knowing all that is going on. What is normal in one situation may not be normal for another family.

We should not insert ourselves into situations we personally have no knowledge of unless it is to pray. If you feel you must ask others to pray it is not your right to share details of the situation you don't have permission to do so. When asking people to pray for a specific person or family just say it is an unspoken request and leave it. Do not utter another word.

In order to understand not being weary in well doing is to first understand Jesus never got weary with us. So, no matter what the situation, no matter how unfair it may be, no matter, just no matter remember Jesus is still Lord of all!

Lastly, let's take an example from the apostles in the book of Acts chapter 16 verse 25. They should have given up. If it had been us, we probably would have. This verse teaches us a big lesson about what to do in the midnight hour.

"And at midnight Paul and Silas prayed, and sang praises unto God: and the prisoners heard them."

Your prayers in your midnight hour will not only affect your situation but will affect others that watch how you handle yourself as a Christian during your time of crisis. The greatest soul winning tool we have is how we live and overcome in the name of Jesus.

So, NEVER GIVE UP!

Tomorrow I will share the journey God has taken me on to learn how to encourage myself in the Lord.

I am waiting on the rest of the doctors to come see Daddy. He's doing better and they have plans to discharge him tomorrow. I will be headed back to Fayetteville about 2:00. I can't wait to go to sleep. I'll be drinking lots of caffeine and eating sugar the whole way home.

Exhausted and headed back to Fayetteville.

I made it home to Fayetteville and I am exhausted. I think I'm getting a little old to be burning the candle at both ends and in the middle. I've been up for somewhere between 36 and 48 hours. I'm going to try and stay up a couple of more hours so that hopefully I can sleep until morning.

FEBRUARY 11, 2014
Depression, Despondency and How to be an Overcomer (Part IIIG of III)

To overcome you must learn how to encourage yourself in the Lord.

Encourage means to give support, confidence or hope.

In the journey God is taking me on He first took me to Job. If any book in the Bible can show us how someone who loses everything and by example shows us how to pick ourselves up with the help of God it is the book of Job. Even with his friends attack him verbally when he would respond you would find a nugget hidden here and there where he encourages himself.

Job 17:9,"*The righteous also shall hold on his way, and he that hath clean hands shall be stronger and stronger.*"

Job 19:25-27, 25. "*For I know that my redeemer liveth, and that he shall stand at the latter day upon the earth.*"26. "*And though after skin worms destroy this body, yet in my flesh I shall see God.*"27. "*Whom I shall see for myself, and mine eyes shall behold, and not another, though my reins be consumed within me.*"

Job 42:2, "*I know that thou canst do every thing, and that no thought can be withholden from thee.*"

The way to encourage yourself in the Lord is to quote scriptures to yourself, read the Word of God and apply it to your situation along with prayer. Then remember every time God supplied your needs and rescued you.

Yes it may be a different situation but the God we serve is the same God that rescued us before and that will be there again and again.

You see, the difference between an overcomer and one who can't overcome is the fact they haven't learned how to stand on the Word of God and its promises. We must hide the Word in our hearts so we can remember His promises to us and encourage ourselves like the greats of the Bible have done.

Let's encourage ourselves no matter our situation!

FEBRUARY 12, 2014
Depression, Despondency and How to Overcome It (Part IIIG of III)

To Overcome You Must Speak Positively.

A few points I will hit today and tomorrow, the most important being that it is definitely Biblical.

First, I will go to some passages that God took me to to remind me about positive thinking and speaking.

Jeremiah 29:12, *"Then shall ye call upon me, and ye shall go and pray unto me, and I will hearken unto you."*

Phillippians 4:13, *"I can do all things through Christ which strengtheneth me."*

Isaiah 55:12, *"For ye shall go out with joy, and be led forth with peace: the mountains and the hills shall break forth before you into singing, and all the trees shall clap their hands."*

Luke 11:9, *"And I say unto you, Ask, and it will be given to you; seek, and ye shall find; knock, and it shall be opened to you."*

Romans 8:28, *"And we know that all things work together for good to them that love God, to them who are the called according to His purpose."*

Galatians 3:9, *"And if ye be Christ's, then are ye Abraham's seed and heirs according to the promise."*

Secondly, today, God wants to remind me and you that we are His!

Because we are His we need to understand that our thoughts need to change. Yes, bad things happen to us but it's what we allow those things to do to us that are the real problem.

When we learn how to stand on the promises of God in our mind and to speak to our situations that's when we will see real change within ourselves.

It is important that you understand this is not a get out of jail free card for those situations we put ourselves into. God will rescue us even out of those situations. It is, however, important to realize how changing our way of thinking will realign us to being so much closer to our God.

You and I need to learn to speak to our situation! We need to remind the devil who our God is!

Most of the time it's not the devil who is the problem but us. That is when we simply need to remind ourselves who our God is!

Today speak and think positively to yourself. Then if you are like me you might need to repent for your thoughts about what God could or could not do in your situation.

****

I think the things I hate most about being widowed is eating alone and not having anyone to talk to but I'm learning to talk to walls...lol.. and I'm probably wearing my closest friends out with frequent calls.

Thanks to those who have stayed close! You know who you are.

And it continues to snow. I guess we will see in the morning if we do indeed get a foot or so of the white stuff. At the rate its coming down unless it suddenly stops we just might have that much when we wake up.

Dad is home from the hospital!

I was blessed to spend some time this evening talking on the phone to my 99 year old Uncle who at one time was a missionary. I love gleaning from an elder's wisdom. I am blessed he is still with us and has such wonderful memories of his life to share.

FEBRUARY 13, 2014
Snow at 1:30 a.m. we have several inches already and still coming down. The road in front of my house is a main road that is now a path. I would say it is a safe bet that no school will happen today.

Depression, Despondency, and How to Overcome It (Part 3I of III)

Why is it so important to think and speak positively?
The Bible tells us why.

Proverbs 18:21, *"Death and life are in the power of the tongue: and they that love it shall eat the fruit thereof."*

Ps. 27:13, *"I had fainted, unless I had believed to see the goodness of the Lord in the land of the living."*

Philippians 2:5, *"Let this mind be in you, which was also in Christ Jesus."*

Psalms 50:15, *"And call upon me in the day of trouble: I will deliver thee, and thou shalt glorify me."*

The Bible is so rich and full on this subject. We tend to shy away from those who speak about positive thinking because so many have taken it to an extreme to justify a rich lifestyle that may or may not have anything to do with Jesus. In reality positive thinking on a spiritual side has so many benefits.

----

1. Positive thinkers don't see problems as problems but as a way to build faith. They see things as they should be not as they are.

Heb. 11:1, *"Now faith is the substance of things hoped for, the evidence of things not seen."*

2. Positive thinkers because of a change of thinking from negative to positive do just as Jesus taught. Then doubt leaves.

Matthew 21:21, *"Jesus answered and said unto them, verily I say unto you, if ye have faith and doubt not, ye shall not only do this which is done to the fig tree, but also if ye shall say to this mountain, Be thou removed and be thou cast into the sea; it shall be done."*

3. Positive thinkers speak positively thereby receiving positive results.

Proverbs 18:21 (partial quote), *"Death and life are in the power of the tongue:"*

I'm only going into three bullet points here but there are so many more. You really should study this on your own and let God speak to you about your situation.

I really believe that positive thinking and positive speaking are so important in our walk with God. So when those times come when things seemingly aren't going our way remember to find the silver lining in the cloudy days.

Yes, we will have trials, valleys, and challenges but if we learn how to look up and say, God I know beyond a shadow of a doubt that you got this it will change your outlook on the problem. Once our outlook is changed we are ripe for a miracle.

Whatever we need, no matter how big or small God will provide. So when you go to pray remember the scriptures above. Sometimes when it is hard for me to be positive I pray the quoted scripture. That will build your faith.

The snow is taller than Brownie. ..lol. I will have to dig her a path in the yard.

We found the road. Not much of a road today. We have about two feet of snow. Check out Brownie making a pass through the two feet of snow so she can get to the road to do her walk.

- I just heard we could get another foot of snow. It's coming down like there is no tomorrow and no end in sight. If we get another foot of snow we will have well over 3 feet of snow. That's just a bit much. Soon I won't even be able to see my chain link fence because it will be completely covered and it's close to 4 feet tall. Sheila Munday, Teresa Mills Stanley, Karen Cochran and 15 others like this.

Can I find my car? LOL

I was trying not to say anything until I get my plane ticket but everything is now falling into place for me to leave for Kenya the second week of March for about a month. When God is in it and orders your footsteps waiting is one of the hardest things to do if you're like me you just want to go already... but sooon in Jesus name. I'M SO EXCITED TO SEE WHAT GOD IS GOING TO DO!

I covet the covering of your prayers for this journey for God.

February 14, 2014
Depression, Despondency, and How to be an Overcomer (Part IIIJ of III)

To truly overcome we have to become more of Jesus, less of us until it is all about Jesus!!!

I know today is Valentine's Day. It is a day we give gifts to those that we love. What greater gift could we give Jesus then to give Him us.

What I mean is by doing what we sing about all the time. Remember, " I will give you all, I will not withhold." By giving Him all so that our lives truly become all about Him so that we are no longer holding anything back.

Let's see what the Bible says:

Galatians 2:20, "I am crucified with Christ: nevertheless I live; yet not I, but Christ liveth in me: and the life which I now live in the flesh I live by the faith of the Son of God, who loved me, and gave himself for me."

Galatians 5:24-25, "And they that are Christ's have crucified the flesh with the affections and lusts. If we live in the Spirit, let us also walk in the Spirit."

II Corinthians 5:15, "And that He died for all, that they which live should not henceforth live unto themselves, but unto Him which died for them and rose again."

Romans 14:7-9, "For none of us liveth to himself, and no man dieth to himself. For whether we live, we live unto the Lord; and whether we die, we die unto the Lord: whether we live therefore, or die, we are the Lord's. For to this end Christ both died, and rose, and revived, that He might be Lord both of the dead and living."

There is so much more in the Bible about this. When we really get it our lives will be revolutionized for Jesus. That is when it will be all about Him.

This is not an easy process. This is not for the faint of heart. . This process requires sacrifice. The most important sacrifice we will ever give is in giving of ourselves to Jesus, complete and whole, holding back nothing.

As a very wise person once told me you think you have sacrificed everything and you haven't yet scratched the surface about a year ago. Look at what you sacrificed. Now, look at what Jesus and the apostles sacrificed.

I think it's time we pray, really pray. And this time we need to really mean the words to that song, "I will give you all, I will not withhold."

Tomorrow I will share part of the journey God has taken me on about Him truly being first in my life.

I am staying in but I will be cooking myself a steak later for dinner. My car is currently buried under 3 feet of snow with more snow and rain coming later this evening. I'm leaving that car buried for now. In a few days I'll get out

FEBRUARY 15, 2014
Depression, Despondency and How to be an Overcomer (Part IIIK of III).

To be an Overcomer you absolutely must put God first!

First means coming before ALL others in time or order.

I could not begin to tell you how many messages I have heard preached on this specific subject. The Bible is very clear on this. We can rationalize our priorities anyway we wish. However, if we truly want to have the overcoming spirit that we should God will be first in our lives.

Let's see what the Bible has to say about this.

Exodus 20:3,"*Thou shalt have no other gods before me.*"

Matthew 6:33, "*But seek ye first the kingdom of God, and His righteousness; and all these things shall be added unto you.*

I believe these two verses make it crystal clear that God must be first. If God is not first we could have made some of those things God blessed us with gods in our life. When we put God first we will have a different mindset about the things of God and the work of God.

Below are a couple of more passages that will give you the idea of what Jesus meant when he spoke and of how the apostles interpreted it.

Matthew 8:21-22,"*And another of his disciples said unto him, Lord, suffer me first to*

go and bury my father. But Jesus said unto him, follow me and let the dead bury their dead."

Romans 8:5, *"For they that are after the flesh do mind the things of the flesh but they that are after the Spirit the things of the Spirit."*

What do these passages mean?

I am a very simplistic person when it comes to the Scriptures. I believe it means what it says it means. Sometimes the Bible in the words of Jesus are strong and hard to understand because of the emphasis we put on things today that are not of the Spirit.

We have to get it!

We really have to get it! We don't have time to play! People are dying and going to hell because we, as Christians, refuse to put God first. We have every excuse in the book.

We can't help out because the house needs cleaned; the kids have activities (not church or God related); we say we cannot spend time in the prayer room before church because the kids will act up; and our excuses go on and on. Well, those kids God blessed you with will never learn how important prayer and a close relationship with God is unless you teach them by example.

Yes, they will act up. However, what you are teaching them every time you take them to a prayer room or a place of prayer is how to enter into the presence of God. After a while they will learn and start having their own conversations with God because they watched you put Him first in all things and not just on Sunday.

When you put God first everything else will just automatically fall into place as long as you do it with the right attitude. Don't put your family last. They come next after God. You love them as Christ loved the church.

So, this Saturday let's examine our priorities and see where God is in that list. If He is not first in your life your priorities need realigned to the Word of God.

Is He Lord of all or not Lord at all?

Another day of snow....

February 16, 2014
Depression, Despondency and How to Overcome (Part IIIL of III)

TO OVERCOME CAST YOUR CARES UPON HIM

DO NOT WORRY!

I can already hear you. What do you know about my problems? You don't have a clue what I'm going through. I have uttered those same words.

Yes, unfortunately, I do have a clue what you're going through and so do many others because we've all been there. Death, cancer, financial crisis, drugs, among other problems have visited our families.

Do not think that just because we are Christians we have a get out of jail free card. The difference between someone who understands overcoming and someone who doesn't is how we allow these problems to affect our futures.

First, let's define a couple of words. These two words are very important to people who want to be an overcomer. I believe we must understand exactly what the Bible tells us to do. All the definitions I have looked up online.

Worry is to give way to anxiety or unease; allow one's mind to dwell on difficulty or troubles.

Cast is to throw forcefully in a specified direction.

What does the Bible tell us to do about our problems, our worries?

I Peter 5:7,*"Casting all your care upon Him, for He careth for you."*

Phillippians 4:6, *"Be careful for nothing; but in every thing by prayer and supplication with thanksgiving let your requests be made known unto God."*

Psalms 55:22, *"Cast thy burden upon the Lord,.."*

None of this is easy to do. That's why some get stuck in depression and despondency while others learn how to overcome in the same situations. We all learn at different speeds. Some of us have to revisit the same lesson again and again. I, for one, am ready to move on and get this.

When we get this then we will understand no matter how big our problems are, our God is bigger! When we worry we are taking God's responsibility away from him.

He wants to take care of our problems and our needs for us but we have to learn how to give those problems and needs to him. We have to cast those problems in the opposite direction from us towards our God and let Him handle them.

Yes, we have to live through it. However, when we know he's taking care of it for us it relieves us as much as we will allow it to.

When we cast our cares on Him Matthew 7:11 makes sense to us.

"If ye then, being evil, I know how to give good gifts until your children, how much more shall your father which is in heaven give good things to them that ask him?"

I know this is lengthy but it's so important that we get it. In our walk with God we have to realize that he is our Father. He only wants to help us. Sometimes we have to go through valleys to grow. While in the valley we have to listen to his still small voice.

Tomorrow, I will share the journey God is taking me on about how we discourage others without realizing it. True overcomers don't discourage others, they encourage them.

February 17, 2014
Depression, Despondency and How to be an Overcomer (Part IIIM of III).

TO BE AN OVERCOMER DO NOT DISCOURAGE OTHERS

Discourage is to make (someone) less determined, hopeful, confident; or to deprive of confidence, hope or spirit
----

Have you done this?

Have I done this?

Let's see what the Bible has to say about this?

Numbers 32:6-7, "And Moses said unto the children of Gad and to the children of Reuben, Shall your brethren go to war, and shall ye sit here? And wherefore discourage ye the heart of the children of Israel from going over into the land which the Lord hath given them?"

Job 16:1-7, "Then Job answered and said, I have heard many such things: miserable conforters are ye all. Shall vain words have an end? Or what emboldenest thee that thou answerest. I also could speak as ye do if your soul were in my souls stead, I could heap up words against you, and shake mine head at you. But I would strengthen you with my mouth, and the moving of my lips should asswage your grief. Though I speak, my grief is not asswaged: and though I forbear, what am I eased. But now he hath made me weary: thou hast made desolate all my company."

Have you or I discouraged someone from following the will of God for their life?

Can you imagine with me, yourself or members of your family, being mentioned in the Bible as miserable comforters. In other words they were discouragers. How many messages have we heard preached on being like Bildad, Eliphaz, Zophar or Job's wife?

Precisely why we do not know who they were is because they were miserable comforters. They had no clue what the word encourage meant but they had an extremely close relationship with the word discourage.

This is why it is so important to think before we speak. Have you or I been a miserable comforter to someone?

What does the Bible say?

Ephesians 4:29, *"Let no corrupt communication proceed out of your mouth, but that which is good to the use of edifying, that it may minister grace unto the hearers."*

Think about this for a minute. If you are a discourager is your communication corrupt?

Tomorrow I will take you on the journey God took me on about the importance of being an encourager.

And another winter storm is raging and the power is out... candles are lit...
A few comments from this post below:

Ronda Dalton Are you feeling the bush calling?
Susan D Wine Smith A few good things to report:
(1) The Wind is blowing again just like on the day of Pentecost (maybe not quite like that but you remember the song).
(2) Brownie is providing my evening amusement by barking at the wind whistling.
(3) I have candles and an oil lamp.
(4) I have matches.
(5) I know how to light candles.
(6) It's almost bedtime and not that many outages have been reported yet.
(7) Most importantly Jesus is with me!
Susan D Wine Smith Yes Ronda Dalton. I knew you couldn't resist saying something. Love and miss you. By the way you made me laugh remembering our stop at the Maryland rest stop a few months ago.
Treasa Dickinson-Dickinson when did ur power go off
Susan D Wine Smith About 8:30

- **Ronda Dalton** I almost called you to meet up today but needed to get home...miss and love you praying for you and brownie...
  Susan D Wine Smith Thanks. I wish you had called. I couldn't have met you. My car is still buried under feet of snow. Thanks f for the prayers.
  David Fitzwater U ok on heat?
- **Susan D Wine Smith** David, thanks for checking on me. Power just came back on.
  David Fitzwater Awesome! Was gonna run you up a little heater.
  ******

Now that it's just me again I think I want a minimalist look for my home... who knows I may even try my hand at building a bed this May. That should be a video for laughs...lol
******

HALLELUJAH!!!!Well, so glad I decided to take a nap. I just woke up to the power coming back on!!! Praise God! Now I think I will go to bed.

FEBRUARY 18, 2014

Today is another day. Twenty-five years ago today I married my soul mate. He's been missing from my life not quite six months and my immediate family has been missing almost that long. Grief affects every person differently.

In my life I have been very fortunate and very blessed but since August 25th it has been like I'm always on the outside looking in at happiness. Happiness at times in our lives can be so elusive. When things happen or seeming exclusions from events its then I am reminded I keep great company.

His name is Jesus and He just wraps His arms around me to comfort me. There is no comfort like the comfort of Jesus on this day my love and I had planned to mark with celebrations of our love.

Do me a favor today hug your families a little closer and let them know how much you love them because none of us are guaranteed a tomorrow.

Depression, Despondency, and How to Overcome (Part IIIN of III)

TO OVERCOME BE AN ENCOURAGER

Encourage is to give support, confidence or hope

Edify is to instruct or improve (someone) morally or intellectually

----

It is not just good enough to be able to encourage yourself in the Lord when you're depressed or despondent. A true overcomer can encourage others when their own world is falling apart before their eyes. You think that is impossible. I did too until I learned how to let God have complete control(most of the time, however, I am still very human).

During the past almost 6 months and today God has sent people into my path from the American Cancer Society, the Pancreatic Cancer Action Network, to just mention a few of the professional organizations I work with to encourage people who are fighting for their lives. Barring a miracle these people are battling illnesses that typically will take their lives.

Today, when I make the call to encourage that person I received a phone call about yesterday I have to be able to step out of my situation and into theirs. I can't let my problems bleed into what I tell them.

True overcomers can put their problems to the side and focus on the person they have to encourage. They need help. No matter who comes to you needing hope you have to forget your problems for a little while to give them hope.

You'll find when you do this you give yourself hope. You think it's a play on words. It is not. That is just how it works. The Bible teaches us that but that's not why. I do it, simply, because I love to help people. We should all love to help others and love like Jesus.

Joshua 1:9, *"Have not I commanded thee? Be strong and of a good courage; be not afraid, neither be thou dismayed: for the LORD thy God is with thee whithersoever thou goest."*

I Thessalonians 5:11
"Wherefore comfort yourselves together, and edify one another, even as also ye do."

Romans 15:4, *"For whatsoever things were written aforetime were written for our learning, that we through patience and comfort of the Scriptures might have hope."*

Knowing the Word of God is a big key to being able to encourage others when our world continues to fall apart. Remember Phillippians 4:8 when you start to focus on your problems. You'll find within those words encouragement and blessing.

"Finally, brethren, whatsoever things are true, whatsoever things are honest, whatsoever things are just, whatsoever things are pure, whatsoever things are lovely, whatsoever things are of good report; of there be any virtue, and if there be any praise, think on these things."
******

So excited... soon...very sooon...

Lord willing I will be home in Mississippi for a few weeks. I can't wait to see my Mississippi family and then before heading out to Kenya I will get to spend about a week in Houston in Jesus name

FEBRUARY 19, 2014
Depression, Despondency and How to Overcome (Part IIIO of III)

TO OVERCOME COMFORT OTHERS

Why? Because the Bible instructs us to do this.

Isaiah 40:1
"Comfort ye, comfort ye my people."

Romans 1:12, *"That is, that I may be comforted together with you by the mutual faith both of you and me."*

II Corinthians 1:3-4, *"Blessed be God, even the Father of our Lord Jesus Christ, the Father of mercies, and the God of all comfort; who comforteth us in all our tribulation, that we may be able to comfort them which are in any trouble, by the comfort wherewith we ourselves are comforted of God."*

I think that's pretty plain. In Romans God lets us know by comforting others we are comforted with mutual faith.

Lastly, we find that God is the God of all comfort. He comforts us so we can then comfort others as He has comforted us.

So, today, when you see someone who needs comfort, comfort them. Let them see Jesus in you through everything you do. Make time in your busy schedule to comfort someone.

It's going to be gorgeous today... in the fifties! Washing all the bedding and hanging it on the line. I love to crawl into a bed with the smell of fresh washed bedding that has been sunkissed. Then washing the rest of the clothes so I can be loaded to start the journey to Mississippi on Friday. Lord willing, I will be there Saturday afternoon late.

February 20, 2014
Depression, Despondency and How to be an Overcomer (Part IIIP of III).

OVERCOMERS LET GOD COMFORT THEM WHEN THEY CAN'T COMFORT THEMSELVES.

Have you ever felt like there was no hope? I know I have. Let's check out Jeremiah.

Jeremiah 1:8, *"When I would comfort myself against sorrow, my heart is faint in me."*

This is a normal human feeling. It's not in feeling of losing hope that is the problem. It's in what we allow this to do to us.

I know, you want me to explain myself. Okay, I will. What God talked to me about through this with my own grief and lost hope went like this.

So, I've given you great blessings, miracles, and so much more that you can't even count in your little mind. Yet you sit there wallowing in self-pity. It's time to get up off your butt and do something for me!

In the beginning of my grief process God's comfort was gentle arms wrapped around me. Because this continued for several months that's when God's comfort changed. Sometimes we need a wake-up call to get us up. A jolt of reality from God talking to us is what we need to get us going.

Let's see what the Bible tells us about God comforting us.

II Thessalonians 2:16-17,"*Now our Lord Jesus Christ himself, and God, even our father, which hath loved us, and hath given us everlasting consolation and good hope through grace, Comfort your hearts, and stablish you in every good word and work.*"

Psalms 147:3, "*He healeth the broken in heart, and bindeth up their wounds.*"

John 14:18, "*I will not leave you comfortless: I will come to you.*"

Remember, today, God's comfort is there but after a while we have to learn how to comfort ourselves in the Word of God.

So, today, get up, brush yourself off, memorize some encouraging scriptures to quote to yourself when depression and despondency come knocking. Then you, with the help of God, can send depression and despondency packing!

Tomorrow I will take you on the journey God took me on about starting to move for Him.

****

It's going to be another busy day today. Laundry, walking Brownie, moving things around so painting can begin soon, packing to leave tomorrow, a trip to Lowes later.... busy, busy!

I am so very thankful to God to be alive. Today is a beautiful day with a temperature in the fifties. I've turned the heat off and opened the windows. I hate having asthma. I still have one more room to clean out but after doing one room and walking Brownie my asthma has said enough. I've medicated and inhaled so now I'm resting praying my chest quits hurting.

And, yes I did pace myself but when you only breathe at 60% of your lungs when it says enough you stop.

Please pray for me. Chest pain has not let up. Called my doctor stopped at their office Blood pressure was up. They sent me to the Emergency Room. Blood pressure here was 156/91. My normal blood pressure is 90/70. I am waiting to see doctor now. They already did an EKG.

My cheering up squad. They are trying to make me laugh. We found out I will be admitted. Abnormal ekg with T wave inversions. Needless to say I'm not taking the news well of being admitted so they're trying to make me laugh. I think they succeeded!

We are having our own small group Bible Study in the Emergency Room with Sis. Joyce McCann, Bro. Randy & Sis. Lois Pitsenbarger.

When did I get old?
My God has got this slight problem of a possible heart attack. On Him I will depend. Praying that the rests of the tests come back negative and the irregularities in the EKG show old damage not new damage to the heart.

February 21, 2014
My primary doctor just came by. Thanking God the cardiac enzymes are negative for a heart attack. A cardiologist will see me later today. I could be at my house tonight in Jesus name.
Thank you Jesus!

Depression, Despondency and How to be an Overcomer (Part IIIQ of III)
TO OVERCOME YOU MUST MOVE!

Did you ever stop to think that what you perceive to be your biggest obstacle could in fact become your way to overcome?
Last night as I was lying in the hospital and they were running tests and I felt God talk to me more about this spiritually. So let me take you on the highlights of the journey God took me on.

Define move
Go in a specified direction or manner; change position.
Define walk
Move at a regular amd fairly slow pace, by lifting and setting down each foot in turn, never having both feet off the ground at once.

Genesis 13:17, "Arise, walk through the land in the length of it and in the breadth of it; for I will give it unto thee."

Exodus 13:15, "And the LORD said unto Moses, wherefore criest thou unto me? Speak unto the children of Israel, that they go forward."

Daniel 3:25, "He answered and said. Lo, I see four men loose, walking in the midst of the fire, and they have no hurt; and the form of the fourth is like the Son of God."

Matthew 14:29, "And He said, Come. And when Peter was come down out of the ship, he walked on the water, to go to Jesus."

John 5:8, "Jesus saith unto him, Rise, take up thy bed, and walk."

Acts 17:28, "For in Him we live, and move, and have our being; as certain also of your own poets have said, For we are also His offspring."

The same type of crisis can happen to two different people with two very different outcomes. The outcome is based on the response of a person to the crisis.

Overcomers don't see a crisis as a crisis but they see it as a bump in the road. They feel that this bump in the road that God is with them. That's why when you look at the passages of Scripture God led me to above you see people's responses and then you see God's response.

When God told Peter to come and walk on the water he could have refused. If he had refused he would have missed one of the greatest miracles of his life. Because he obeyed he literally walked on water.
It's the same with us. I could go on and on there are so many examples but think about the ones I have above. Sometimes it is hard when you're the one laying in a hospital bed. An overcomer is one whose trust is in God and knows that their trust is just simply in God no matter what.

I want to define one more word from google.

Stagnant is having no current or flow and often having an unpleasant smell as a consequence.

What you need to do today is look at yourself the problems you've had. How have you dealt with them? Have you included God in every aspect of your life? Do you overcome your problems or do you allow your problems to overcome you? Do problems and crisis stop you?
If they do look at the definition above of stagnant. As Christians we should not be stagnant. We should move and flow in the presence of God. We should not stink in the presence of God or be unmoved.

Lastly lets go to one more scripture.

II CORINTHIANS 5:7, "(For we walk by faith, not by sight:)"

Think about it. Examine your own life. Let the Bible talk to you. Let it change you. No matter what situation we have in our lives we simply walk by faith.
****

Well, evidently I can't get sick like normal folks. When I take to my sick bed it is an event. I had another episode with my heart. Needless to say I won't be getting out of the hospital this weekend.

They are keeping me on a Nitroglycerin drip because my blood pressure and heart keep doing strange things. When it starts doing strange things then they come with nitroglycerin pills and patches. I'm learning that a headache is staying with me.

I'm scheduled for a stress test Monday. The cardiologist was very concerned about the irregularities in my EKG. He said I'm at intermediate risk to have a heart attack. Just what everyone wants to hear.

Jesus has got this! On Him I depend. This is just another bump in the road. I will worship and praise Him for all His blessings on me!

February 22, 2014
Depression, Despondency, and How to be an Overcomer (Part IIIR of III)
TO OVERCOME YOU NEED TO HAVE A TESTIMONY

How do you get a testimony?
Well, you have to have a test.
First, let's look at the definition of testimony as found on dictionary.com.

Testimony
1. the statement or declaration of a witness under oath or affirmation, usually in court.
2. evidence in support of a fact or statement; proof.
3. open declaration or profession, as of faith.

Looking at this definition God is showing me that I can't produce evidence if I have never been through anything. In order to share what God can do some of us have to go through some things.
Let's look at what the Bible has to say about a testimony. The Bible tells us what we're supposed to do with ours.

Psalms 81:5, *"This he ordained in Joseph for a testimony, when he went out through the land of Egypt: where I heard a language that I understood not."*

Mark 5:19, *"Howbeit, Jesus suffered him not, but saith unto him, go home to thy friends, and tell them how great things the Lord has done for thee and have had compassion on thee."*

Luke 21:12-14, *"But before all these, they shall lay their hands on you, and persecute you, delivering you up to the synagogue, and into prisons being brought before kings and rulers for my name's sake. And it shall turn to you for a testimony. Settle it*

therefore in your hearts, not to meditate before what ye shall answer."

So, think about the tribulations of Joseph, being thrown into prison and then being recognized was always a part of God's plan for his life. Let's calmly take a look at our own life, could it all be part of a bigger purpose?

If you have a testimony of God doing great things in your life and you never share it are you disobeying God? There are so many people that need encouraged. Have you ever thought that your testimony could be life changing for someone else? Perhaps bring them to God.

It is time we quit hiding our light under a bushel and share it with others! So no matter what situation you may find yourself in look for an opportunity to share the greatness of our God.

Tomorrow, I will take you on the journey God took me on about the value of our individual testimonies to God.
*****
So I'm getting a lot of messages and texts wanting to know how I am. Well, I'm still in the hospital and will be here until Monday. No episodes with my heart since yesterday afternoon. I am just waiting for the stress test on Monday.

Hospital food....blech... For those that know me know this is so unappetizing. I know I will eat the roll, turkey and maybe the pears... the green gunk looks like baby food.... ugh....and the potatoes well need some gravy and/or lots of butter....

If I was just anybody I'd say it's all good, but I know better It's all God! Tonight, even in the hospital there is no reason for me not to worship my God and remember that no matter what It's simply all God!

I already know it's going to be alright!

I had never heard this song until tonight. Awesome! Love it! Lord, hear my voice when I lift my hands to thee!

BLESS THE LORD BECAUSE HE HAS HEARD MY VOICE EVERY TIME I CRY! EVERY TIME!!!

There is just something about the name of Jesus! Everything we need.... everything... is in the name of Jesus! I love the song, Alabaster Box. Tonight I can see my daughter, Leah, signing to it with such anointing as she did years ago. How, I would love to hear her voice but God knows and God has got this and my heart problem in the palms of His hands. So I'm laying this at His feet and just going to worship Him!

Tomorrow morning I can't go to church and worship so worship for me. I will be worshiping in my hospital room tonight and tomorrow because you see I simply love Him. Jesus has done so very much for me. I am so very blessed. No matter what happens to me I've been blessed far more than I ever deserve. Thank you Jesus for blessing me!

FEBRUARY 23, 2014
Depression, Despondency, and How to be an Overcomer (Part IIIS of III).
THE VALUE OF OUR INDIVIDUAL TESTIMONIES TO GOD.

Define Value:
1. the regard that something is held to deserve; the importance, worth, or usefulness of something.
2. a person's principles or standards of behavior; one's judgment of what is important in life.

In the journey God took me on about the value of our individual testimonies I have been overwhelmed at the value God places on them. In Exodus we see it where it is referring to the tablets of the covenant. However, it was a testimony given to Moses from God. Think about that. God was teaching us by example.

Exodus 25:16, "And thou shalt put into the ark the testimony which I shall give thee."
Exodus 30:6, "And thou shalt put it before the vail that is by the ark of the testimony, before the mercy seat that is over the testimony, where I will meet with thee."

Look where it is placed. It is placed before the veil that is by the ark of the testimony but before the mercy seat that is over the testimony. Then God says I will meet you there. I am still trembling when I think of this. So if you don't think your testimony is valuable think about the example God Himself gave us by what He did so that we would know.

I am not a great Bible Scholar. I am a very simple person when it comes to this. However, it awes me to know how much God values our testimonies. Another example is Job 1:8. You see God knew Job's testimony.

I wonder does He know your testimony? Mine?

Job 1:8,. "And the Lord said unto Satan, Hast thou considered my servant Job, that there is none like him in the earth, a perfect and an upright man, one that feareth God and escheweth evil?"

Do we have this testimony before God?

I think it's time to examine some more of those dark corners in our heart we hold in reserve just for us. All of our hearts have to be given to Him. No Holding Back if we truly want to have a testimony like Job that God would use him as an example to the devil.

Tomorrow I will continue to take you on the journey God has taken me on about our testimonies by sharing with you the benefits a testimony gives us when we share it

Yes, today I am still at the hospital in Oak Hill. This morning my blood pressure is going up but I have messaged many to pray. I know My God Has Got This!

Today when you go to church worship for me. If I could I would be worshiping because you see I simply love God no matter what.
I'll be watching Royalwood Church online. I can't wait to be part of their service even from the hospital.

While watching Royalwood live streaming I got kicked off at a very important part of the message. Below is a message Sister Macey sent me and my response.

Yes!! Did you hear what Bro Macey said about The Lord telling him that someone watching was going to be healed? He did not know you had written me or that you were in the hospital or that you would be watching. I thought of you immediately!!!! Praise The Lord!

My reply a few minutes later.

No I didn't hear that but Sis. Lawanda shared it with me. I had gotten bumped off the hospital server and evidently missed a couple of very important minutes. But I'm still claiming it as my miracle! A good stress test tomorrow. They just came in and took off my telemetry monitor. Praise God!

Thanking and praising God for the prayers. My blood pressure has dropped to 129/67. All glory and honor to God. Again, Thanks for the prayers!!!

I'm a Worshipper EVERY DAY!

They just came in and took off the heart monitor. I have a place ready for IV's but no IV's!!!! God is working on me. Believing for a great stress test tomorrow and in Jesus name I will be out of the hospital!

FEBRUARY 24, 2014
Depression, Despondency, and How to Overcome (Part III T of III)

Benefits of Having a Testimony

Benefit is an advantage or profit gained from something

Think about that definition in relationship to your walk with God. To have a testimony you have benefits. I know it doesn't seem that way when you're being tested but oh, the relationship when you learn how to depend on God for everything.

Did you ever think that having a test has a great benefit to you as a Christian?

Let's see what the Bible has to say about it.

Job 2:3, *"And the Lord said unto Satan, Hast thou considered my servant Job, that there is none like him in the earth, a perfect and an upright man, one that feareth God and escheweth evil? And still he holdeth fast his integrity, although thou movedst against him to destroy him without cause."*

Psalms 19:7, *"The law of the Lord is perfect, converting the soul: the testimony of the Lord is sure making wise the simple."*

Hebrews 11:5, *"By faith Enoch was translated that he should not see death; and was not found because God had translated him: for before his translation he had this testimony, that he pleased God."*

Revelation 12:11, *"And they overcame him by the blood of the Lamb, and by the word of their testimony; and they loved not their lives unto the death."*

Five things I see in these four passages as benefits of your test and testimony:

1. You keep your integrity before God.
2. You have a testimony before God.
3. Testimony of the Lord makes wise the simple.
4. You please God.
5. You overcome by the word of your testimony.

Just think about these benefits!
WOW!

As I as reading these passages I kept getting more and more excited about my relationship with God and my testimony. I'm nothing great just a normal everyday person. Most of the people in the Bible didn't think of themselves as anything extraordinary. It's not in being extraordinary it's in not letting situations or circumstances define your outcome but letting your walk with God define the outcome.

So today, if you're being tested, count yourself blessed and highly favored of God. Then look at what you can accomplish with your testimony. You never know how many lives your test will ultimately help and touch if you learn how to be a victor instead of always a victim.

Praise God in your valley!

Watch Him do miraculous things in your life. Sometimes the process is slow and sometimes it is fast but however long your valley is to know that Jesus is with you and on Him you can depend.

Let's be Victors not Victims!

Continuing to believe... Just got up and was moving around. They came and took my blood pressure 151/110. Pray folks, please pray. I still believe. I still know my God has got this! Oxygen level was at 96% so that's good news. All is well with my soul. In Jesus name. The stress test will tell the tale and Jesus will be there!
It is well with my soul! That is really all that matters. God's will be done.
First part of the stress test is done which was taking pictures. Waiting to be hooked up and do the treadmill.

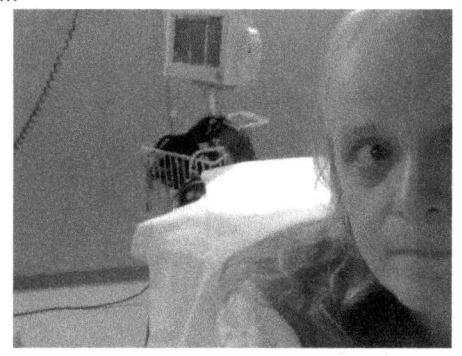

February 24, 2014
A Thank you from my heart to the many who are lifting me up in prayer!

While all this has been going on with this little heart problem because to God this is a little thing I have been blessed. Bro. & Sis. Tommy Craft have stayed close on the phone along with countless friends and pastors from around the U.S.

Pastor Greg Hurley and the folks from Solid Rock in Oak Hill have loved me, prayed for me and been with me through this. I so appreciate the visits and prayers especially Bro. Smith, my friend Wilden's pastor and a call from Pastor David Bounds. Lastly, my son is waiting while they are doing the stress test. God blessed me with a few minutes with him before the test started.

There are so many to mention that I hope you understand how much I love and appreciate all you have done for me.

While I was waiting on the stress test the doctor had informed me they knew what they were looking for and that I would probably have to be transported via life flight to either Charleston, West Virginia or Huntington, West Virginia where they would do a heart catheterization and open heart surgery. Therefore, I had called my son because he was unfortunate enough to be my next of kin. It was time for an end of life discussion. It may not have been that serious but the doctors seemed very worried which ratcheted my concern up. I still believed God had given me a miracle I just wondered how far I would have to travel this road.

I remember lying on the table after they had taken the before pictures for the stress test. Bro. Smith had prayed for me and Bro. Bounds had called. Then I was alone. I placed my hands on my chest and began rubbing it. I looked up and said, "God, I thought I heard you tell me to go to Africa. This problem with my heart shouldn't be a problem. You can massage out any blood clots or blockages. I trust you to take care of me. I trust you to make my blood pressure be normal and heal my heart. I only want to do your will. I can't do it if something is wrong with my heart."

When the cardiologist came in I sat up and he immediately pushed me back down on the bed. He did not want me to get up. He told me, "Do you not realize you could have another major heart attack during the stress test with your blood pressure and chest pains?"

I insisted to get on the treadmill. They surrounded me. I was able to go 9 ½ minutes even jogging. After I got done they let me know my blood pressure had reacted as it should. So then they put me through the machine for the after pictures. They put me through the machine three times!!! Each time they went a little slower! 45 minutes later I was discharged!

Whatever they had seen was GONE!!!

HALLELUJAH!!! My stress test was fine!!!

The miracle Bro. Macey said that someone watching online yesterday was getting their miracle. I, along, with many friends, claimed that miracle for me.

Thank everyone for their prayers!

HALLELUJAH!!! TO GOD BE THE GLORY!!!

Monday's To Do List
1. Study the Word of God - check
2. Pray - check
3. Believe for my miracles -check
4. Spend the day with my son - check
5. Be discharged from the hospital with NO NEW MEDICATIONS - Check
6. Dinner and part of the evening with my son. - Check
7. Rejoice for my miracles - Check
8. Run errands - Check
9. Wash clothes - Check
10. Counsel/encourage Cancer patient - check
11. Bathe Brownie - Check
12. Put clothes away - check
13. Trim Brownies toenails (so not looking forward to that one.
14. Rejoice in the Lord - coming soon
15. Go to bed -

Depression, Despondency and How to be an Overcomer (Part IIIU of III)
--TO OVERCOME YOU MUST BE A GIVER

I can hear you already thinking she's going to talk about offering and tithes. That is required Biblically and useful but not where I'm going this morning. God talked to me about being a giver to others to truly overcome in my own life.

Let's see where God took me on this journey through the Bible on giving.

Acts 20:35, *"I have shewed you all things, how that so laboring ye ought to support the weak, and to remember the words of the Lord Jesus, how he said it is more blessed to give than to receive."*

II Cor 9:6, *"But this (I say), He which soweth sparingly shall reap also sparingly; and he which soweth bountifully shall reap also bountifully."*

We have all heard it seemingly a million times, "it is more blessed to give than to receive". It is so important to understand the concept of giving no matter our situation or circumstances.

We have to quit focusing on our problems and learn how to focus on others. Not only will this help others but it will ultimately help us more. I've found when I reach out to help someone whether it's to bless them with something or my time to encourage others I usually walk away having received more than I gave.

To receive is not the reason to give. We should give simply because that's what we should do.

No matter what your situation today find someone you can give to. Everyone has something to give.

Watch and see how it will change your life!

Tomorrow I will talk about the journey God has taken me on about how to give Biblically to be an overcomer.

A busy day today! I am so blessed not to be in the hospital. My partial to do list below:
1. Finish returning calls.
2. Breakfast! (Yes I am going to try and eat three small meals today).
3. Go to Lowes
4. Pick up dry cleaning.
5. Take keys to friends.
6. Walk Brownie
7. Take out the trash
8. Finish laundry
9. Finish packing
10. Walk Brownie
11. Pray and rejoice all day!!!!
And a few other things that will be mentioned later.

Brownie and I just crossed the Virginia state line.

When I crossed the Virginia state line God swept in the car. I'll never forget it. I heard God speak to me and say, "I'm going to restore the years the cankerworm has ate."

I started crying, praying and talking in that heavenly language worshipping God as I continued to drive. The whole trip would be one of much rejoicing and prayer.

Depression, Despondency and How to be an Overcomer (Part IIIUii of Part III)
How to give according to the Bible.
Giving according to the Bible is very important.
1. Give in secret.
2. Give as God has purposed in your heart.
3. Give abundantly.
4. Give cheerfully.

God brought these three points to my mind this morning from the following three scriptures. Come on this journey with me that God is taking me on.

Matthew 6:1-4, *"Take heed that ye do not your alms before men, to be seen of them: otherwise you have no reward of your father which is in heaven. Therefore when thou doest thine alms, do not sound a trumpet before thee, as the hypocrites do in the synagogues and the streets, that they may have glory of men. Verily I say unto you, They have their reward. That thine alms may be in secret: and thy Father which seeth in secret himself shall reward thee openly. "*

Luke 6:38
"Give and it shall be given unto you: good measure pressed down, and shaken together, and running over, shall men give unto your bosom. For with the same measure that ye mete withal that shall be measured to you again."

II Corinthians 9:7, *"Every man according as he purposeth in his heart, (so let him give); not grudgingly, or of necessity: for God loveth a cheerful giver."*

True overcomers learn how. They apply themselves to wanting to have the mind of Christ. This is usually unpopular especially among Americans. We want the easy way out. The easy way out is not how you get close to God.

As we have heard said many times if you don't stand for something you will fall for anything. So, when you sing, "I will give you all, I will not withhold," think about those words and what they really mean.
If God should ask of you all do it with a smile.

Don't be upset. God will bless you. God will take care of you.
Think about your giving and what God has asked of you. Have you done what He asked?

A Note from the Author

I have let you take a peek inside my life. There are many things that are not included in this book but know that over 40 things have happened in the past eight years to get me to where I am today. Do not expect to have the faith of giants in the Word of God if you haven't slayed any giants in your own life.

March 2014

This month I was privileged to spend part of it in Jackson, Mississippi in much counsel with my pastor the Bishop Tommy L. Craft and his wife Sister Diane as I prepared to leave for Kenya, Africa for a month.

I flew to Houston, Texas where I spent a week with friends gathering the things I needed to take with me. Taking that flight was a miracle. The first book in the "Just Tagging Along with Jesus" series has been published. The second book in the series is due out in January.

April 2014

In April 2014 on my way home from Africa the breaking continued with the death of my father. I remember standing in line at the airport waiting to check in for my flight back when I called to see how my dad was doing. I spoke to my mom and she let me know Dad was on a ventilator. I got off the phone with her and I prayed.

I said, "God if he's not going to be Daddy, please take him. Don't make him suffer. No matter what problems we have had no one deserves to suffer. You let me spend time with him at the hospital. I've said my goodbyes. Your will be done in Jesus name."

Then I started calling friends in the area to go to the hospital to support my mother during this time. I am so grateful for Bro. Doug Joseph and his family, Sis. Cheri Sandy and her family, Bro. & Sis. Ray Frankhouser, and Sis. Ronda Dalton. They all supported my mother during this time.

I caught the plane and when I landed in Qatar I called home and found he had revived and pulled out the ventilator tubing. He was sitting up talking to them. I thought he would be okay.

When I landed in Houston 18 hours later it was to be greeted with the news on Facebook that my father had passed away a few hours after my flight had taken off. When I saw that, yes I was upset but I was relieved because I knew his suffering was not over. My father may have had his issues but he was a hard worker his whole life and provided for our family. It is from him I get this work ethic.

Upon my return from Kenya I was extremely ill so I was unable to travel further than Houston, Texas. I spent the week of my father's death mainly in bed regaining my strength with Sister Haygood providing food while I recovered because I had overworked while I was in Africa.

Then I went to West Virginia in April to the West Virginia Ladies Conference. I flew in because physically I was unable to drive. Sister Ronda Dalton picked me up at the Pittsburgh Airport. On Friday afternoon after I spoke Sister Ronda graciously took me to see my mother and to see my Daddy's grave before heading back to church that night. While I was recovering emotionally I was still a loose cannon because of my husband's death over seven months prior to this. When you lose your best friend who you've spent over half of your life with you go through cycles of grief.

While I am moving forward I am still healing. There are some things that take time to recover from. In those times you have to treat yourself with tender loving care. You have to realize your limitations and not push yourself too quickly. Grief takes time and has no specific timetable.

When I am in West Virginia I take photographs and that is part of my offering to the conference. This year I was also privileged to be one of the ministers on Friday morning. Thursday night, however, I was taking pictures when the unthinkable happened.

So, the story I haven't told because I wanted to tell it firsthand to a few folks near and dear to me but the whole WV District Ladies Conference heard it and now are saying, "Are you wet?"

Last night I thought it would be a good idea to get some pictures from the baptistry of the conference. The door on the men's side automatically locks and the door on the women's side had a doorstop and would stay open. So it was decided to go in from the women's side. Well, I had not been in from the women's side until I went to take pictures during the first worship song.

As soon as you step through the door on the women's side, you step into the baptistry. They had foam board over the baptistry. So when I stepped in from the women's side. My heel went down and down I went. I didn't think anyone had seen me. I was almost completely immersed, LOL. As I went down I thought, "Ok, God what are you trying to teach me here. I really thought Kenya had taken care of the pride thing?"

The sound man and the folks in the balcony saw it happen. A few people on the floor saw but most were worshiping I hope. When the sound man saw me go down he said, In Jesus name so I got rebaptized! He watched to make sure I came up. I crawled out praying no one saw me.... however, that was false hope...

I took my clothes off in the women's bathroom and wrung them out several times because they were dripping so bad. Then I redressed and headed down hoping to avoid anyone I knew. Well, luck was not on my side. Walking down the hallway by Bro. Hudson's office I heard footsteps then Bro. Hudson said, "Susan, did you get the pictures? Oh, my, what happened? Did you fall in the baptistry? Oh, my you fell in the baptistry!"

We went into his office and I asked him if the church had a clothes dryer. He went in his bathroom and came out with this little hairdryer, a mini travel one I believe. I looked at it and I said, "I don't think that's going to help." So he sent for his Children's minister's wife and she came and took me to their apartment where I wore one of her t-shirt's until my clothes were dry enough to wear and we went back to church. Well, she went back to church. I went into Bro. Hudson's office and hid.

Bro. Hudson's son had gone to get rice and brought in this huge box full of rice. We packed my phone and the digital cameras in rice. The jury is still out on the cameras. I really thought the phone had survived. Well, it is another casualty so if you're trying to call me I promise I'm not being rude. The phone is not working.

After church I went in and told a few people once I found out some young people in the balcony had seen what happened so it's better to be laughed with than at....

Before ministering this morning Sis. Hudson was introducing me and she told the story about the baptistry to the conference. I had planned to if she hadn't. Everyone loved it. Then Sis. Mickey Mangun has followed up with stories of where is Sis. Susie. Is she in the baptistry?

It's all in good fun. If you can't laugh at yourself I don't know how you can accomplish anything because embarrassing things will eventually happen to people who take risks. In order to accomplish something with your life you have to take a risk. Those who don't step out have no idea of the freedom that comes with being liberated by God to do His will and His bidding for His good pleasure!

I want to please Him and I crave a double of the double portion!!!!

Everything that has happened to me this past year prepared me for a dive in the baptistery. When my foot caught I just knew God would catch me. I turned so I would fall backwards and when I did it was like I felt gentle arms holding me and laying me down in the baptistery. Bro. Davenport says I went completely under yet somehow my hair did not get messed up and the hat I had on only had a drop of water on it.

Now that it has been months since this happened I realize how big a miracle God gave me. I could have hit my back on the seat in the baptistery, broke my neck or drowned. Nothing bad happened. I was able to slither out.

You see, God sees our end from our beginning. He knows what faith we will need before we need it and he lovingly prepares the way for us to be trained. I have been in God's bootcamp for the past few years. I have been trained to be His servant. I always want to be in training ever learning about service to the King of Kings and Lord of Lords. I truly want to be a servant of servants.

David had to fight on the field with the sheep by himself fighting a lion and a bear before he fought Goliath. Faith has to be built by daily making choices to build your faith. You do that by the choices you make. You do that when you choose to spend time reading your Bible, time in the prayer room, and when you choose to worship whether anyone else is worshipping or not.

I said all that to say, that is why, when I fell in the baptistry I just knew God was going to catch me. We have that type of relationship. What type of relationship do you have with Jesus? Is it a surface relationship or is it that of a best friend?

While my breaking was not over it was time to bring this book to a close. I hope this book changes you as it has changed me. In reading over all the things that have happened I am humbled that God loves me enough to trust me to be broken and to lead me to become closer still to Him.

In finishing this book I have one last picture. I want to be so busy in the kingdom of God that I never have time to think about what I don't have. I want everything I have to bring glory and honor to God.

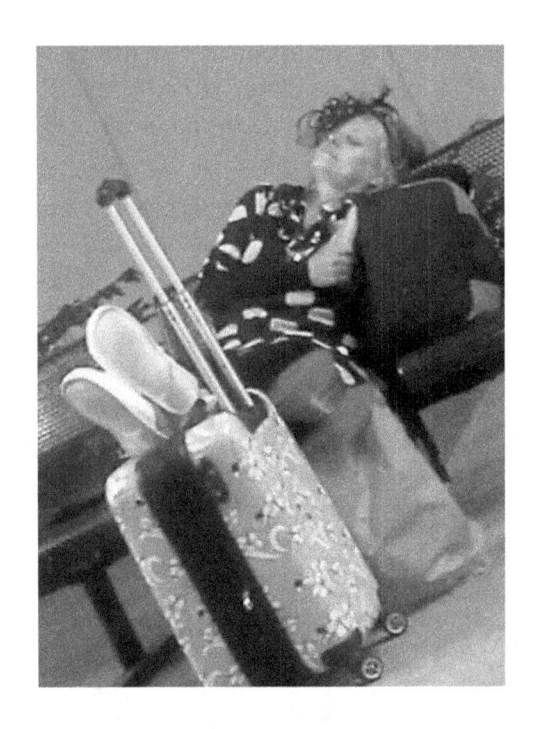

Exhausted working for Jesus I can sleep anywhere even waiting to be picked up outside an airport.

Just a few of the curve balls life has thrown me...

Below is the incomplete list (some things were left out to protect those I love) in order:

(1) My deceased husband's brush with possible colon cancer;
(2) A major surgery and two weeks in the hospital for him;
(3) I became septic having emergency gallbladder surgery;
(4) 2008 diagnosed with pancreatic cancer;
(5) many surgeries, almost two years of hospital stays and a few near death experiences;
(6) finding out my husband was taking my prescription dilaudid out of my IV bags and putting water in them because he was in pain and addicted to prescription drugs, beginning the process to get him help;
(7) hearing him fire a gun in the wall to scare us wanting us to think he had committed suicide,
(8) having him arrested, appearing before a judge with him in shackles,
(9) three stays in drug rehabilitation, one stay in detox,
(10) taking a position as #2 in a small company, consequently being fired supposed inadequate leadership skills while income and employee morale increased as payables decreased;
(11) a rock hitting my oil pan causing two weeks without a car while a specialty dealer replaced the oil pan for $1,100.
(12) extreme pain from bad teeth
(13) being told I could have possible lung cancer
(14) On the evangelism field in Houston my car springing a leak in the radiator. No money with repair costs of over $1,200
(15) my husband dying from a prescription drug overdose;
(16) forced to have his body cremated because of a family situation.
(17) being interrogated by the State Police for his possible murder;
(18) Homeowners insurance being cancelled; having a yard sale selling everything I could to come up with the money to pay the policy after convincing them to issue it in my name since the deed had not been changed yet.

(19) being attacked verbally by a friend of my son's and her mother regarding our family situation;
(20) my son unexpectedly moving out and in with his former girlfriends family.
(21) both vehicles breaking down within two weeks of each other.
(22) refrigerator quit working in the middle of winter.
(23) Christmas alone,
(24) commode messed up, learned how to turn the water off;
(25) water pipes freezing and bursting (thank God for homeowners insurance)
(26) Bishop James L. Kilgore dying unexpectedly - 2nd most influential man in my life other than my husband and father;
(27) My dad becoming ill, spending three days with him in the hospital;
(28) having a heart attack;
(29) Becoming extremely ill my last day in Africa
(30) Dad dying while I was on a plane coming home from Africa
(31) mentally and physically incapable of attending my fathers funeral
(32) falling into a baptistry
(33) verbally being attacked by friends who are like family(jealousy is a horrible disease)
(34) staying subsequently with a someone who had challenges
(35) keys to car disappearing, called a locksmith, new keys made
(36) Someone doing everything to destroy me and my ministry

The secret to continuing no matter what is to remain still standing... Still praying.... Still putting God first regardless. Yes, I have made missteps and mistakes but I know how to go to my knees in prayer. I know how to repent, do you?

Most have not learned the two most important secrets of success.... Repentance first and then Worship regardless of your situation or problem! Worship through it! Call on Jesus first when reeling from shock. In the beginning you just reel than you call on the name of the one who will rescue you.

Other Books by Susan D. Smith

Surprised by God with Pancreatic Cancer

My Child, I've Got This

Living the Miracle

The Blood

Depressed? What does the Bible say about it?

COMING SOON

Just Tagging Along With Jesus, Adventures in Kenya (Spring 2015)

Write it On the Doorposts of My Heart (Spring 2015)

Two Destiny's One Outcome (Spring 2015)

Adventures of the Yellow Convertible Bug (Winter 2015)

Cherry Blossoms
(Spring 2015)

AVAILABLE

Sister Susan D. Smith

To come to your church

Or

Civic organization

To build faith and hope

(304) 640-5717

Facebook: Susan D Wine Smith

CPSIA information can be obtained
at www.ICGtesting.com
Printed in the USA
BVHW011708300321
603735BV00005B/46